AF758162

LOST IN NEWFOUNDLAND

VOLUME 2

WITH PHOTOGRAPHER MICHAEL WINSOR

At twilight, the Atlantic moves in slow rhythm around Green Point Lighthouse, softening the rocks beneath fading light.

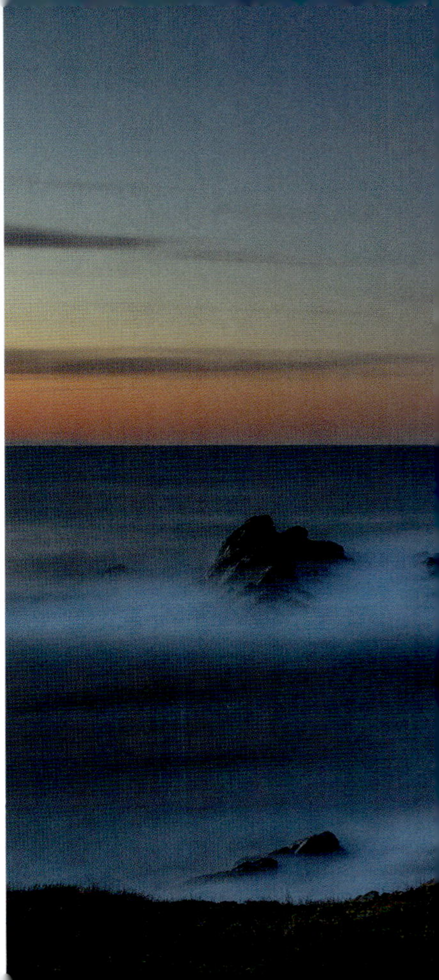

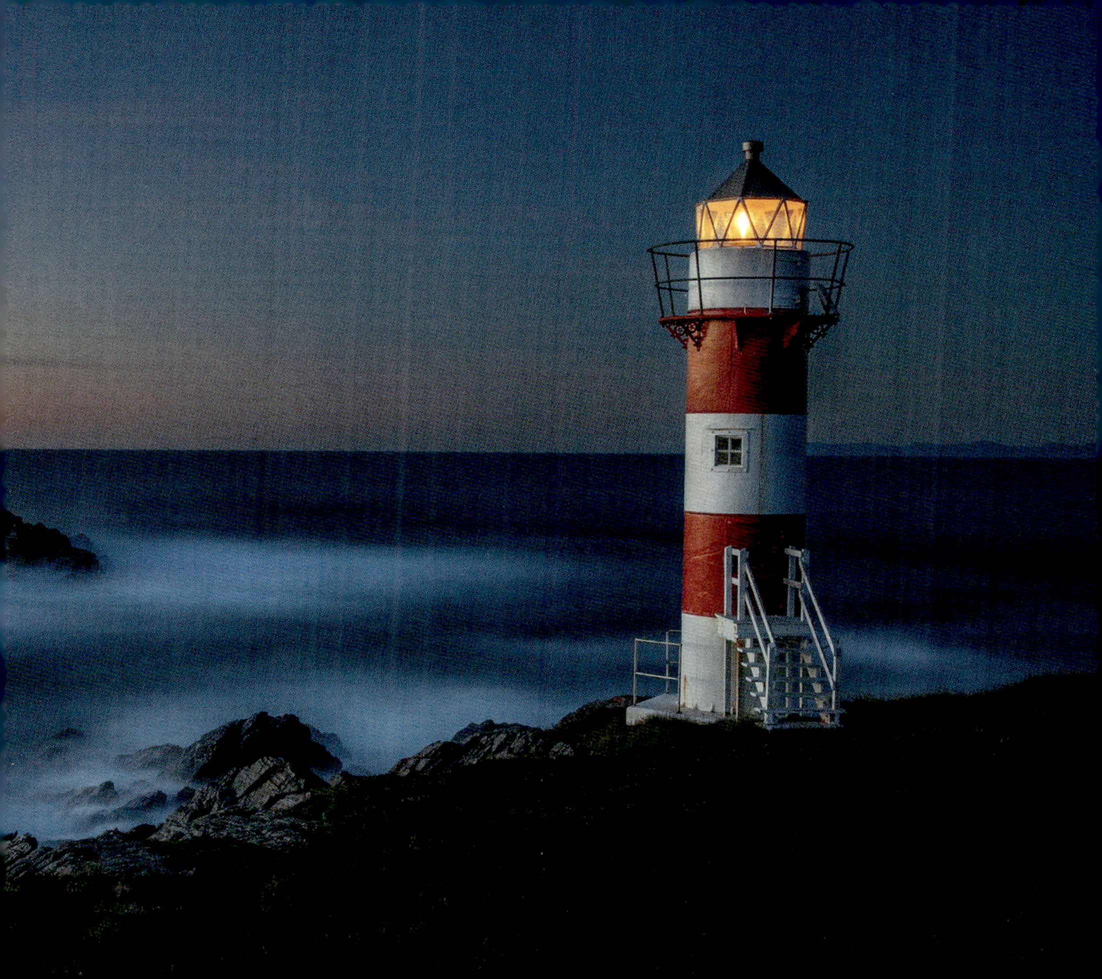

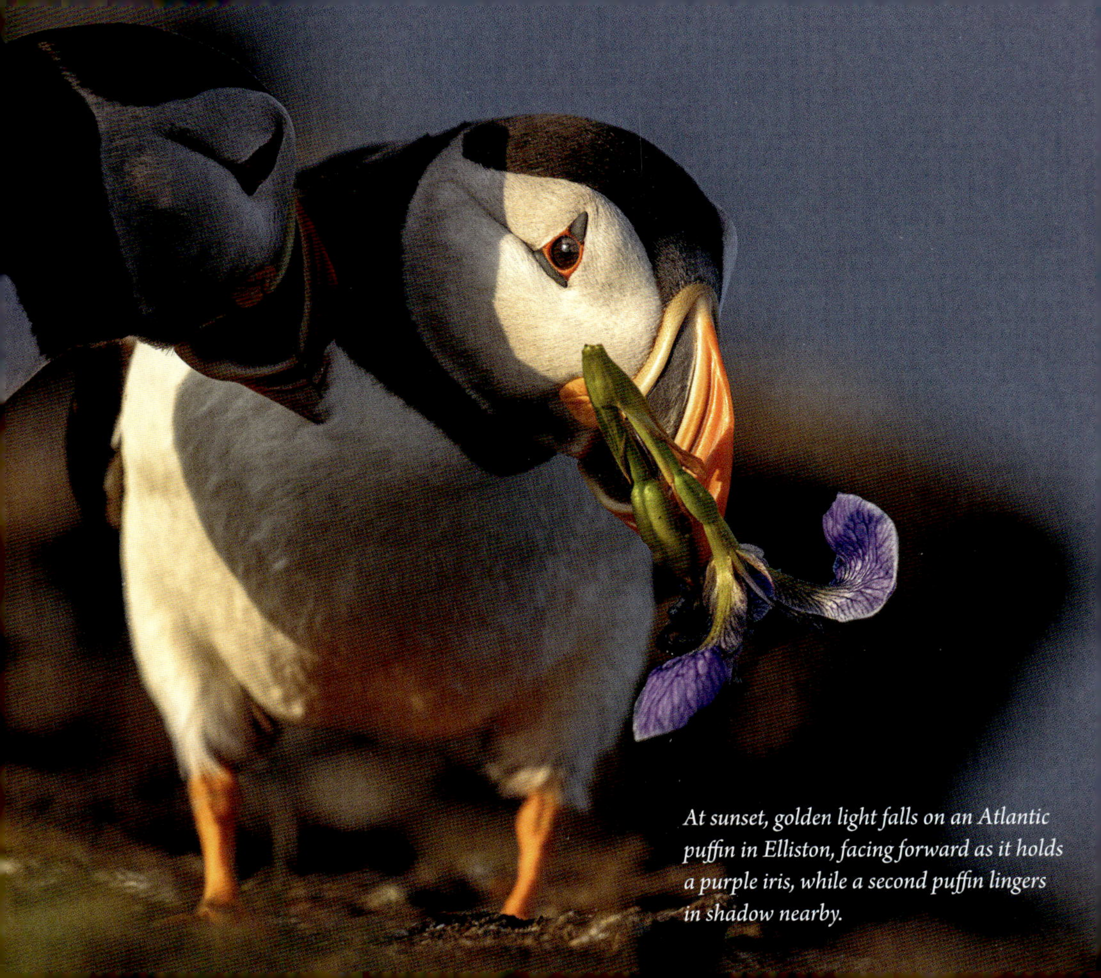

At sunset, golden light falls on an Atlantic puffin in Elliston, facing forward as it holds a purple iris, while a second puffin lingers in shadow nearby.

Newfoundland and Labrador is not a place you rush through. Over time and through experience, my connection to this land has deepened. I've come to realize that I am still lost in Newfoundland—in the rugged landscapes, majestic wildlife, and deep history that continue to define it. This place asks you to slow down, to listen, and to pay attention to the quiet moments in between. Moments like standing beneath a lighthouse at night, stars hanging overhead, and the ocean rolling in steady and calm. Moments like an Atlantic puffin pausing with a purple iris held gently in its beak, light falling across its face. A simple moment, unannounced, where nothing needs to happen—because it already has.

When I first began photographing Newfoundland, my goal was simply to share this place with the world. I wanted people to see the dramatic coastlines, the variety of wildlife, and the raw beauty that shapes life here. Over time, after travelling from Africa to the Arctic and many places in between, I came to understand something deeper. What makes Newfoundland and Labrador truly special is not just how it looks, but how it makes you feel.

There is a rare sense of openness here, revealed by roads that seem to lead nowhere in particular, communities where time moves a little slower, and landscapes that make you feel small in the best possible way. You can stand on a cliff's edge watching humpback whales leap out of the ocean and feel completely alone, without ever feeling lonely. You have room to breathe, to think, and to simply exist, without expectation.

Photography has a way of teaching patience, and Newfoundland is the perfect classroom. The light is never guaranteed, the weather can change in an instant, and sometimes the best moments happen when you stop chasing them. Some of my favourite images were made when plans fell apart, when I waited longer than expected, or when I trusted the moment instead of the schedule. The photograph isn't always about what you see through the lens, but about what you feel while standing there.

To become lost in Newfoundland and Labrador is not to be confused or directionless; it is to let go. To step away from noise, crowds, and constant motion. It is to trade certainty for discovery and deadlines for adventure. The best photographs often begin when the camera is set down and you take a moment to be fully present with the land. When you experience a place first, the images will follow. In taking time to experience this place, many people find something they didn't know they were looking for—a sense of calm, of perspective, or even of themselves. It's a quiet reminder that not all journeys are meant to be rushed.

This book is an invitation—not just to explore a place, but to experience it fully. To slow down, to wander, and to allow Newfoundland and Labrador to reveal themselves in their own time. If you arrive with an open mind and a patient heart, you may leave with more than photographs. You may leave changed, carrying a little piece of this place with you long after the road disappears behind you. And maybe, just maybe, you'll find that by becoming lost in Newfoundland, you've finally found your way.

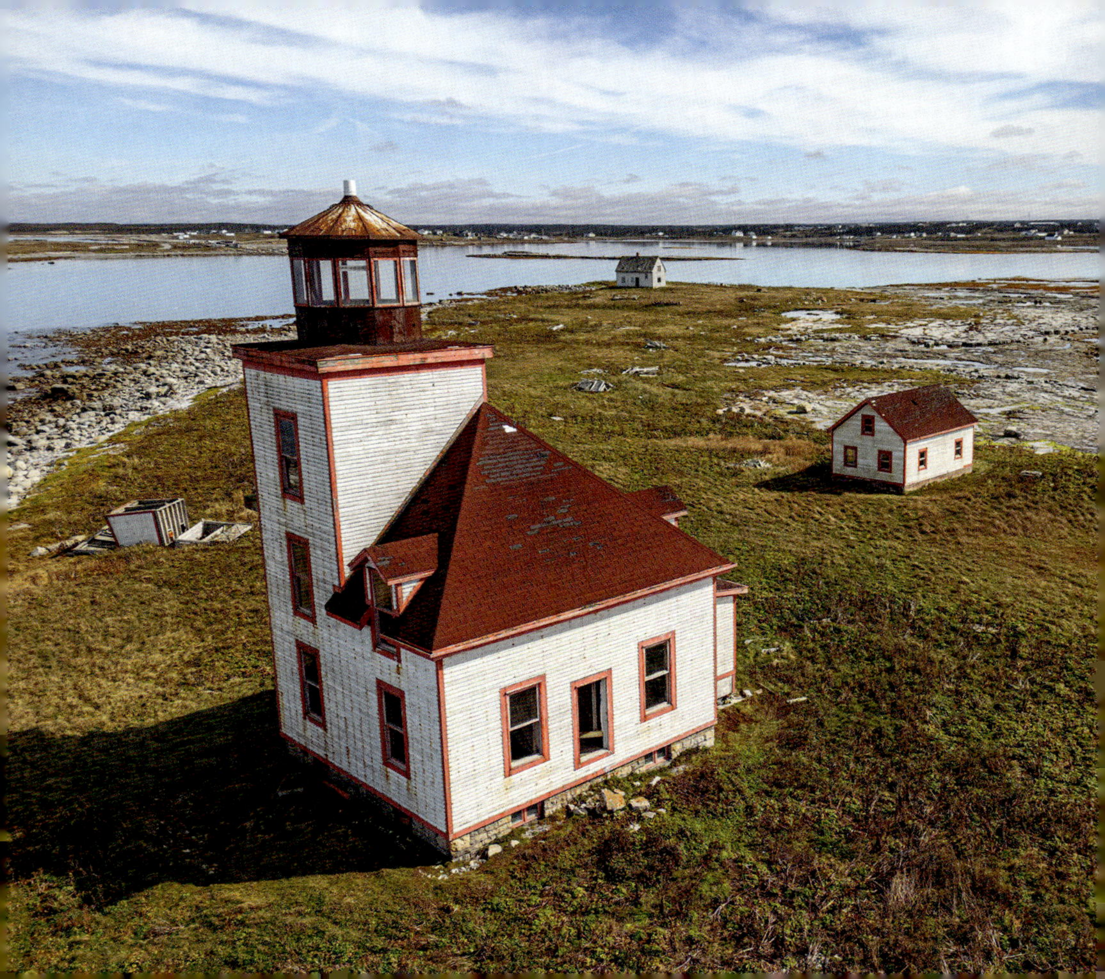

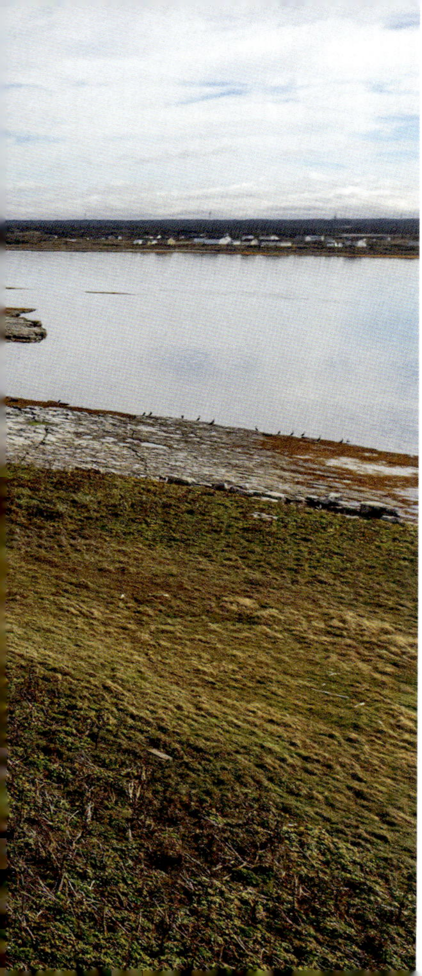

In bright midday light, Flowers Island Lighthouse stands above the island as the community of Flowers Cove stretches along the coast in the distance.

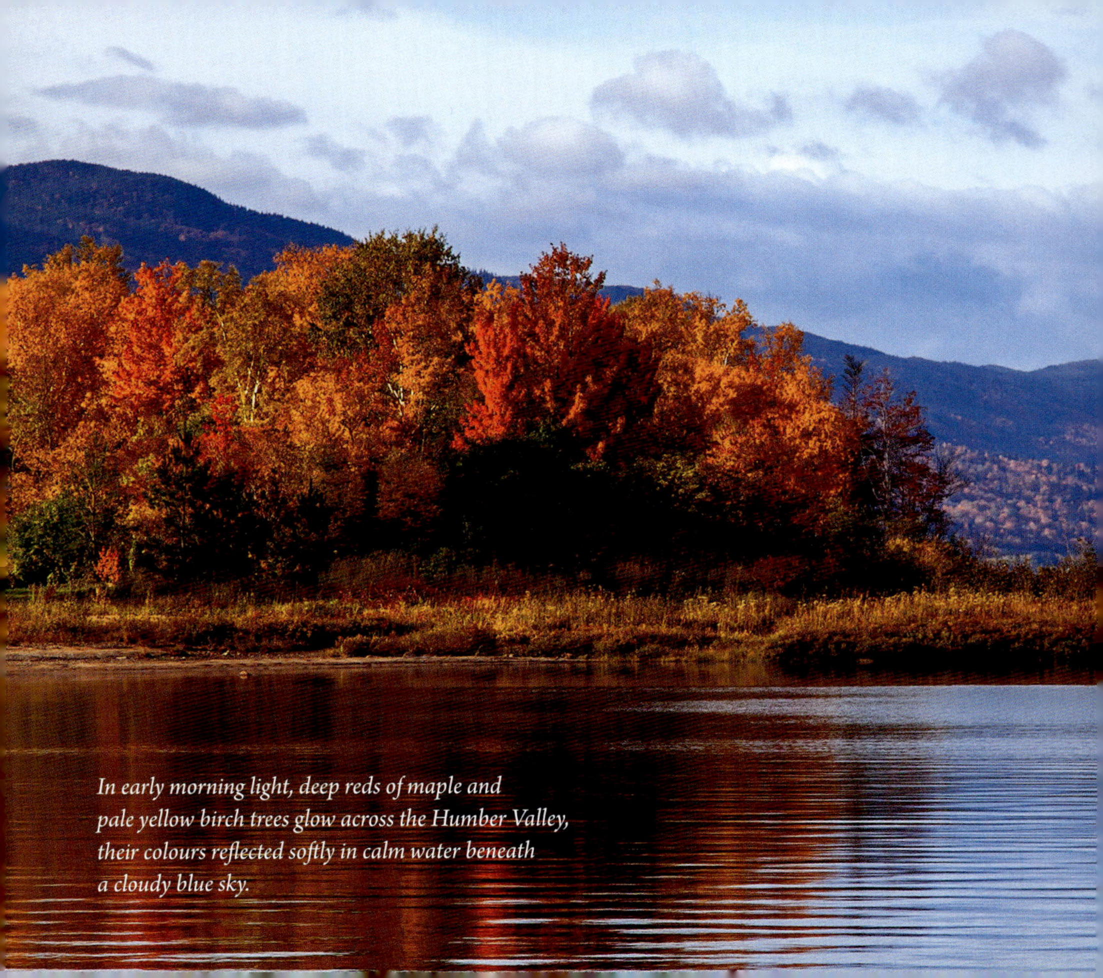

In early morning light, deep reds of maple and pale yellow birch trees glow across the Humber Valley, their colours reflected softly in calm water beneath a cloudy blue sky.

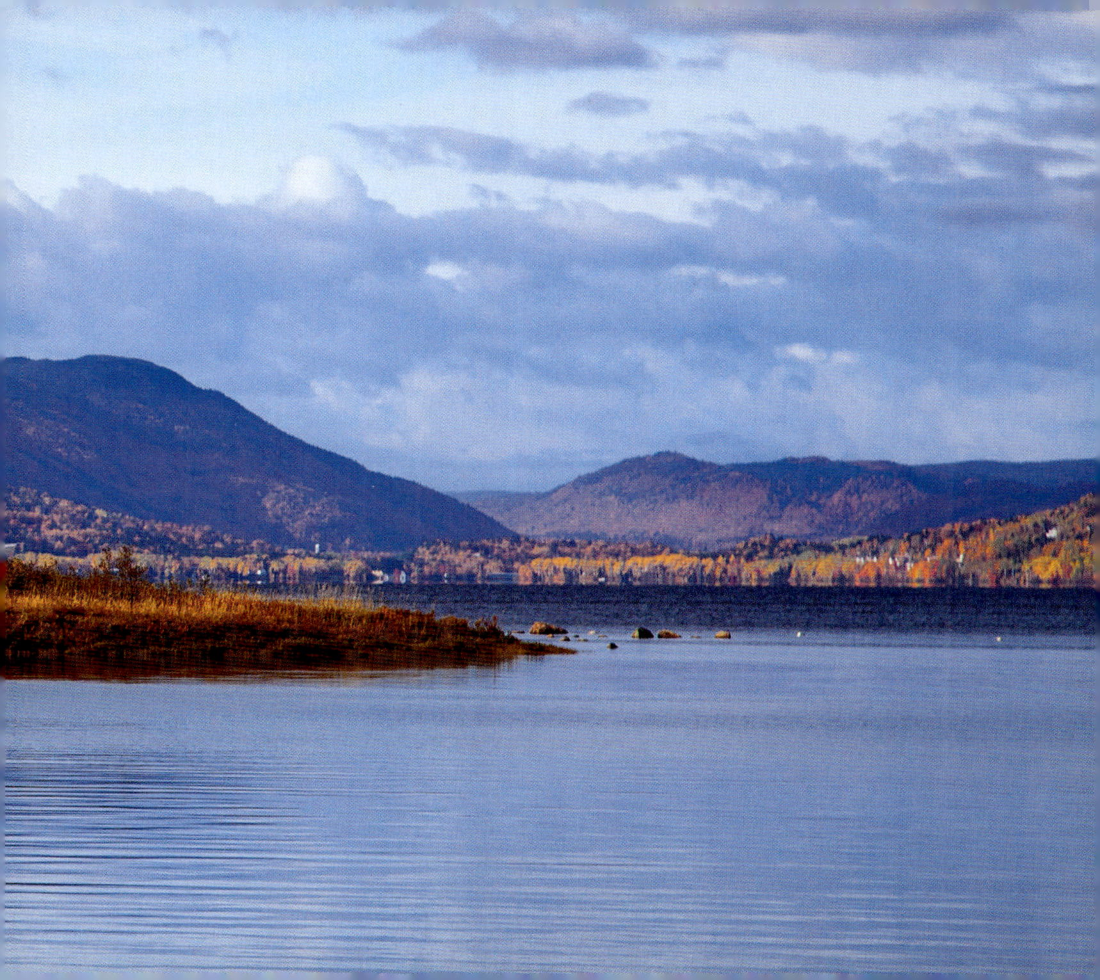

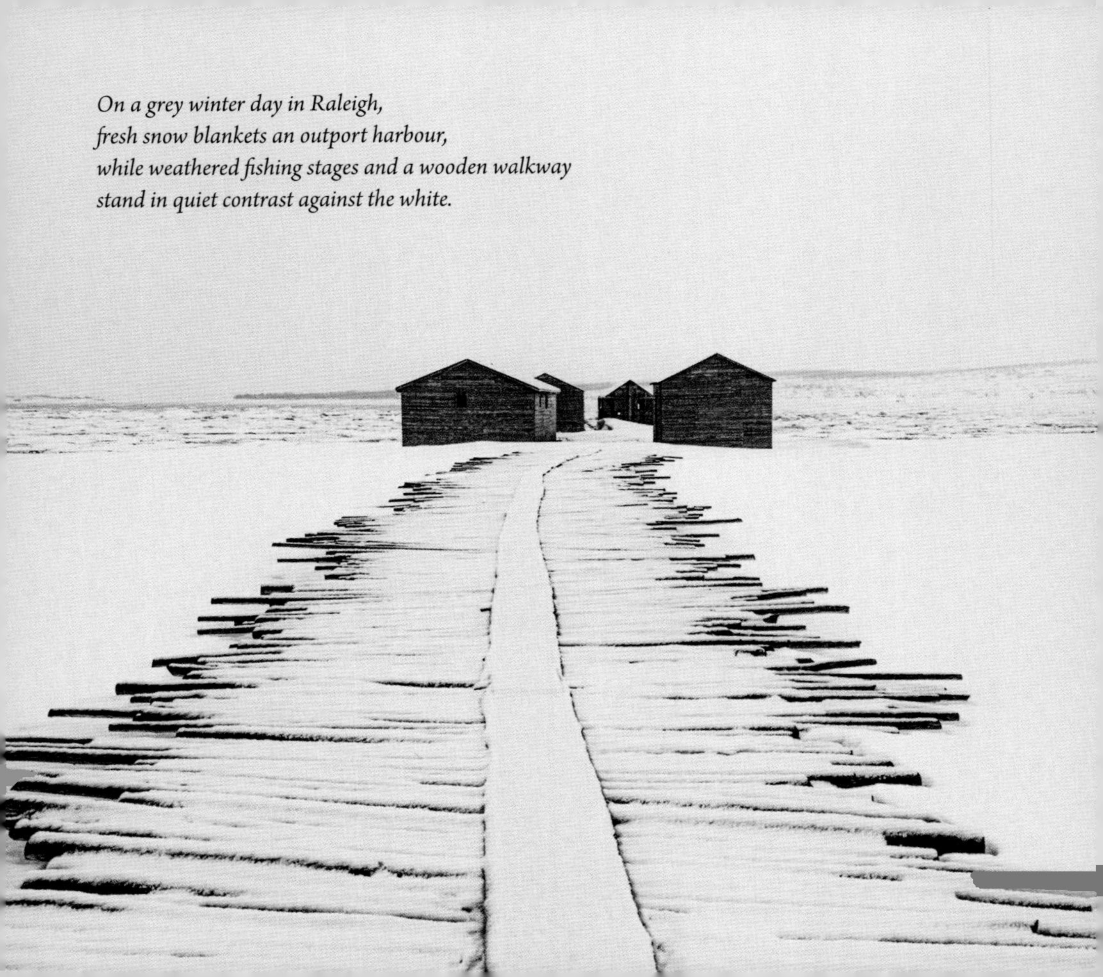

On a grey winter day in Raleigh,
fresh snow blankets an outport harbour,
while weathered fishing stages and a wooden walkway
stand in quiet contrast against the white.

After release at Cape Norman, a young polar bear steps free from its transport and makes its way into the Strait of Belle Isle, washing clean in the cold waters of the Atlantic.

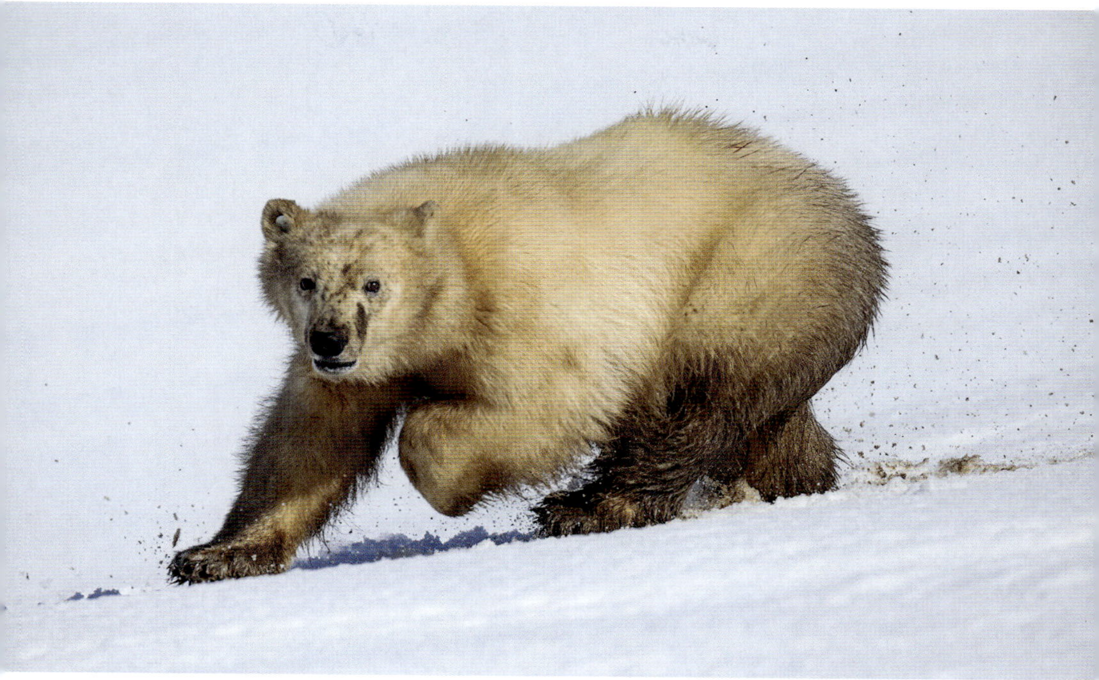

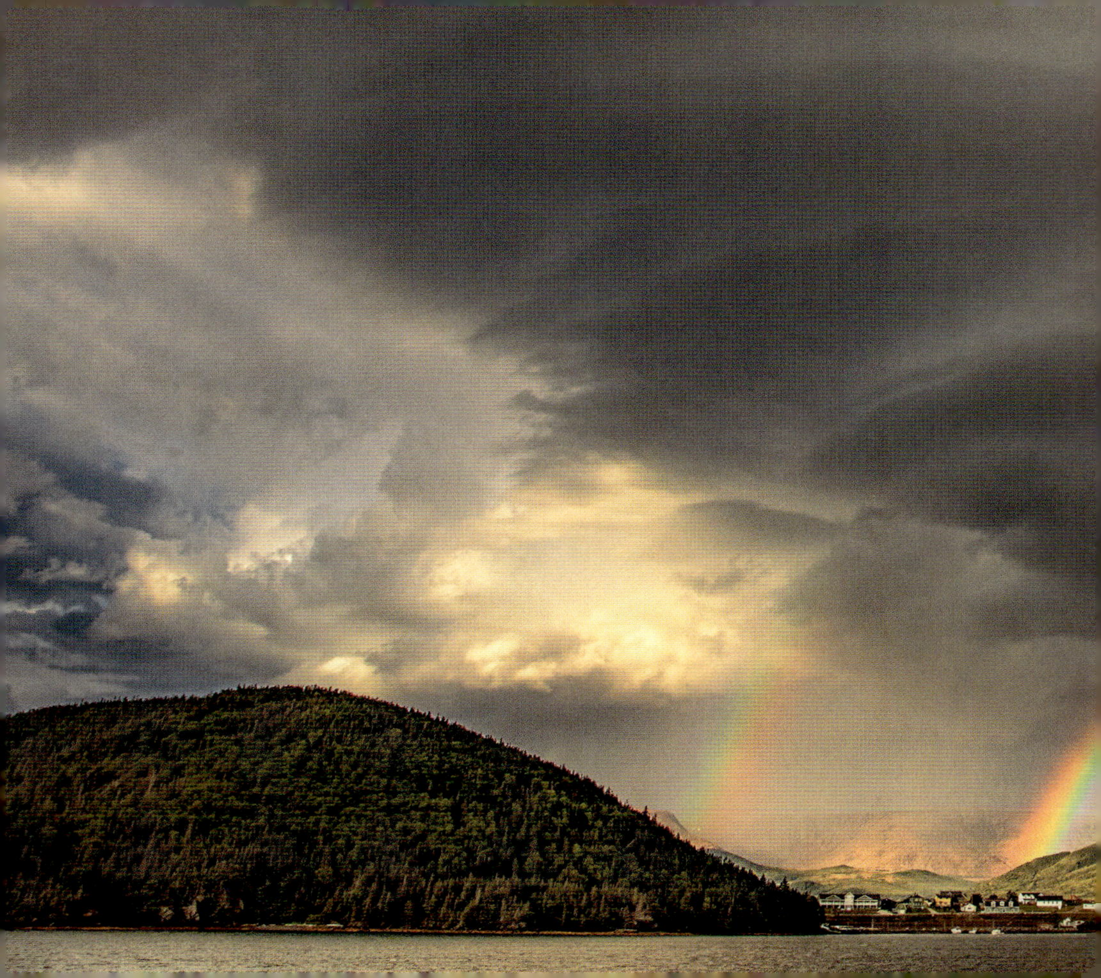

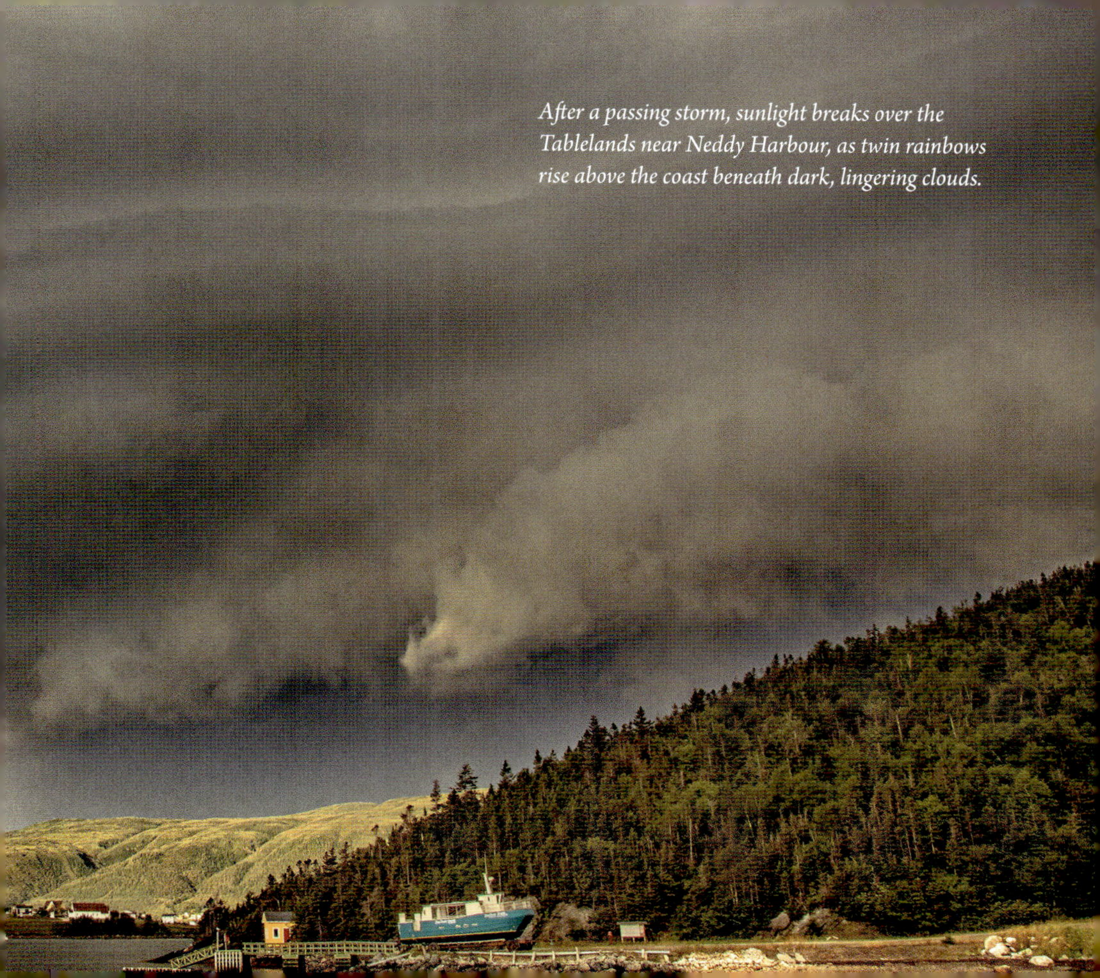

After a passing storm, sunlight breaks over the Tablelands near Neddy Harbour, as twin rainbows rise above the coast beneath dark, lingering clouds.

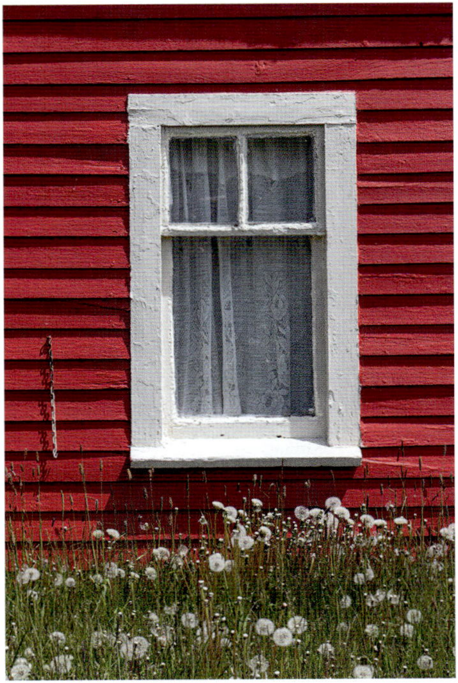

In warm sunlight, a single white-framed window glows on a red saltbox home in Tor's Cove, with green grass and dandelions resting below.

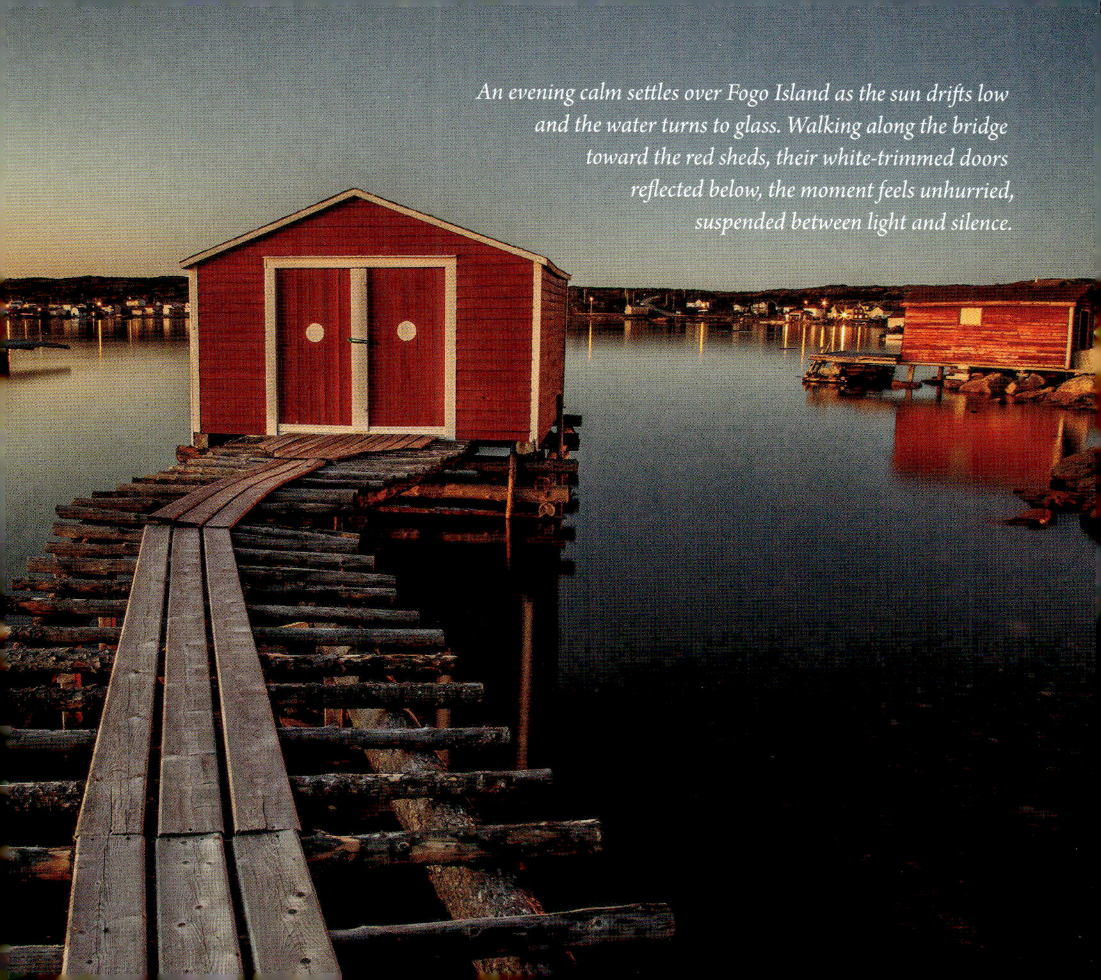

An evening calm settles over Fogo Island as the sun drifts low and the water turns to glass. Walking along the bridge toward the red sheds, their white-trimmed doors reflected below, the moment feels unhurried, suspended between light and silence.

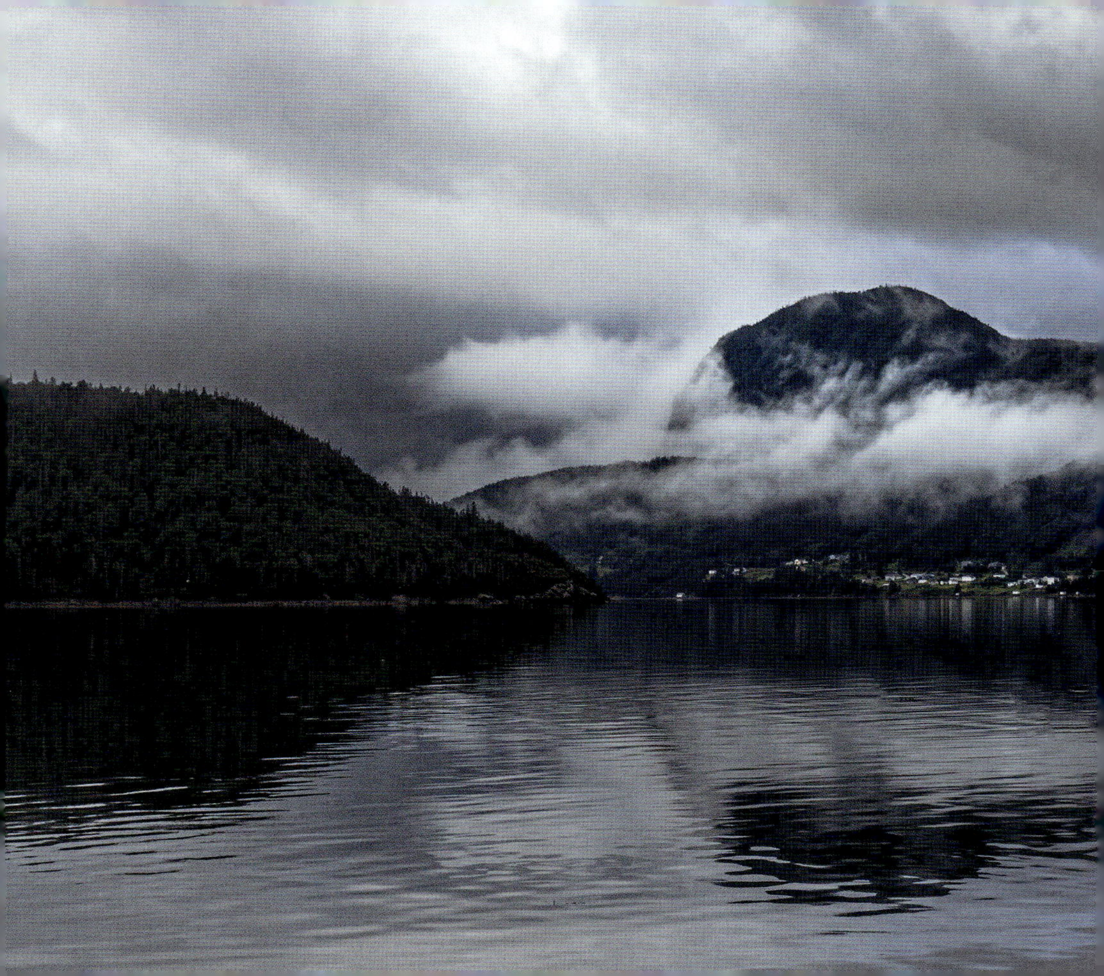

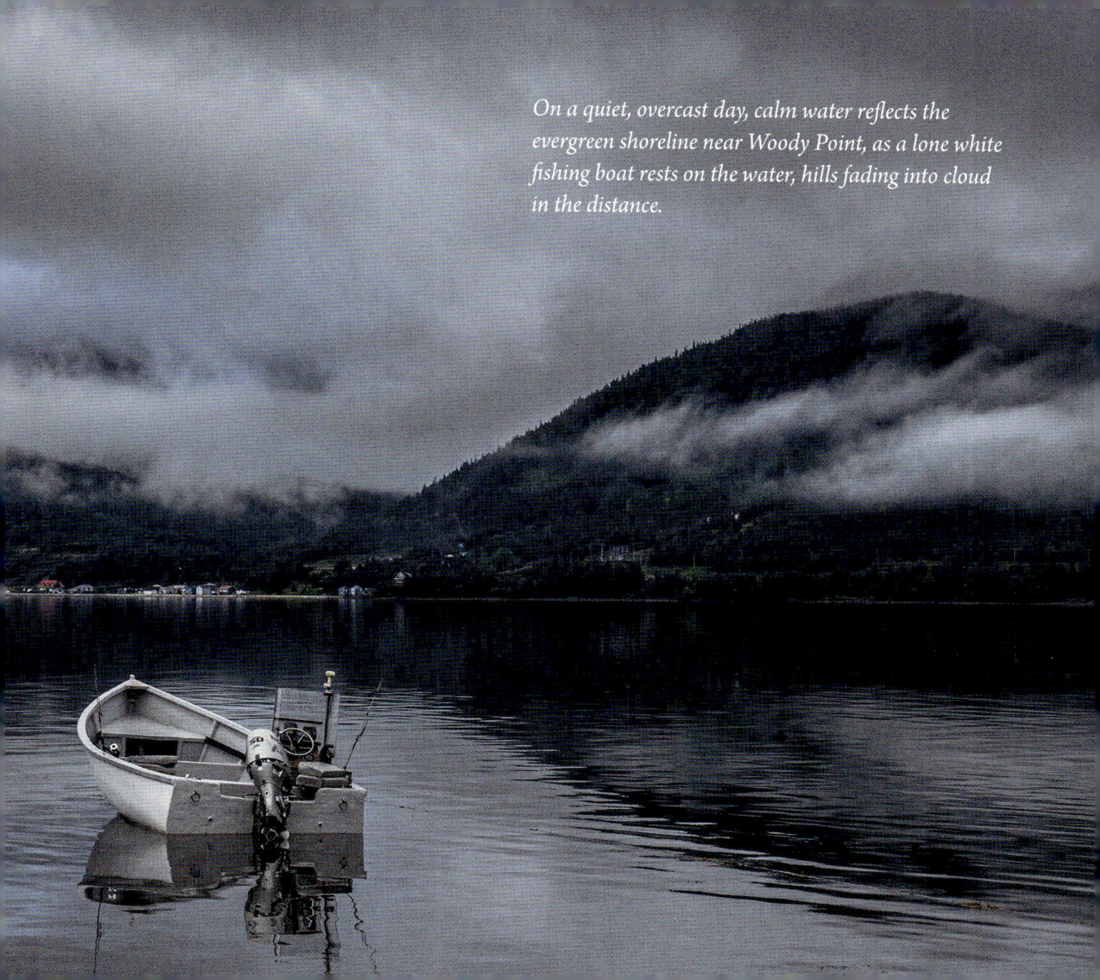

On a quiet, overcast day, calm water reflects the evergreen shoreline near Woody Point, as a lone white fishing boat rests on the water, hills fading into cloud in the distance.

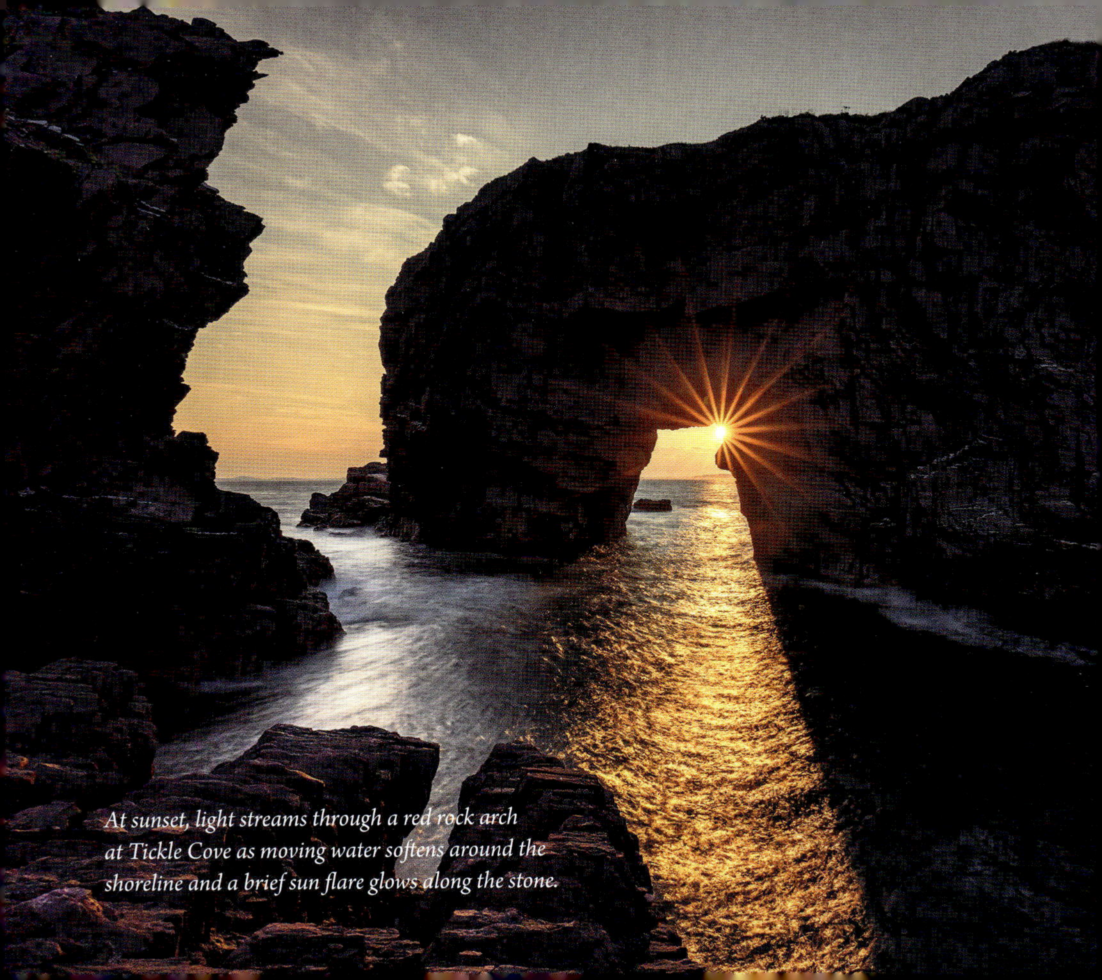

At sunset, light streams through a red rock arch at Tickle Cove as moving water softens around the shoreline and a brief sun flare glows along the stone.

In golden evening light, a humpback whale slips beneath the surface off the coast of Newfoundland, as water falls from its tail and glows orange against dark rock and sea.

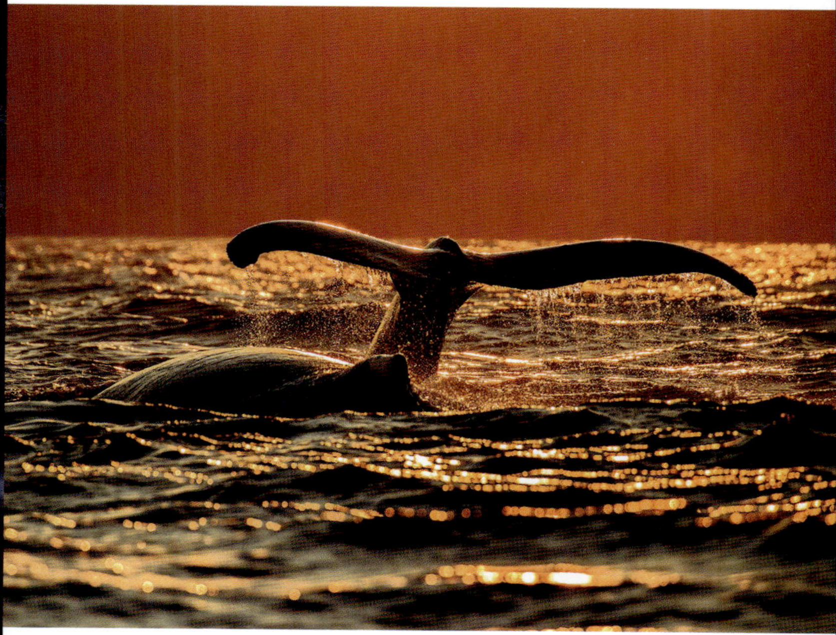

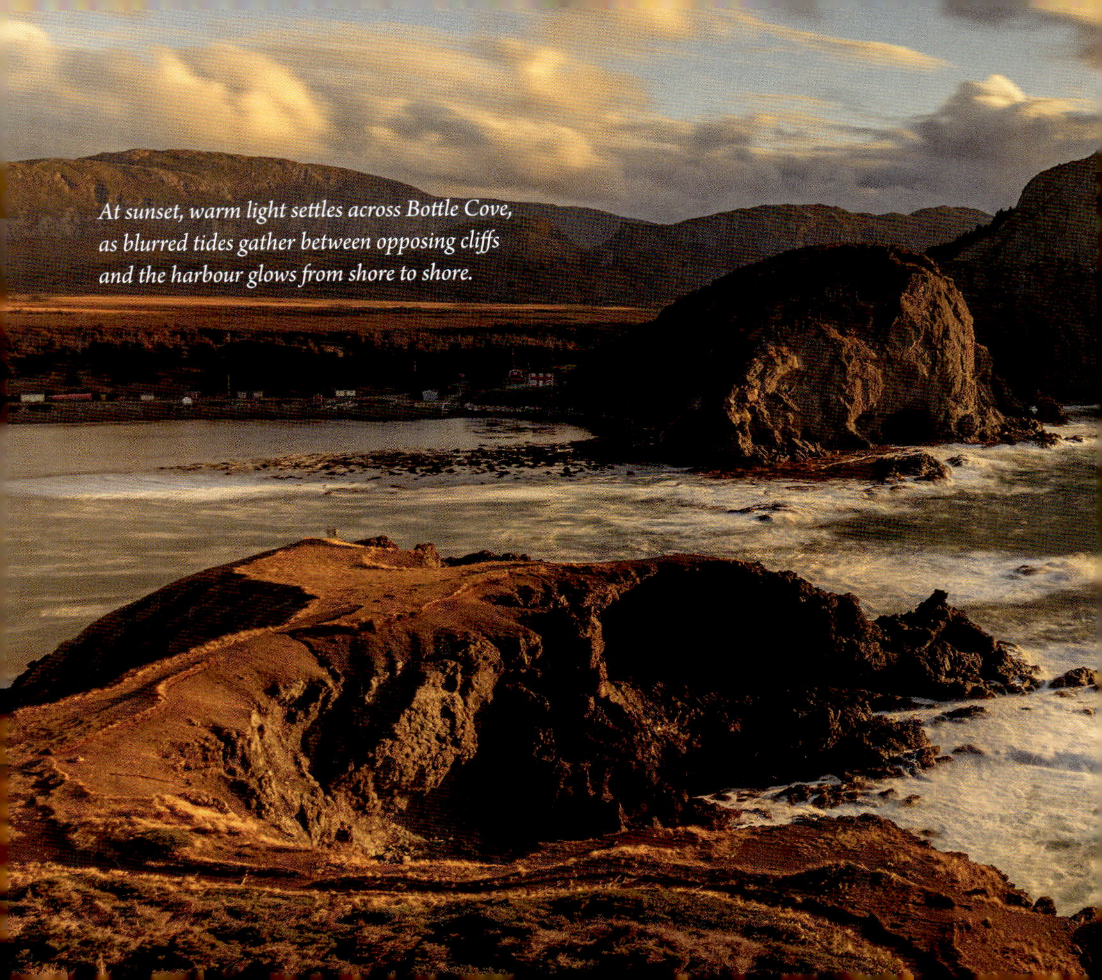

At sunset, warm light settles across Bottle Cove, as blurred tides gather between opposing cliffs and the harbour glows from shore to shore.

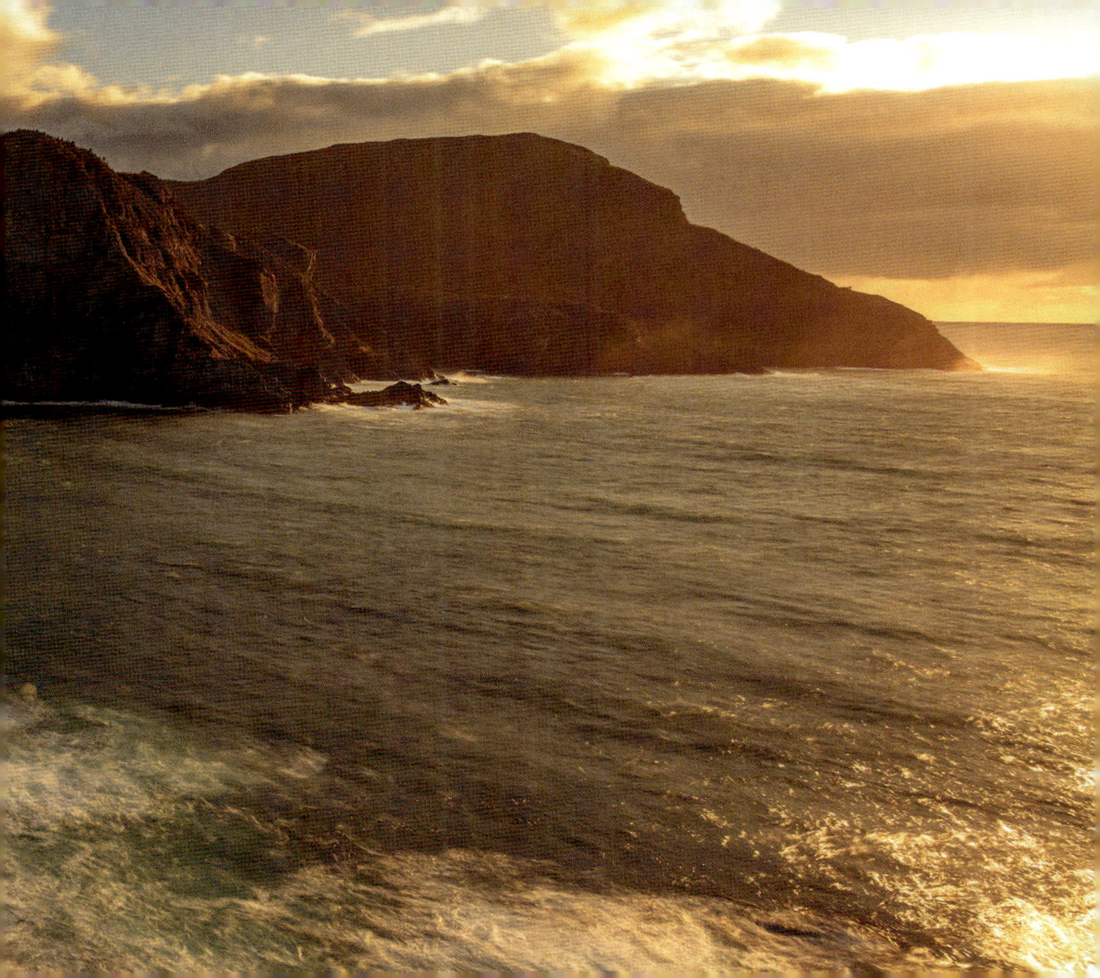

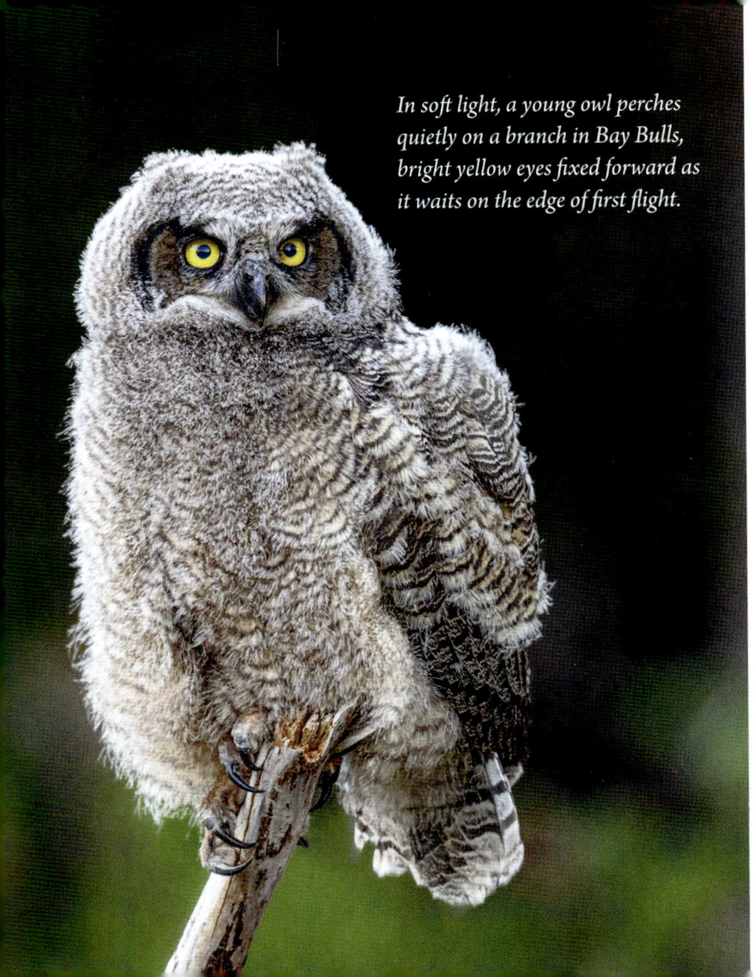

In soft light, a young owl perches quietly on a branch in Bay Bulls, bright yellow eyes fixed forward as it waits on the edge of first flight.

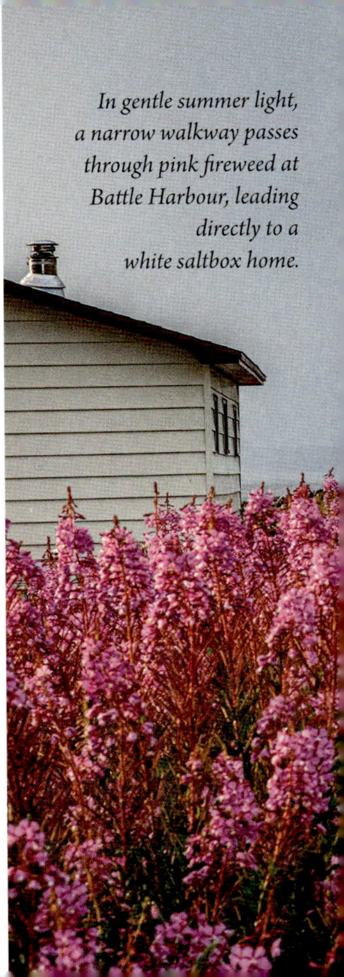

In gentle summer light, a narrow walkway passes through pink fireweed at Battle Harbour, leading directly to a white saltbox home.

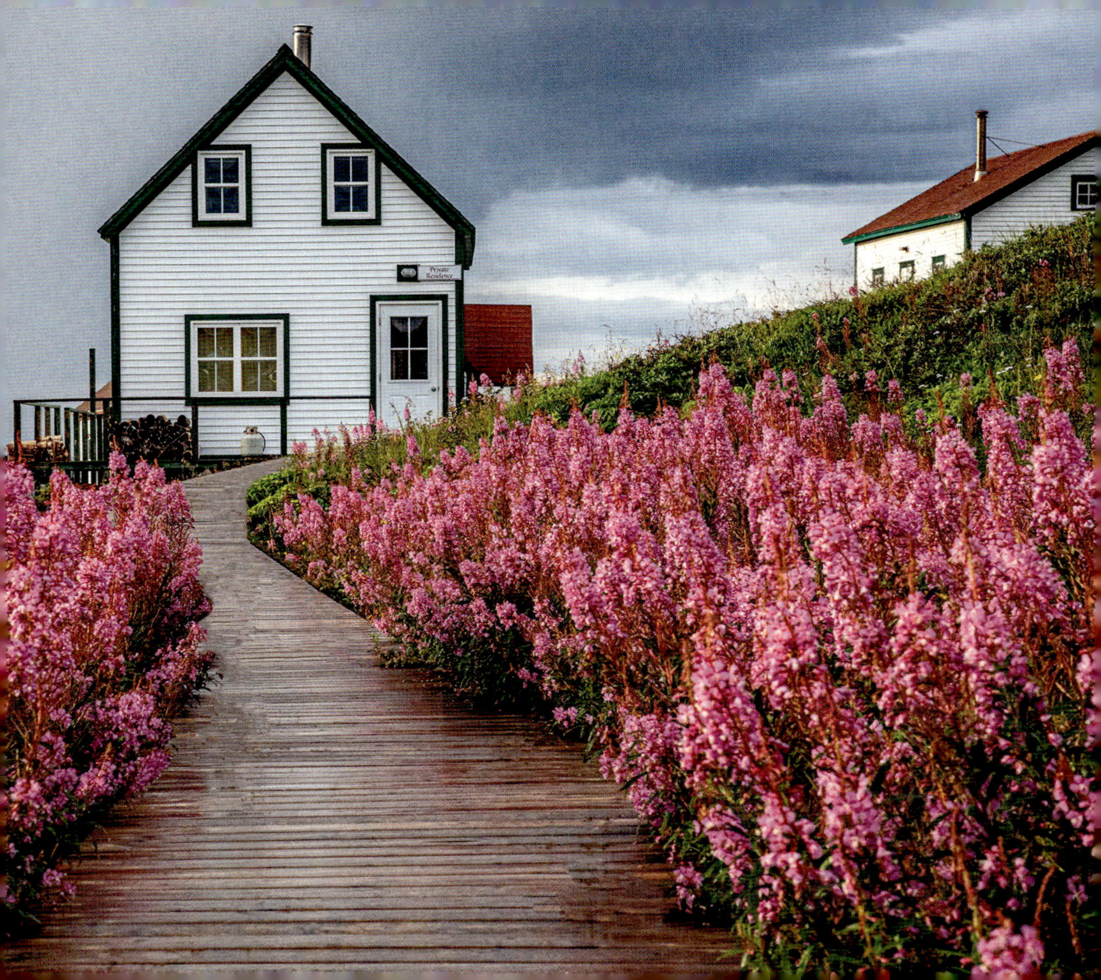
Private
Residence

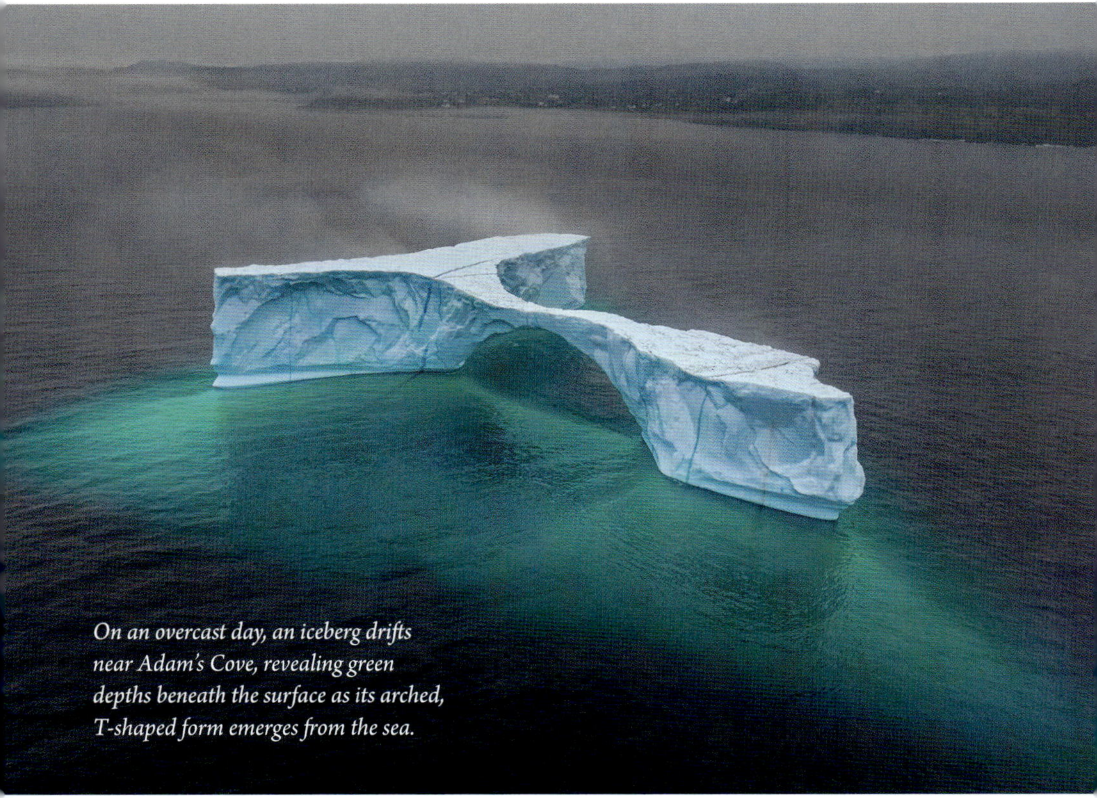

On an overcast day, an iceberg drifts near Adam's Cove, revealing green depths beneath the surface as its arched, T-shaped form emerges from the sea.

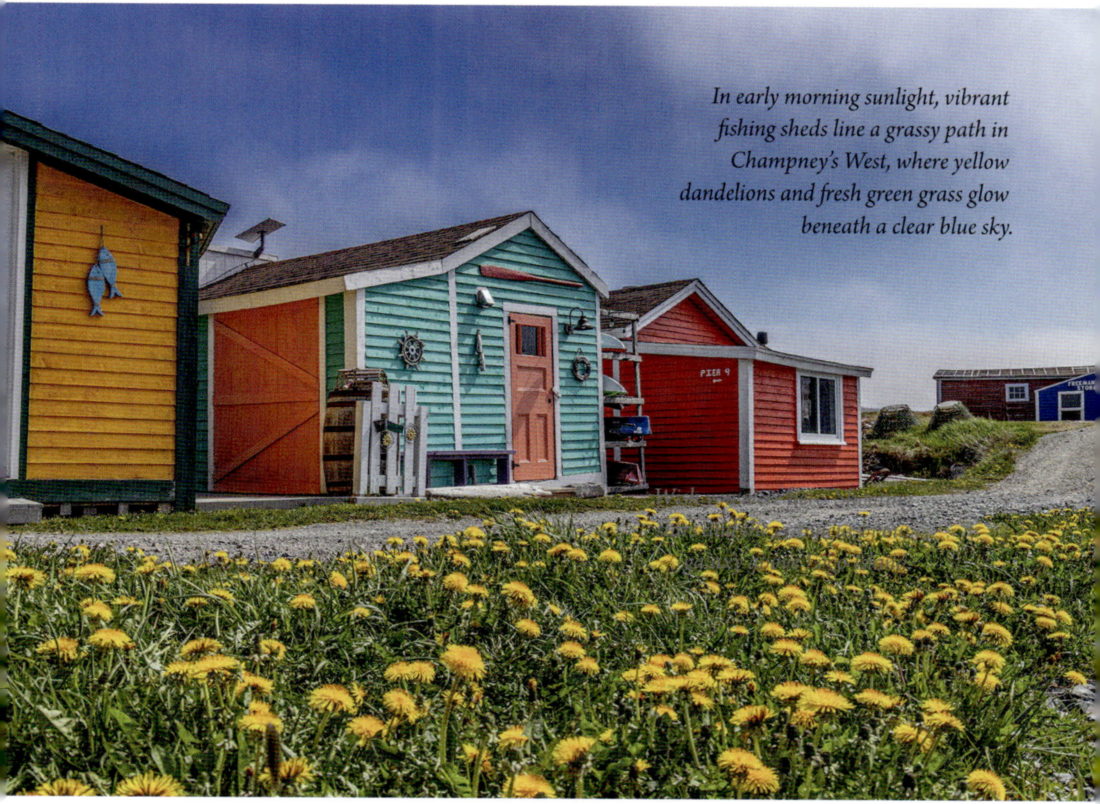

In early morning sunlight, vibrant fishing sheds line a grassy path in Champney's West, where yellow dandelions and fresh green grass glow beneath a clear blue sky.

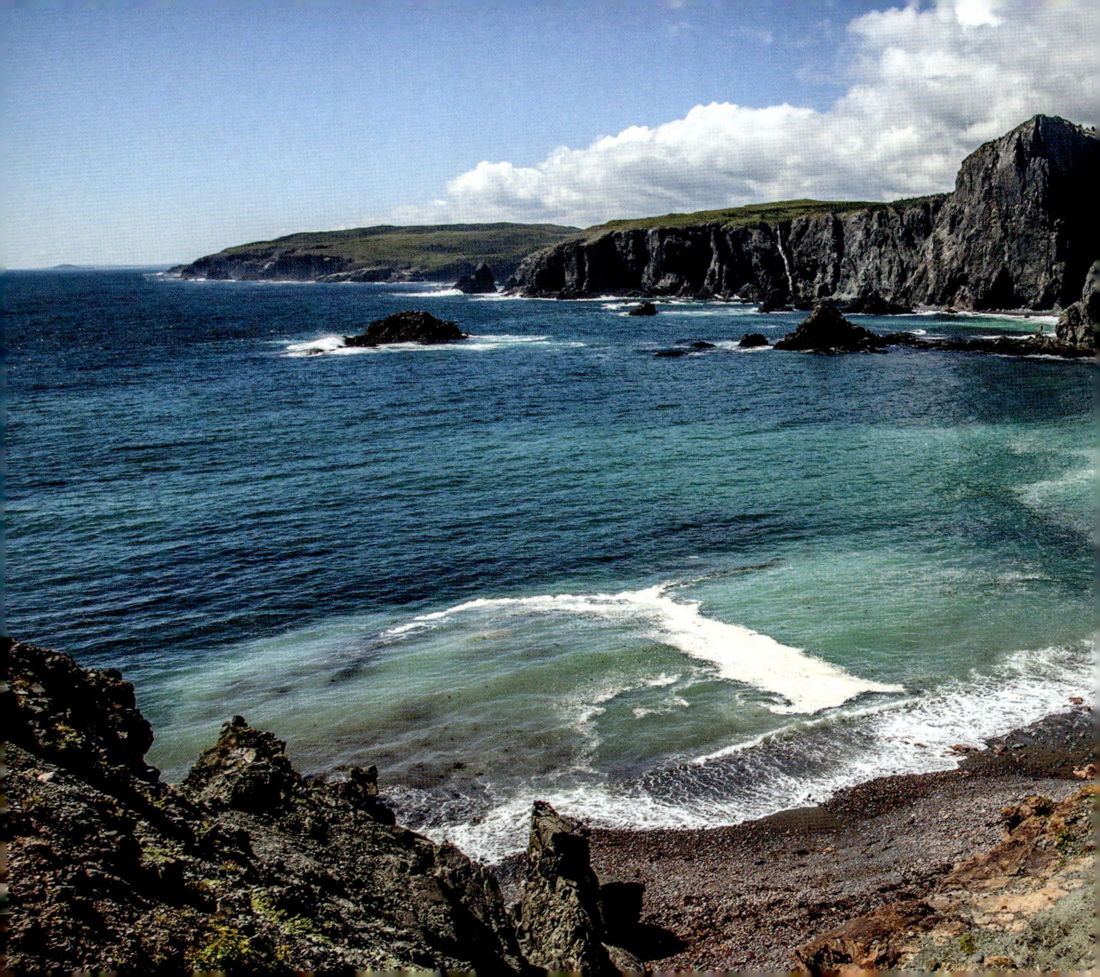

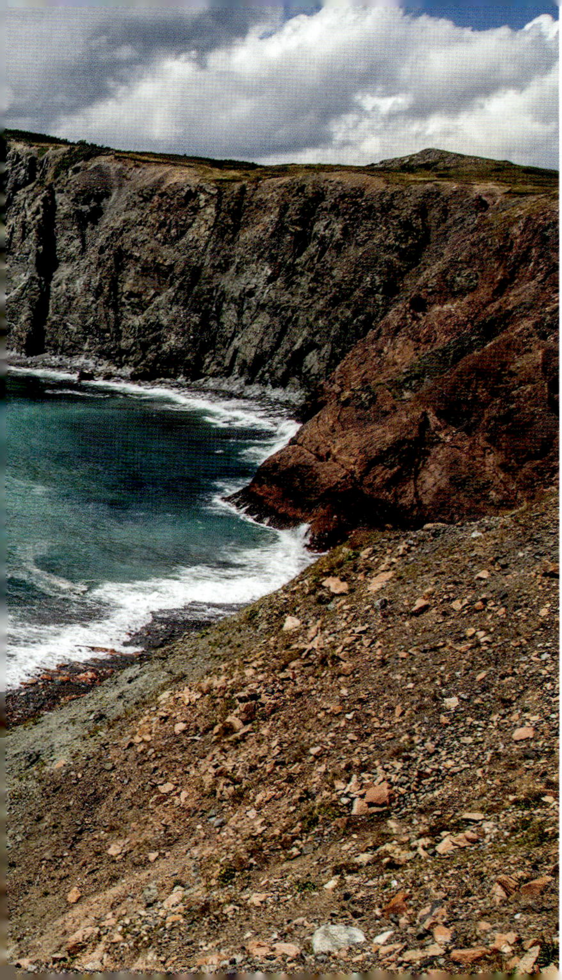

In bright sunlight, rugged cliffs rise above Chambers Cove, standing in stark contrast to the winter night when US Navy ships were wrecked along this shore.

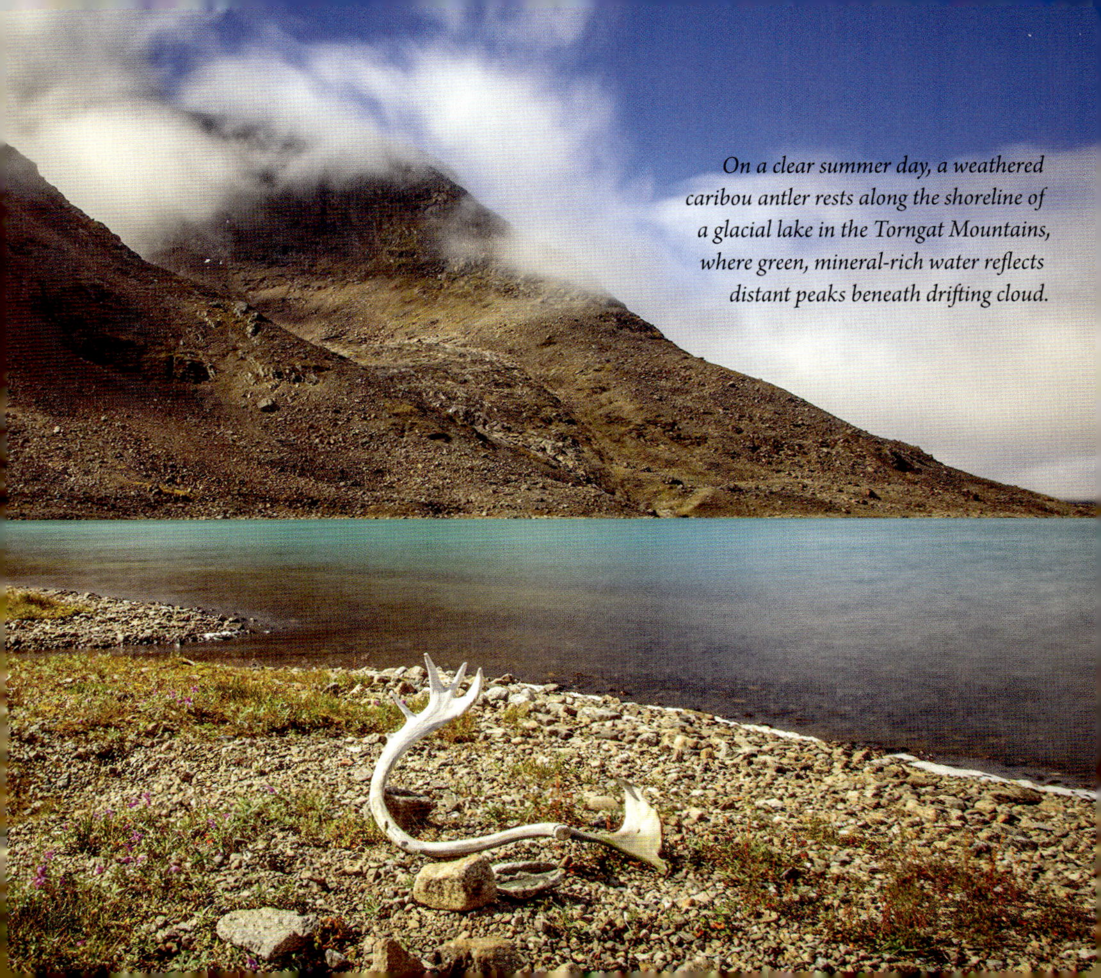

On a clear summer day, a weathered caribou antler rests along the shoreline of a glacial lake in the Torngat Mountains, where green, mineral-rich water reflects distant peaks beneath drifting cloud.

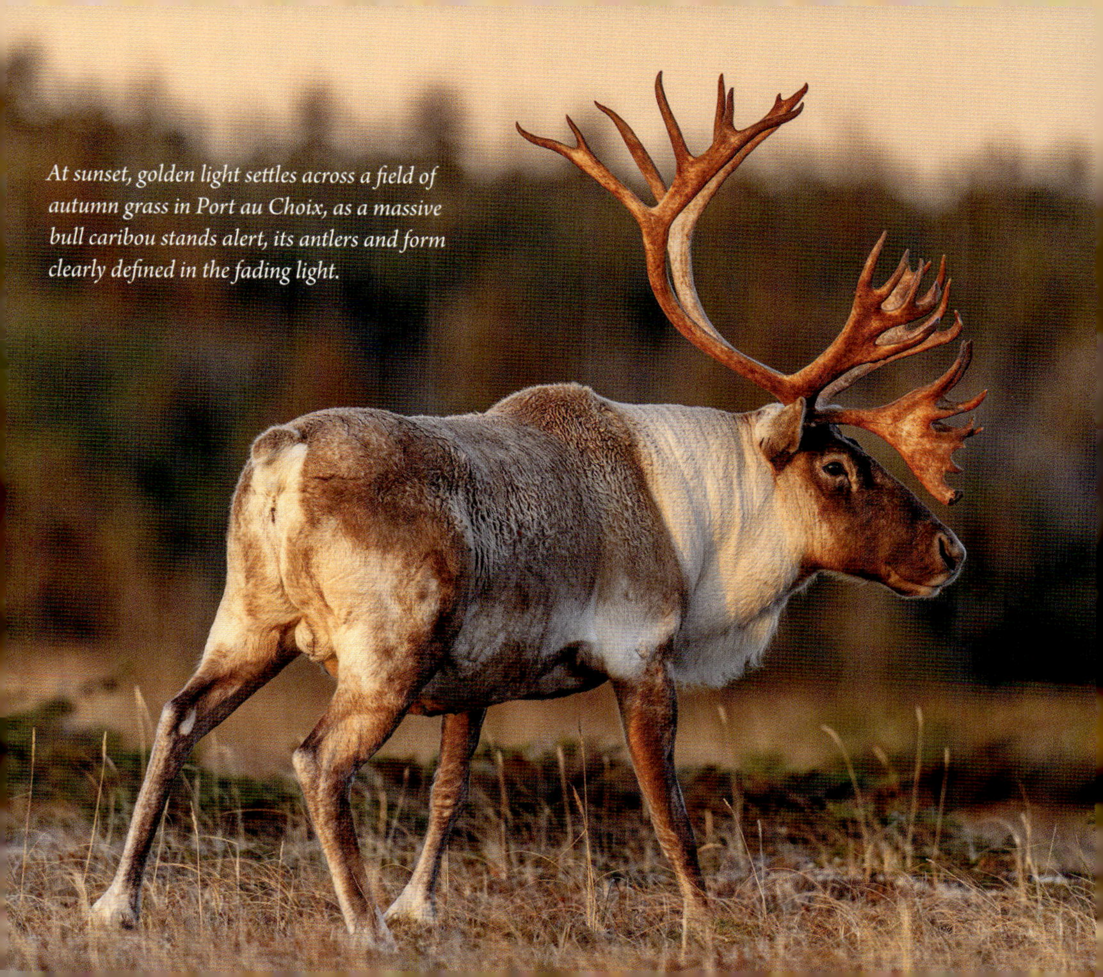

At sunset, golden light settles across a field of autumn grass in Port au Choix, as a massive bull caribou stands alert, its antlers and form clearly defined in the fading light.

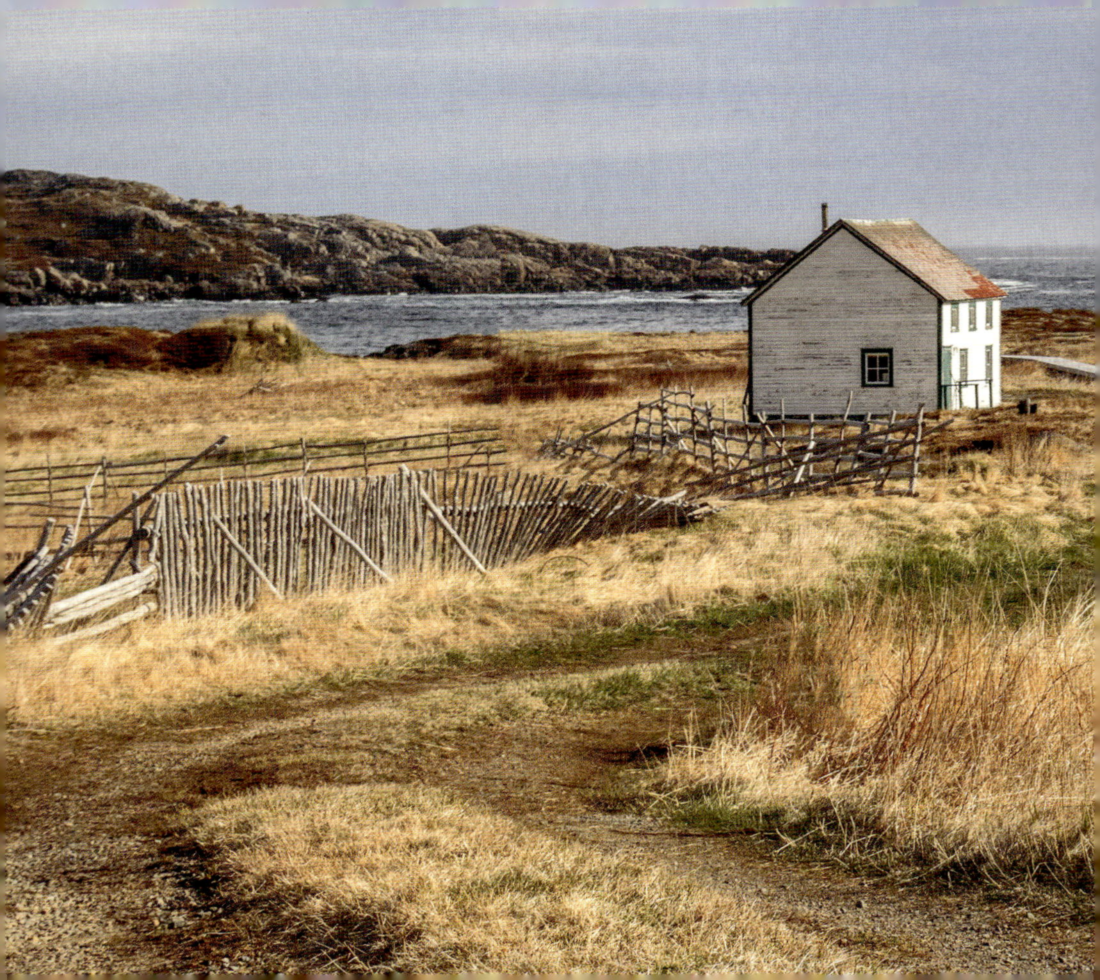

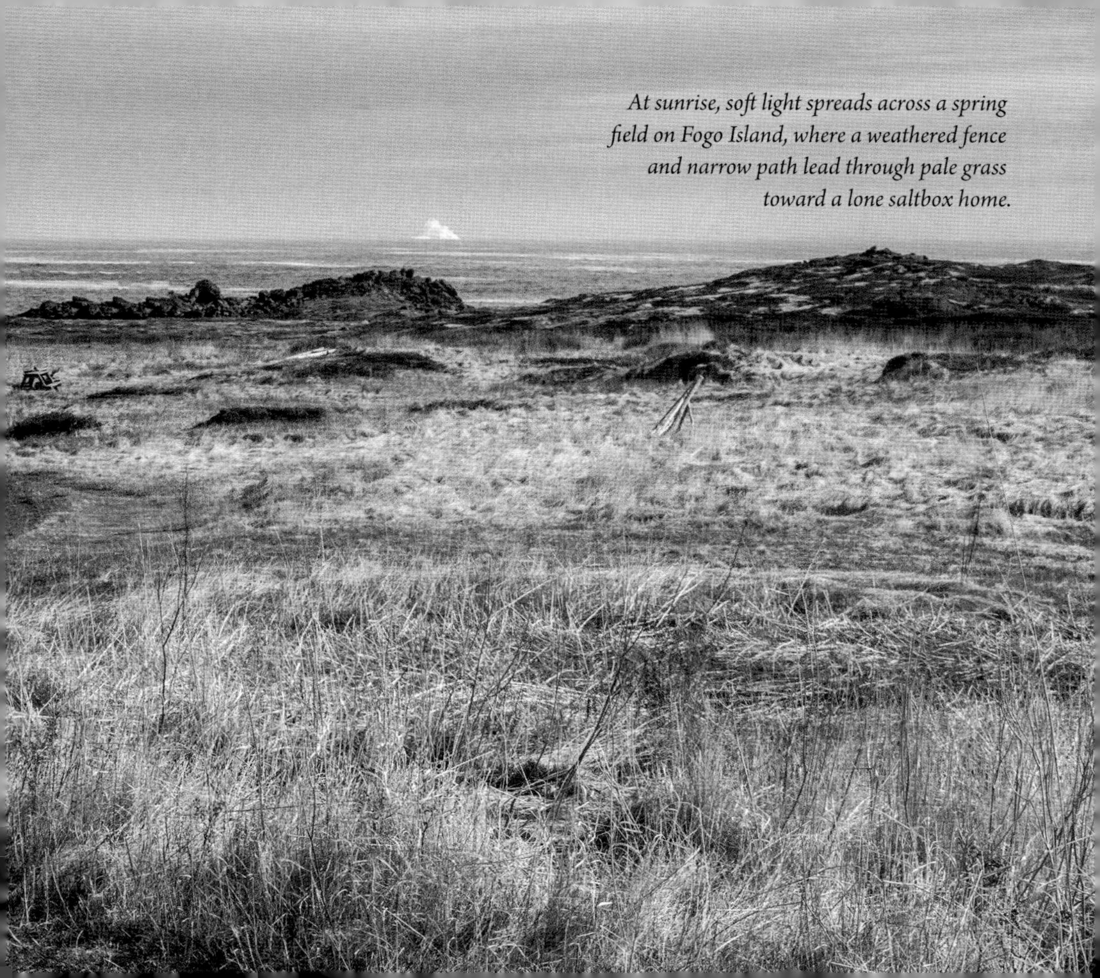

At sunrise, soft light spreads across a spring field on Fogo Island, where a weathered fence and narrow path lead through pale grass toward a lone saltbox home.

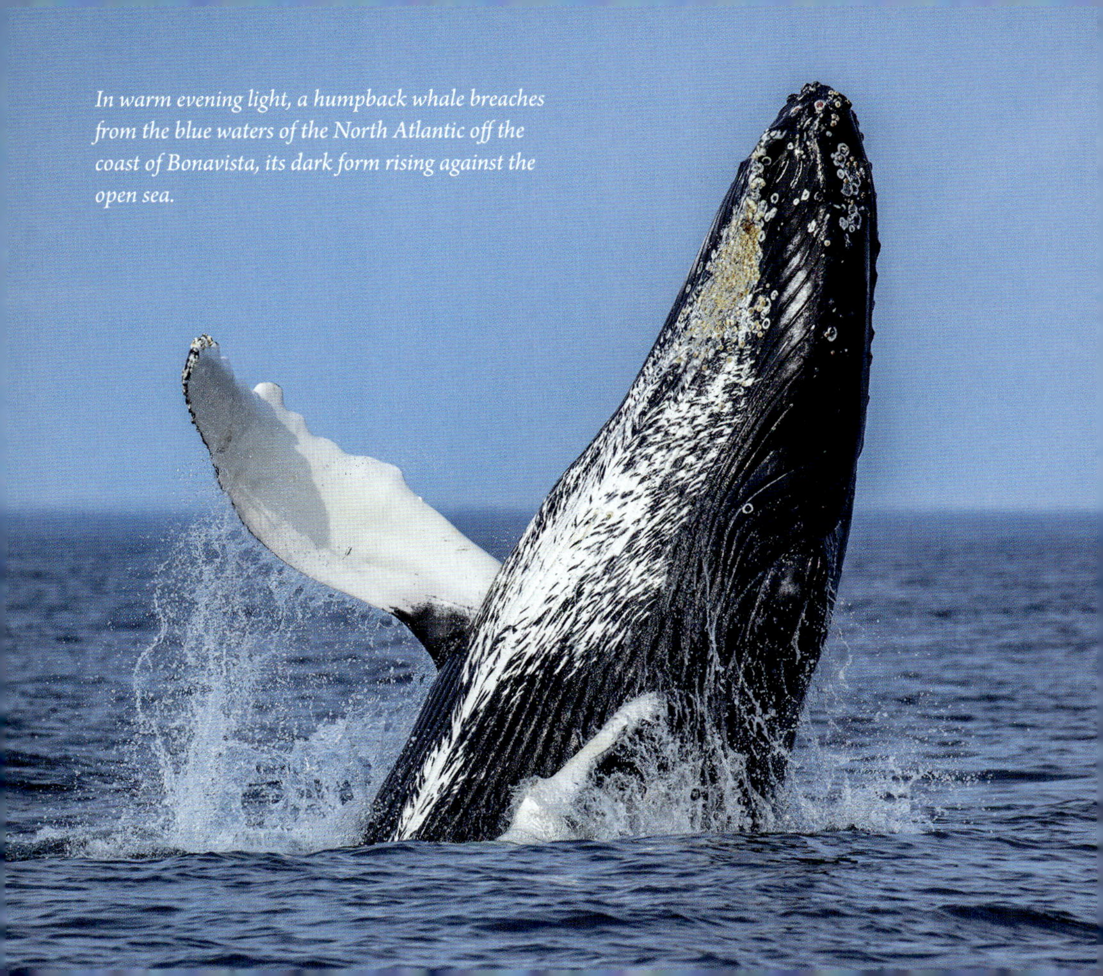

In warm evening light, a humpback whale breaches from the blue waters of the North Atlantic off the coast of Bonavista, its dark form rising against the open sea.

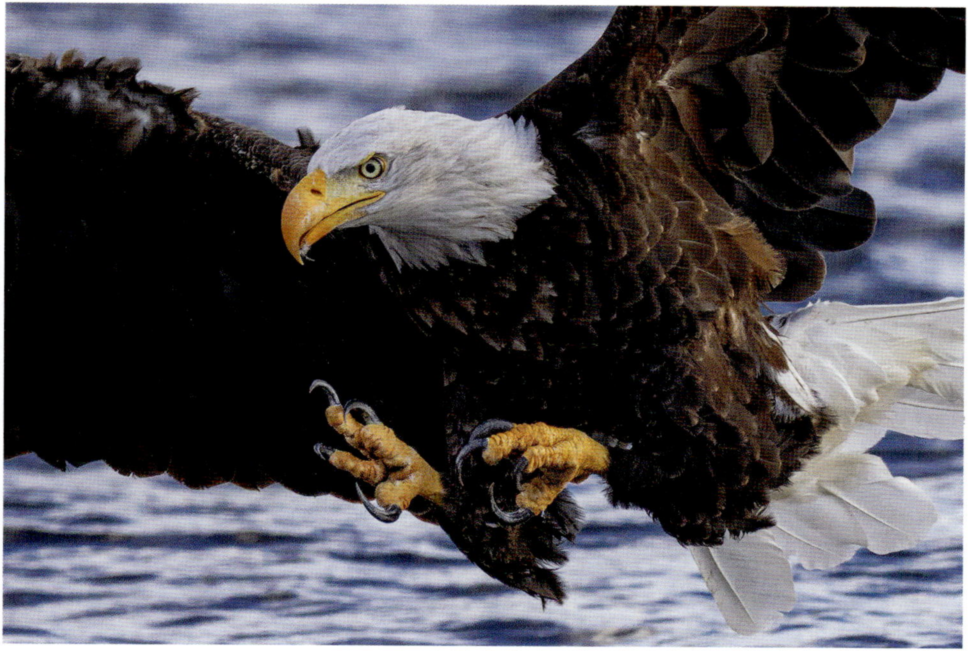

At sunrise, a bald eagle descends toward the ocean in Cox's Cove, its talons extended and gaze fixed as it reaches for prey beneath the surface.

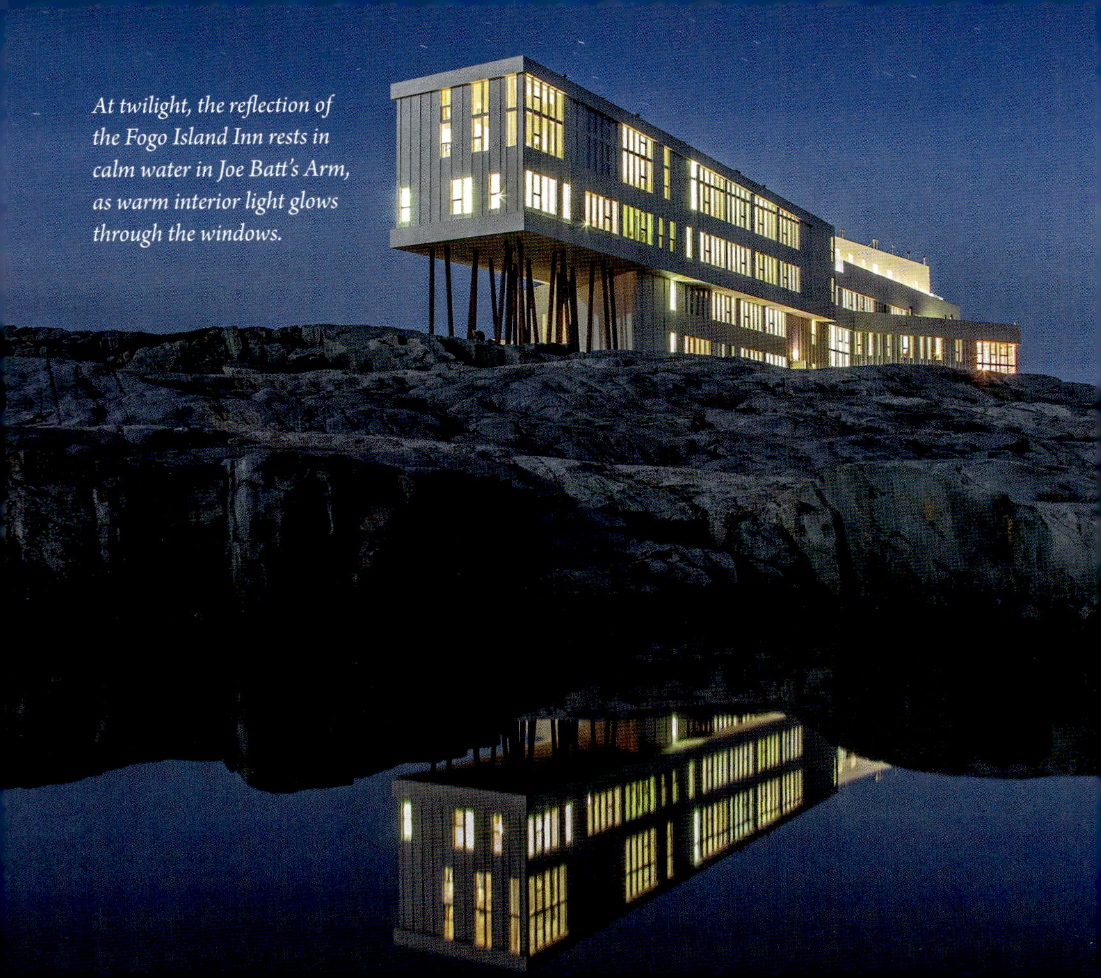

At twilight, the reflection of the Fogo Island Inn rests in calm water in Joe Batt's Arm, as warm interior light glows through the windows.

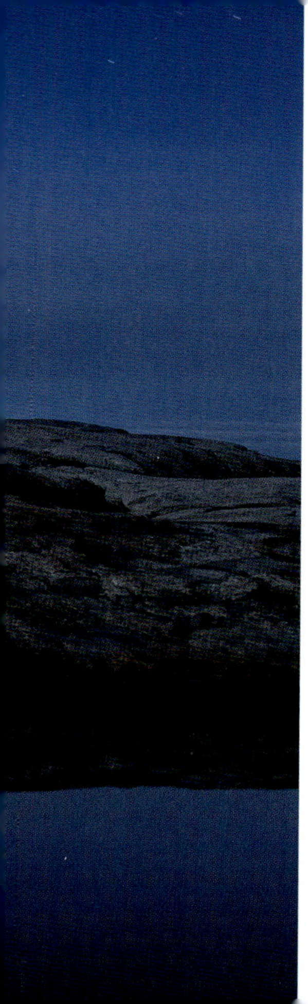

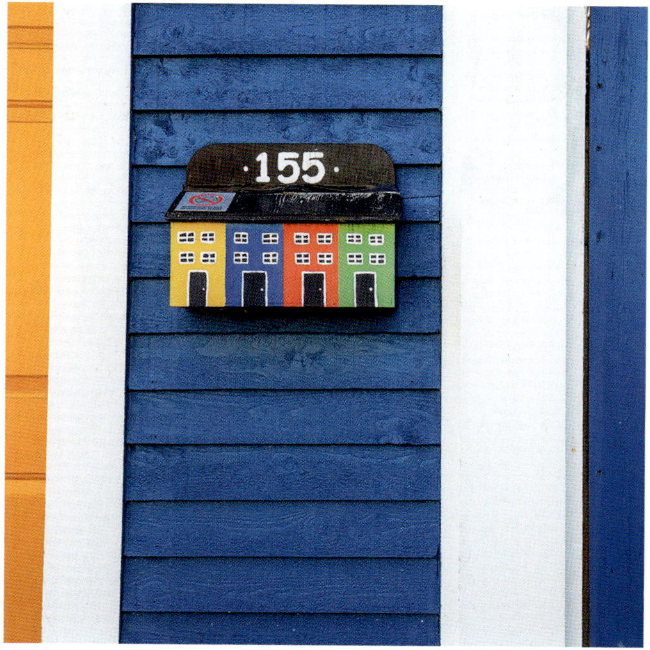

On the blue clapboard of a downtown home in St. John's, a brightly painted wooden mailbox mimics the smallest details of the playful palette of the city's well-known houses.

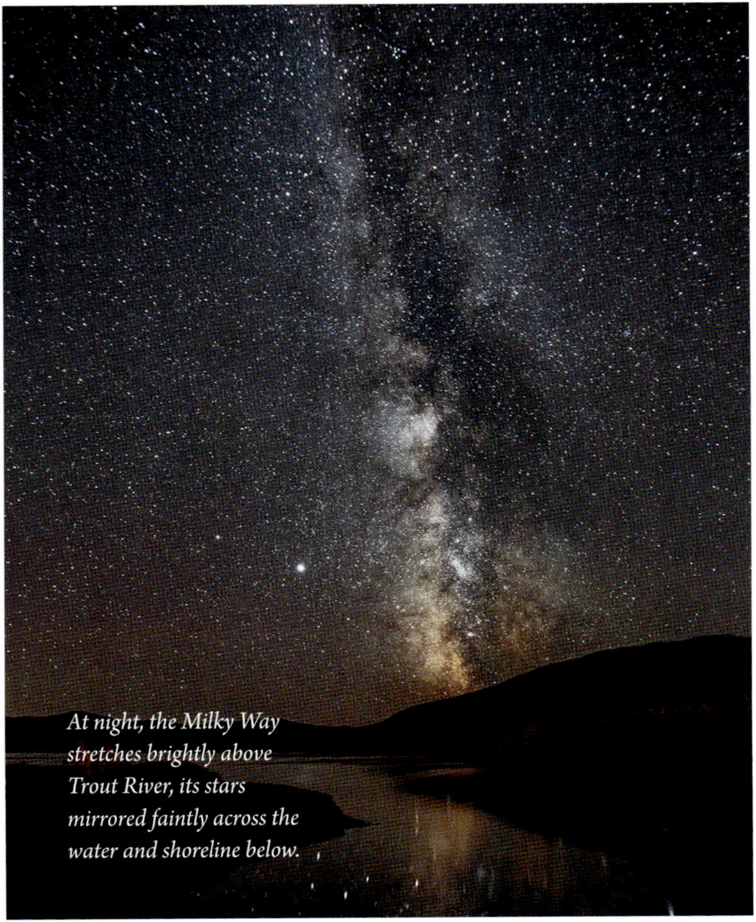

At night, the Milky Way stretches brightly above Trout River, its stars mirrored faintly across the water and shoreline below.

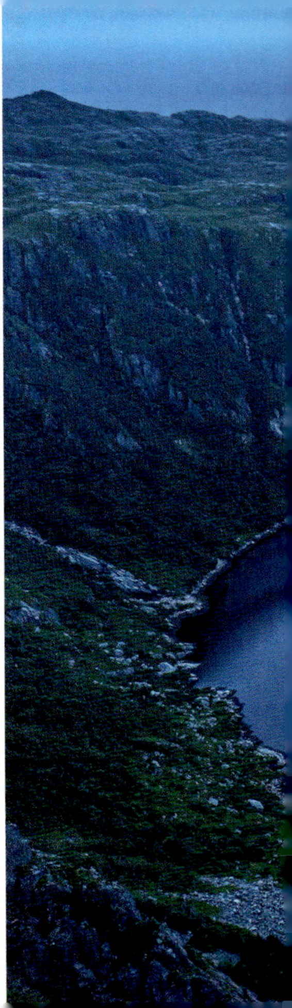

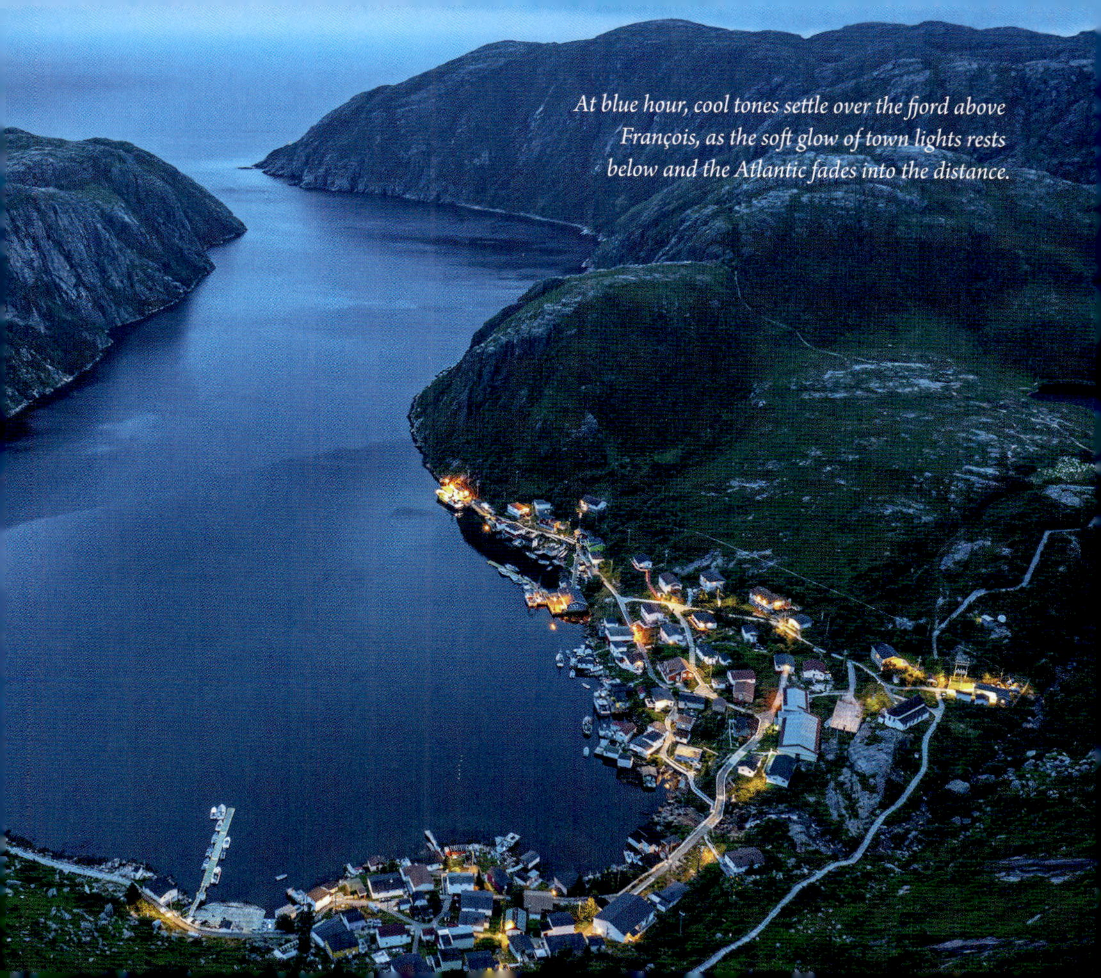

At blue hour, cool tones settle over the fjord above François, as the soft glow of town lights rests below and the Atlantic fades into the distance.

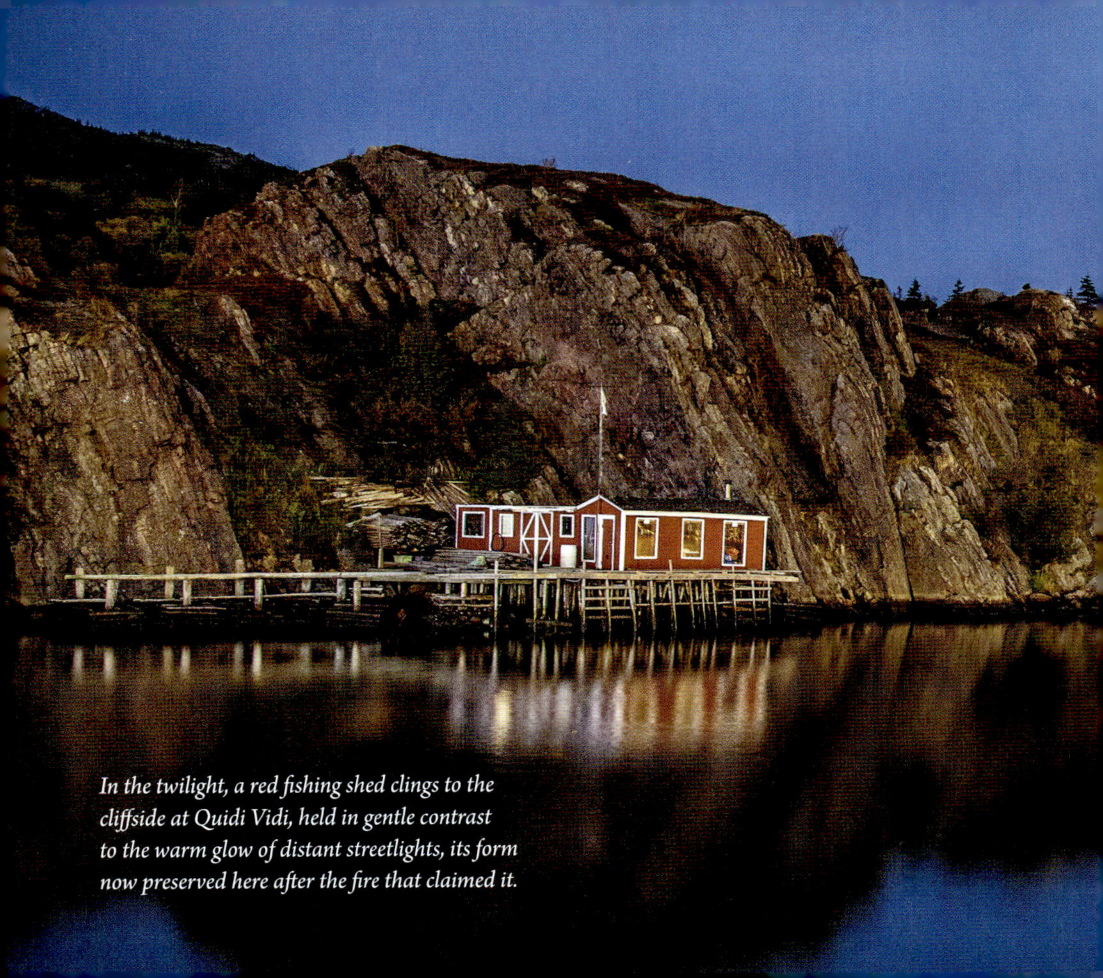

In the twilight, a red fishing shed clings to the cliffside at Quidi Vidi, held in gentle contrast to the warm glow of distant streetlights, its form now preserved here after the fire that claimed it.

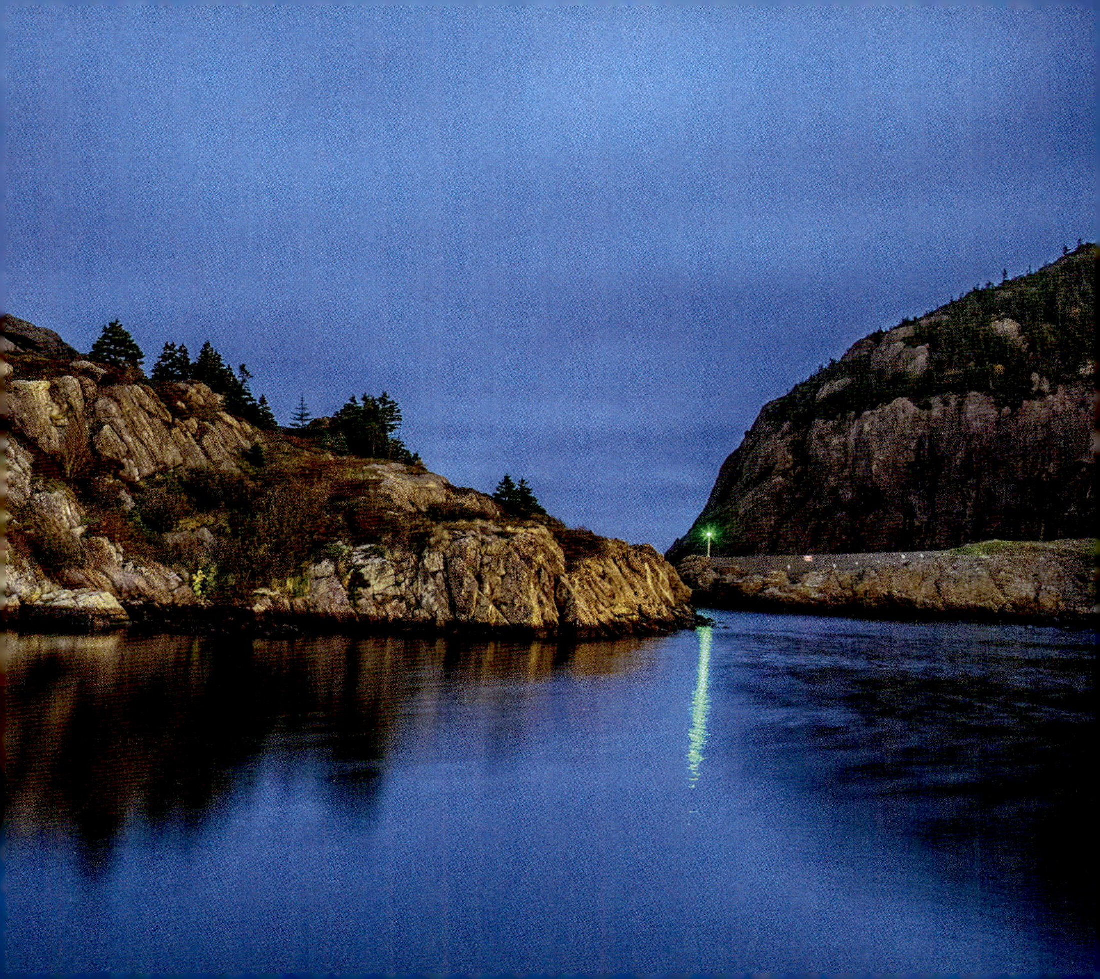

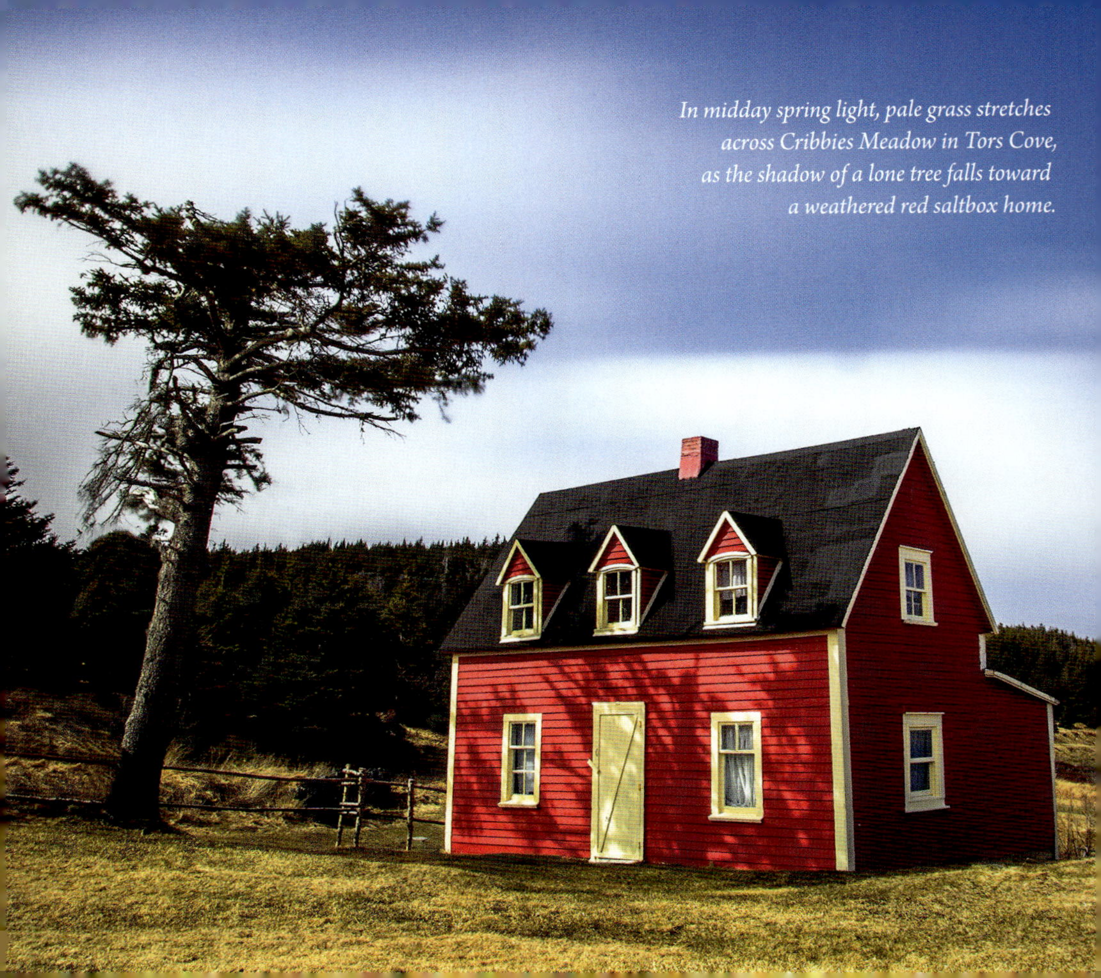

In midday spring light, pale grass stretches across Cribbies Meadow in Tors Cove, as the shadow of a lone tree falls toward a weathered red saltbox home.

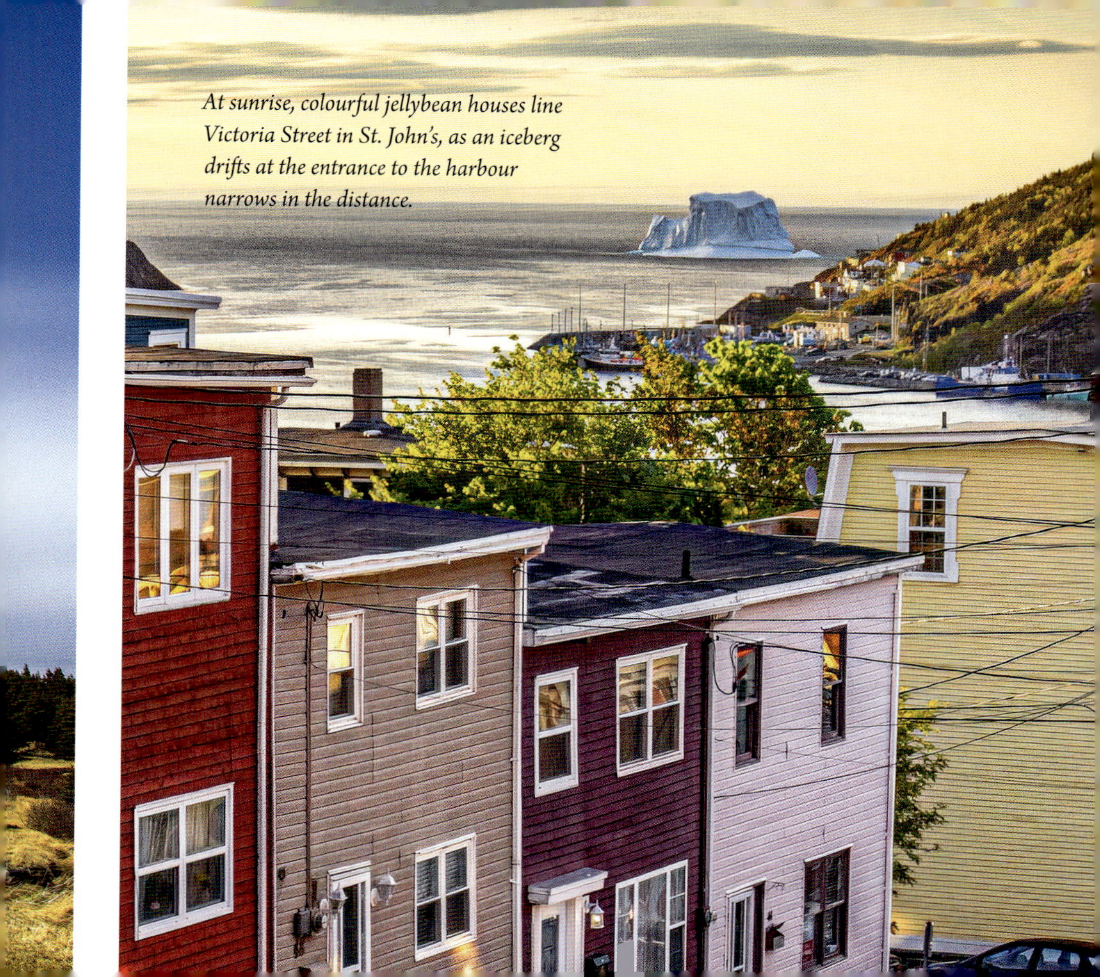

At sunrise, colourful jellybean houses line Victoria Street in St. John's, as an iceberg drifts at the entrance to the harbour narrows in the distance.

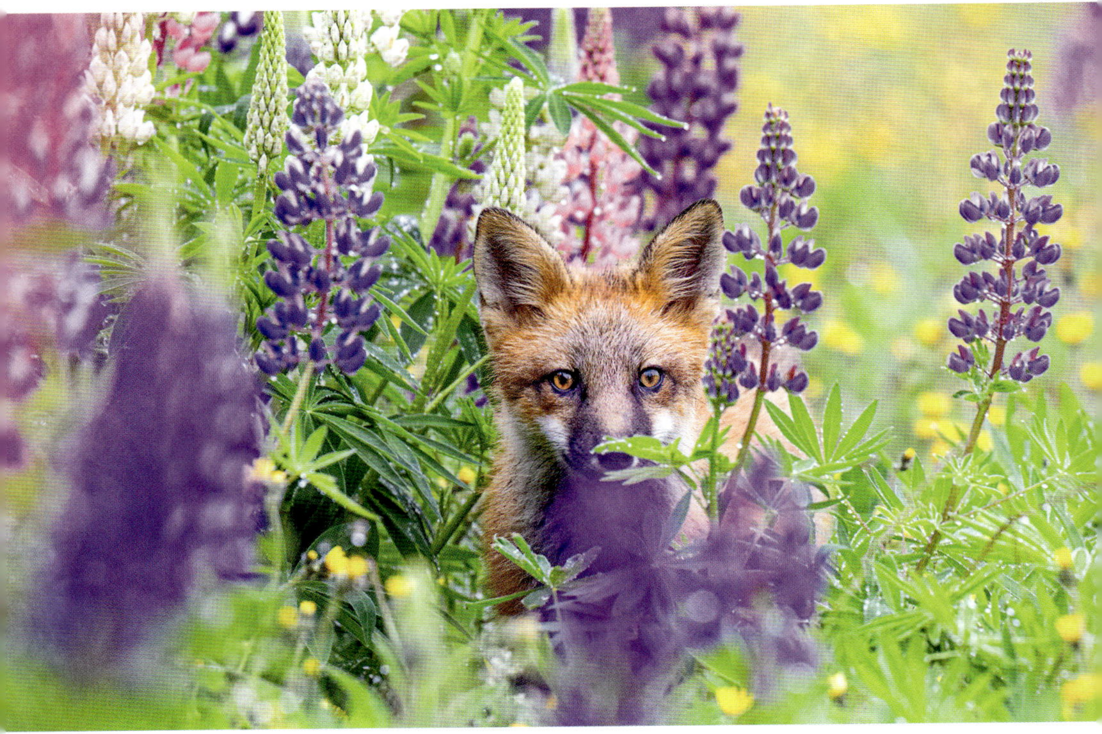

In soft summer light, a red fox pauses among blooming lupins in Catalina, its gaze fixed forward amid purple, pink, and green fields.

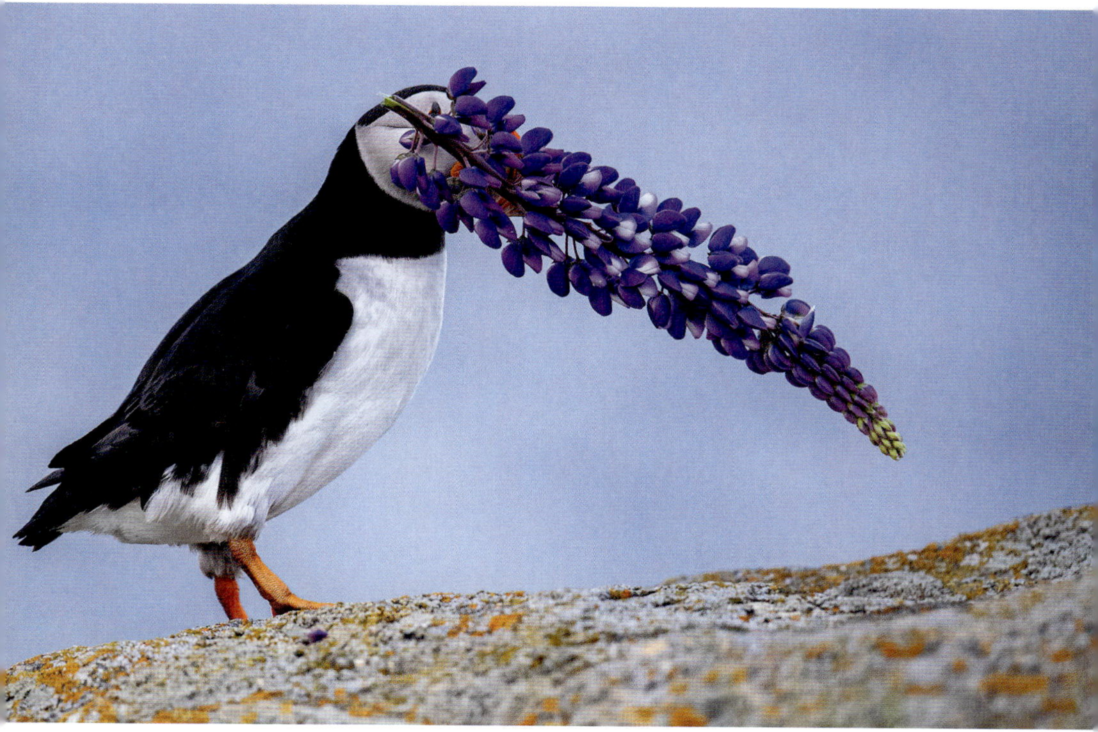

Against a clear blue sky, an Atlantic puffin stands at the edge of a cliff in Elliston, holding a purple lupin stem that rests brightly against its dark plumage.

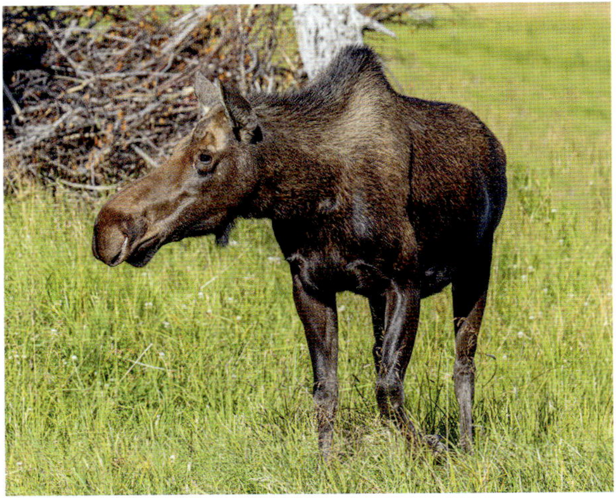

In bright sunlight, a moose stands quietly in tall grass—a species introduced to the island in the early 1900s that has since become deeply woven into the landscape.

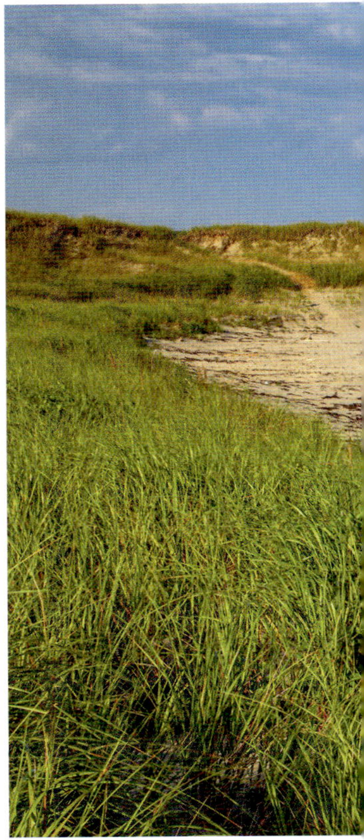

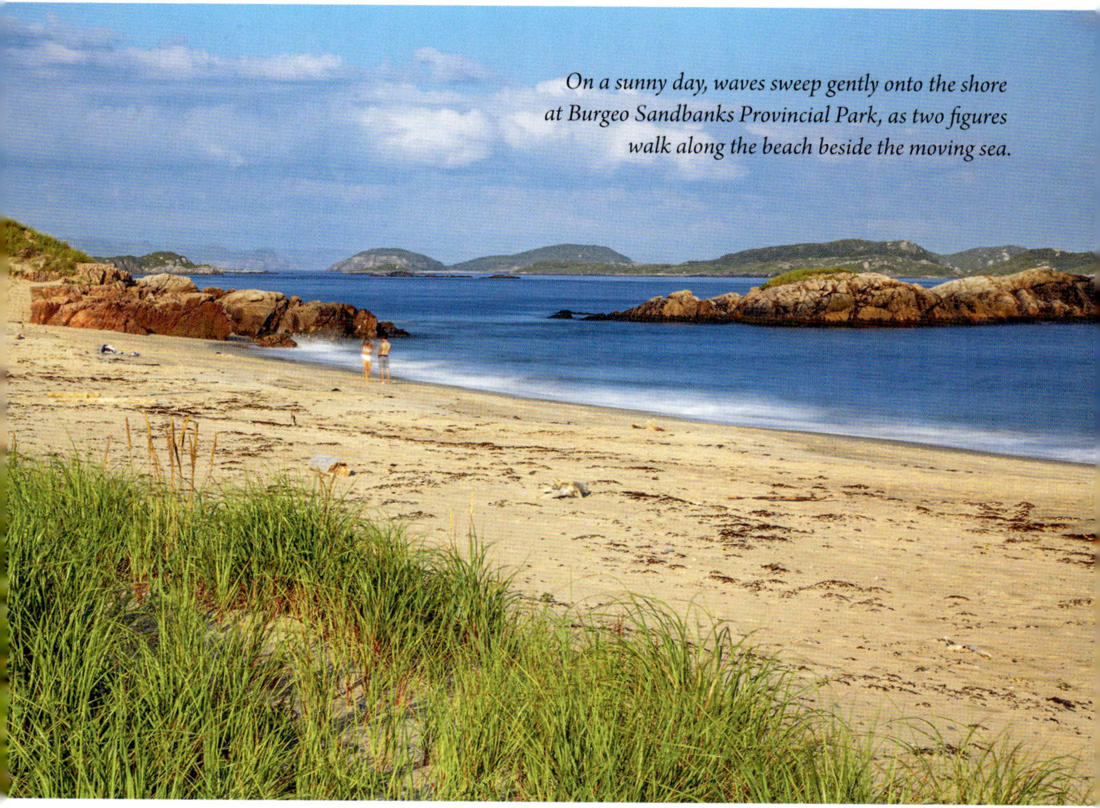

On a sunny day, waves sweep gently onto the shore at Burgeo Sandbanks Provincial Park, as two figures walk along the beach beside the moving sea.

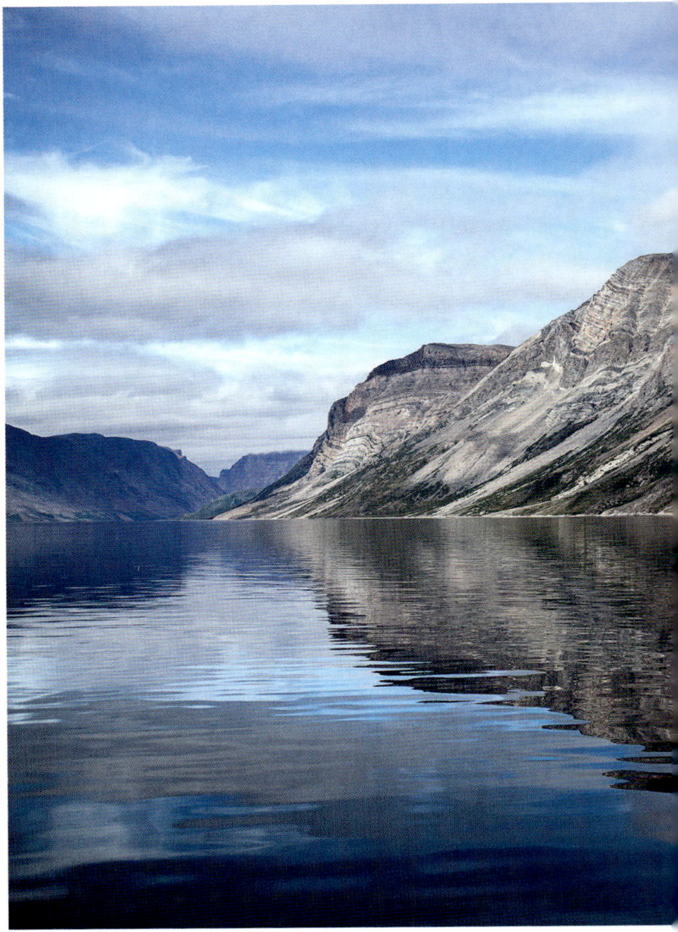

On a clear blue day, a barren Arctic landscape stretches across the Torngat Mountains, where rock and sky reflect in still water far above the treeline, in a place few ever reach.

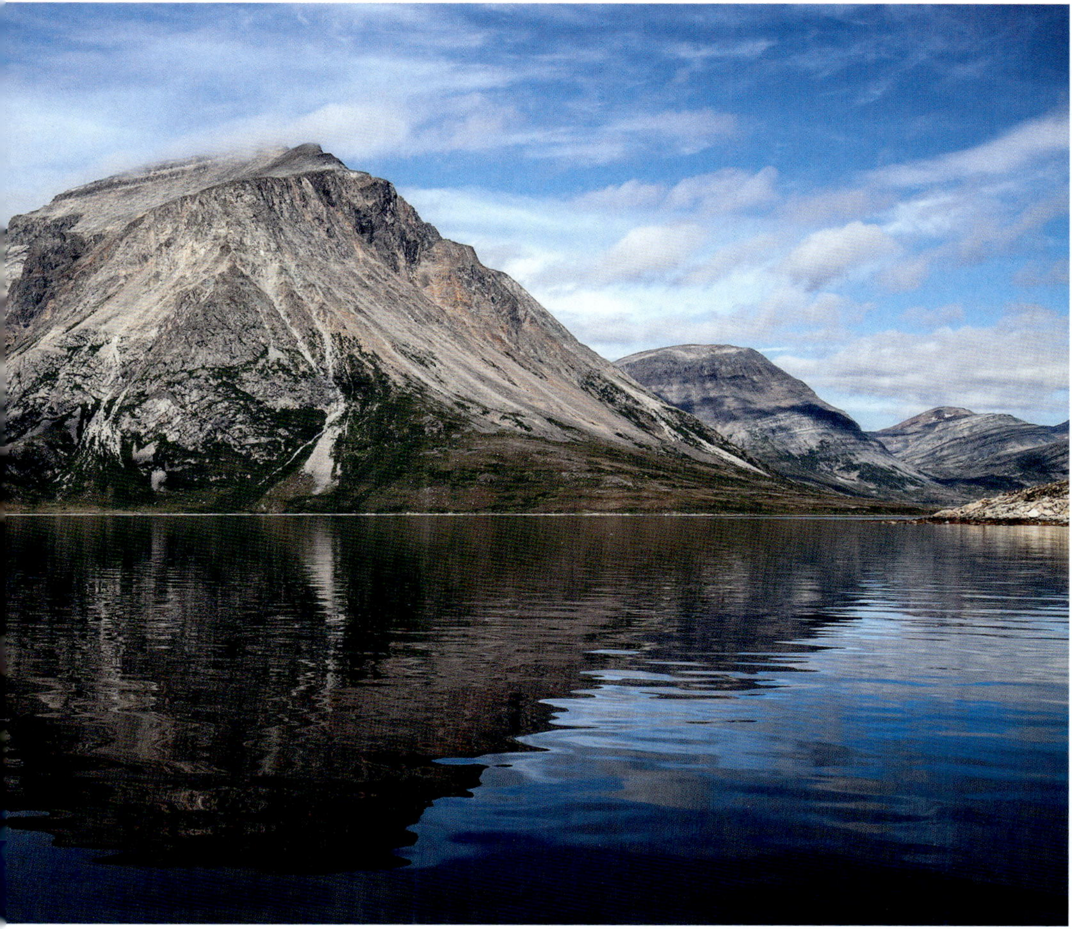

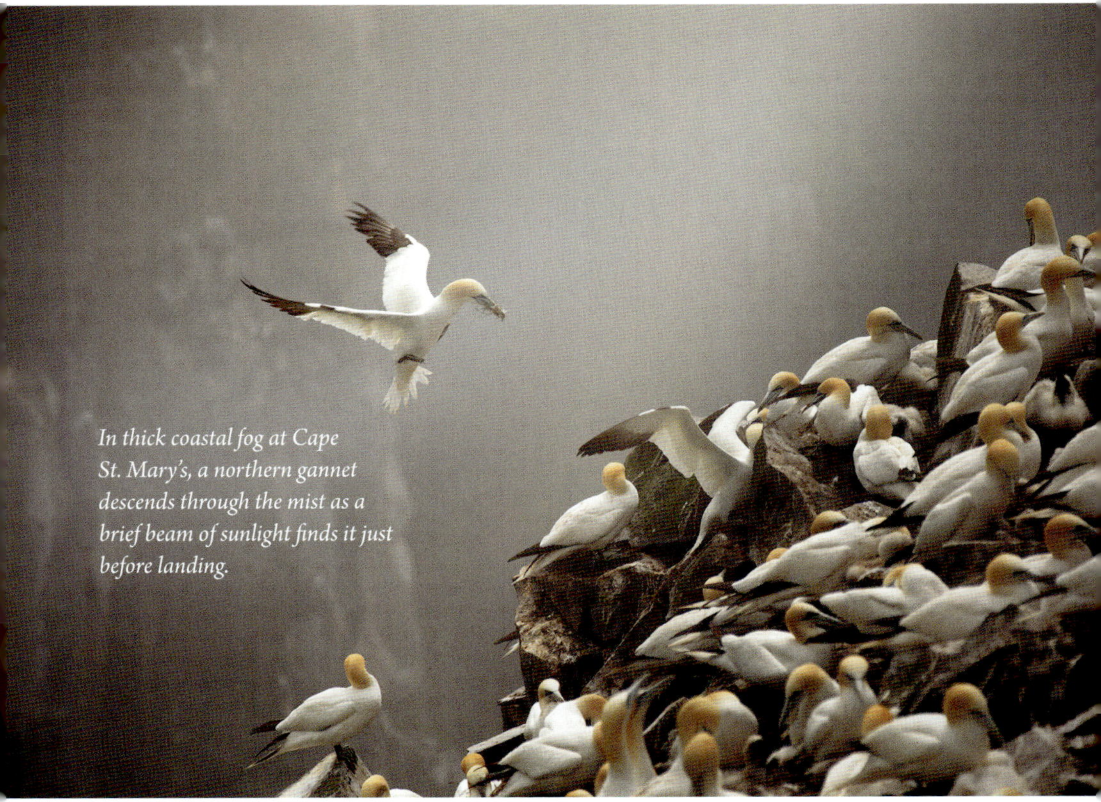

In thick coastal fog at Cape St. Mary's, a northern gannet descends through the mist as a brief beam of sunlight finds it just before landing.

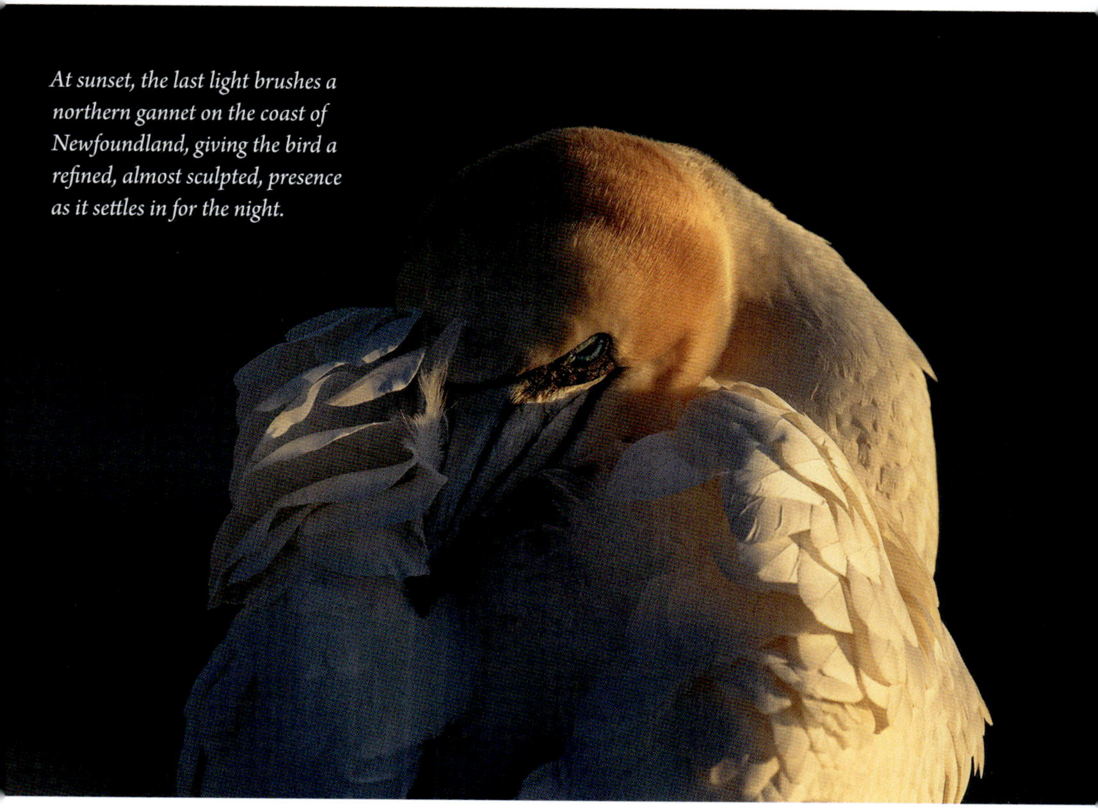

At sunset, the last light brushes a northern gannet on the coast of Newfoundland, giving the bird a refined, almost sculpted, presence as it settles in for the night.

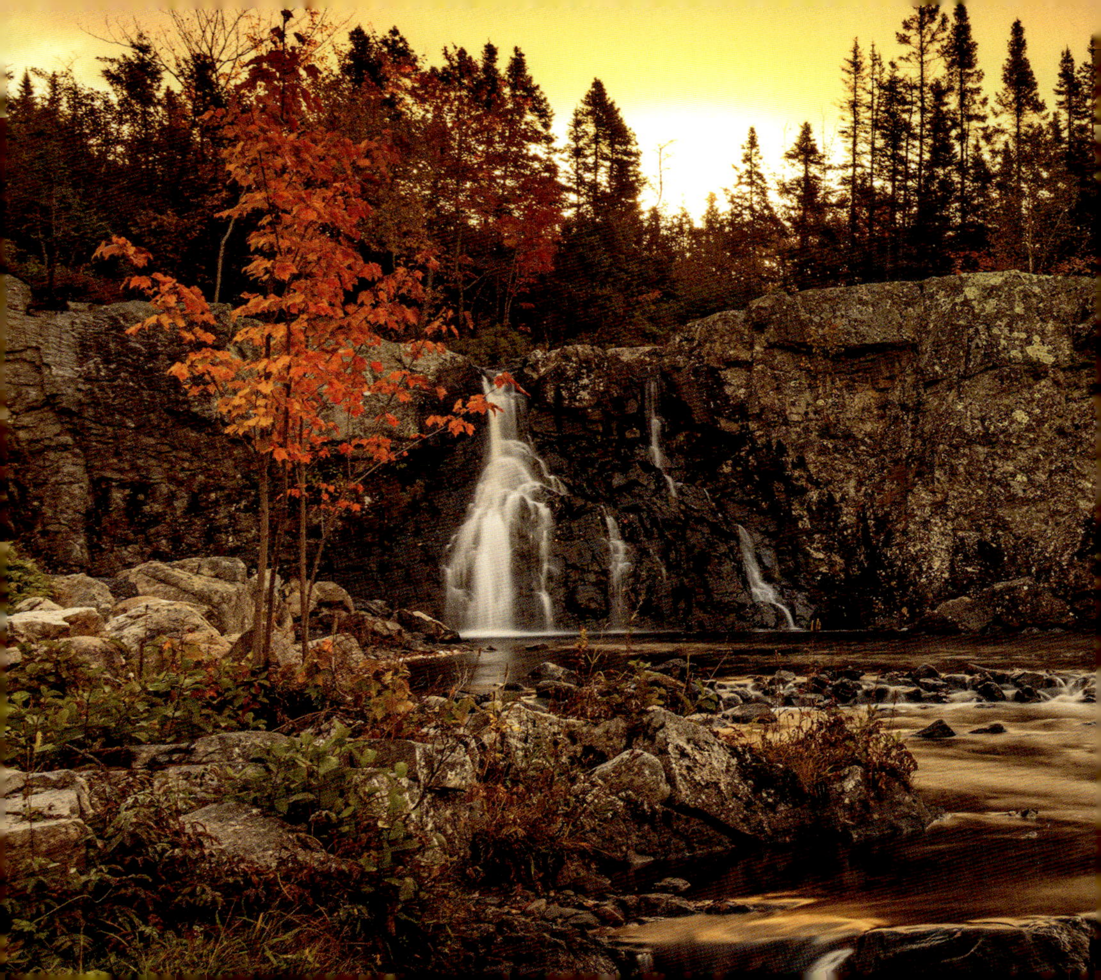

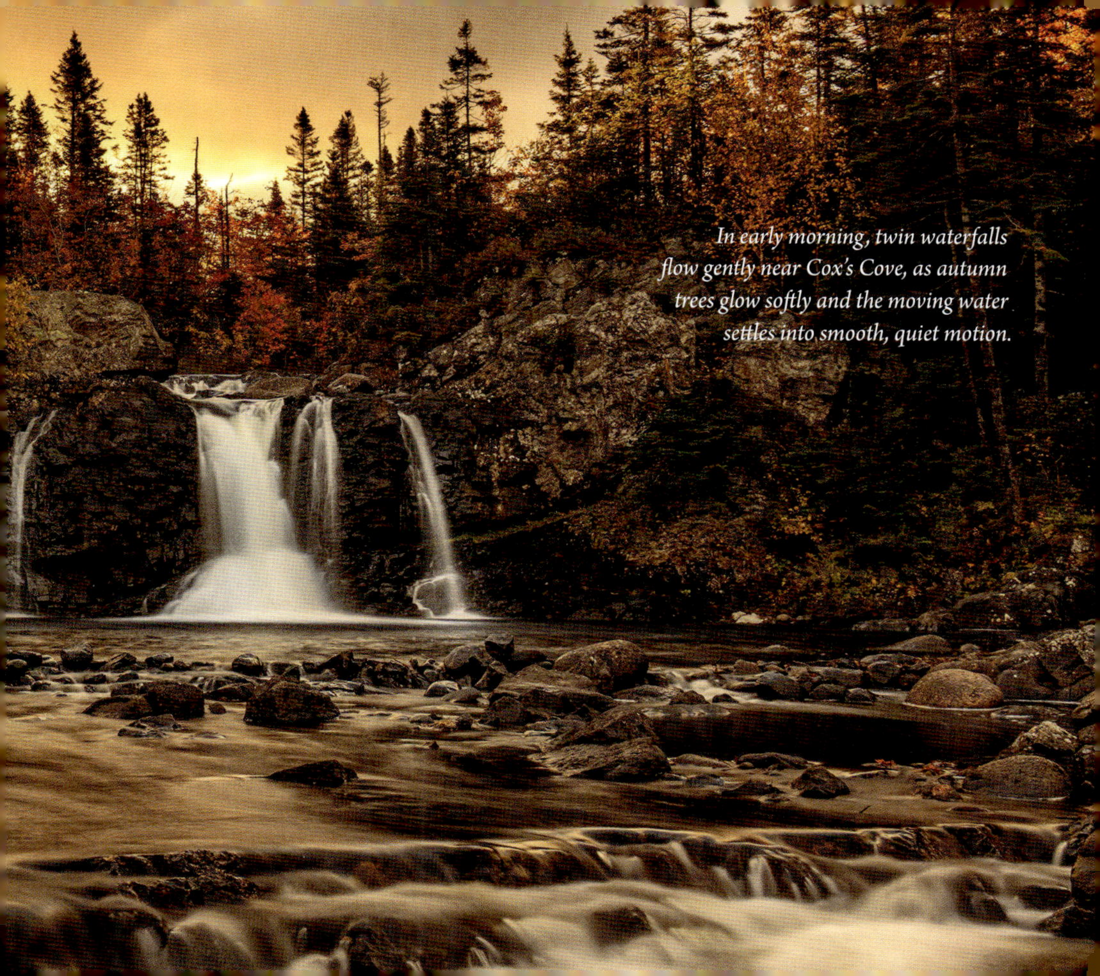

In early morning, twin waterfalls flow gently near Cox's Cove, as autumn trees glow softly and the moving water settles into smooth, quiet motion.

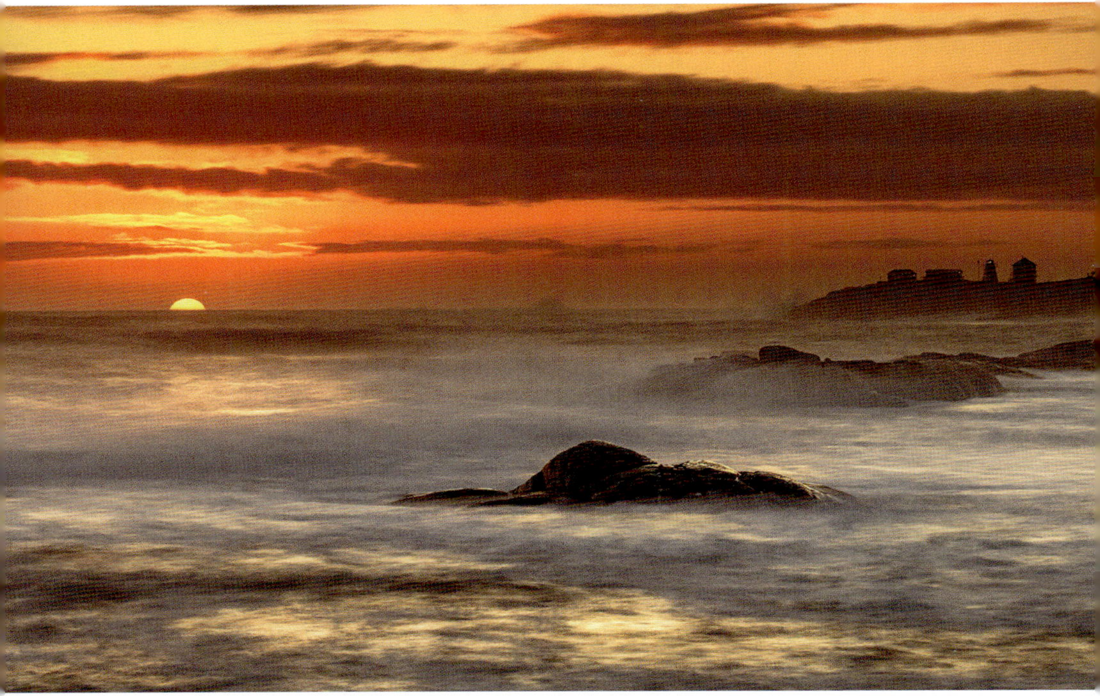

At sunrise, the Atlantic surges against the rocks at Greenspond, as rough seas blur into motion beneath an orange sky and the sun breaks the horizon.

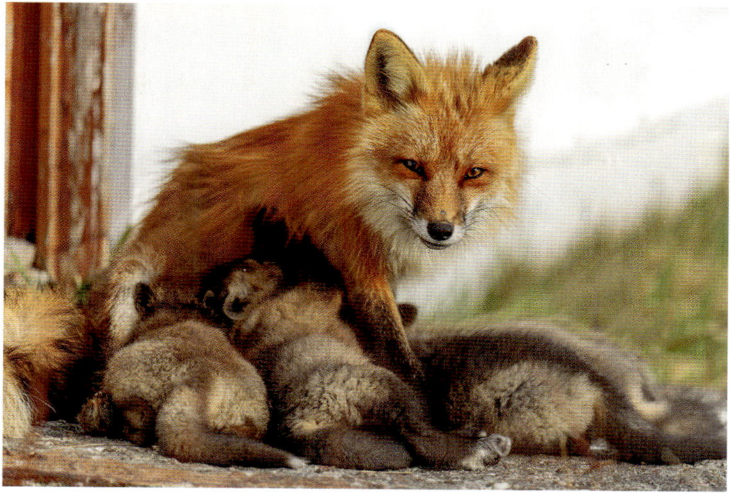

Warm light settles on a red fox in Bonavista,
as she pauses while feeding her kits
and fixes an intense gaze
through the golden morning air.

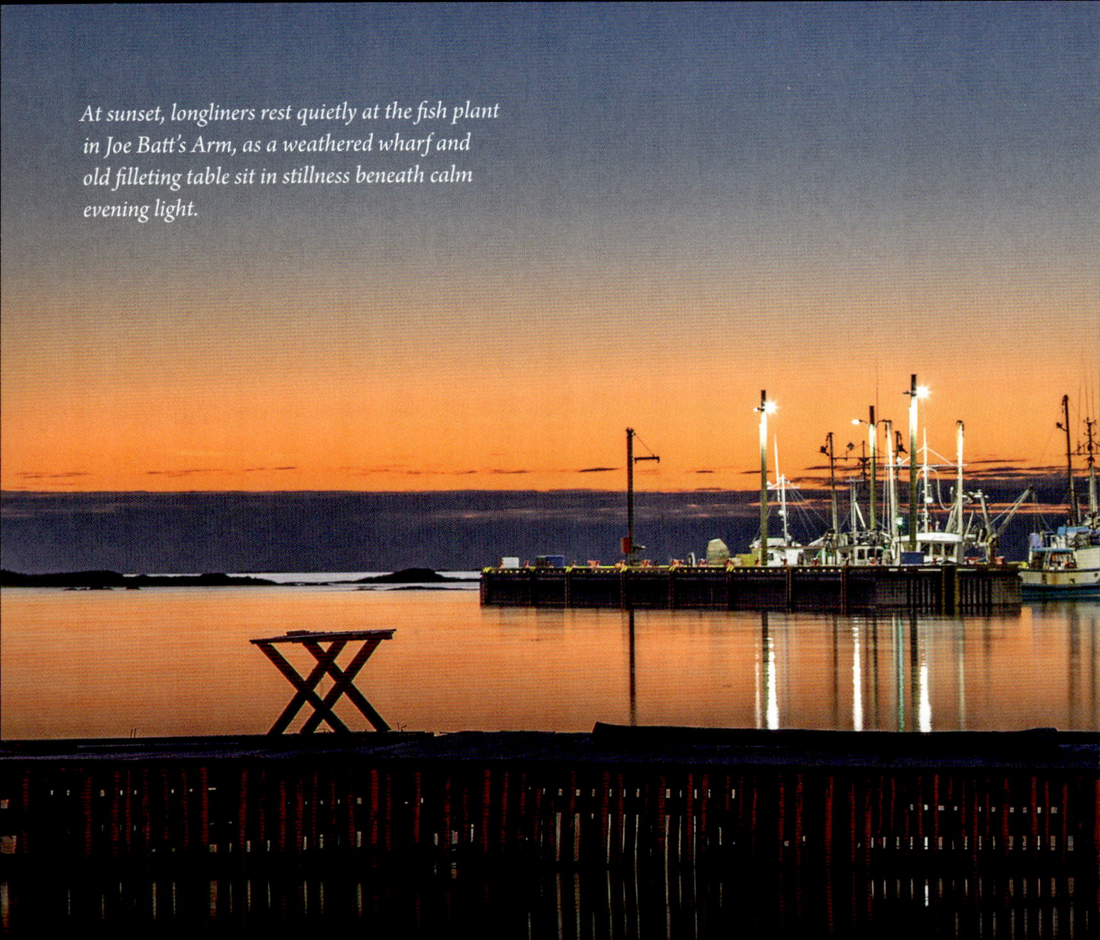

At sunset, longliners rest quietly at the fish plant in Joe Batt's Arm, as a weathered wharf and old filleting table sit in stillness beneath calm evening light.

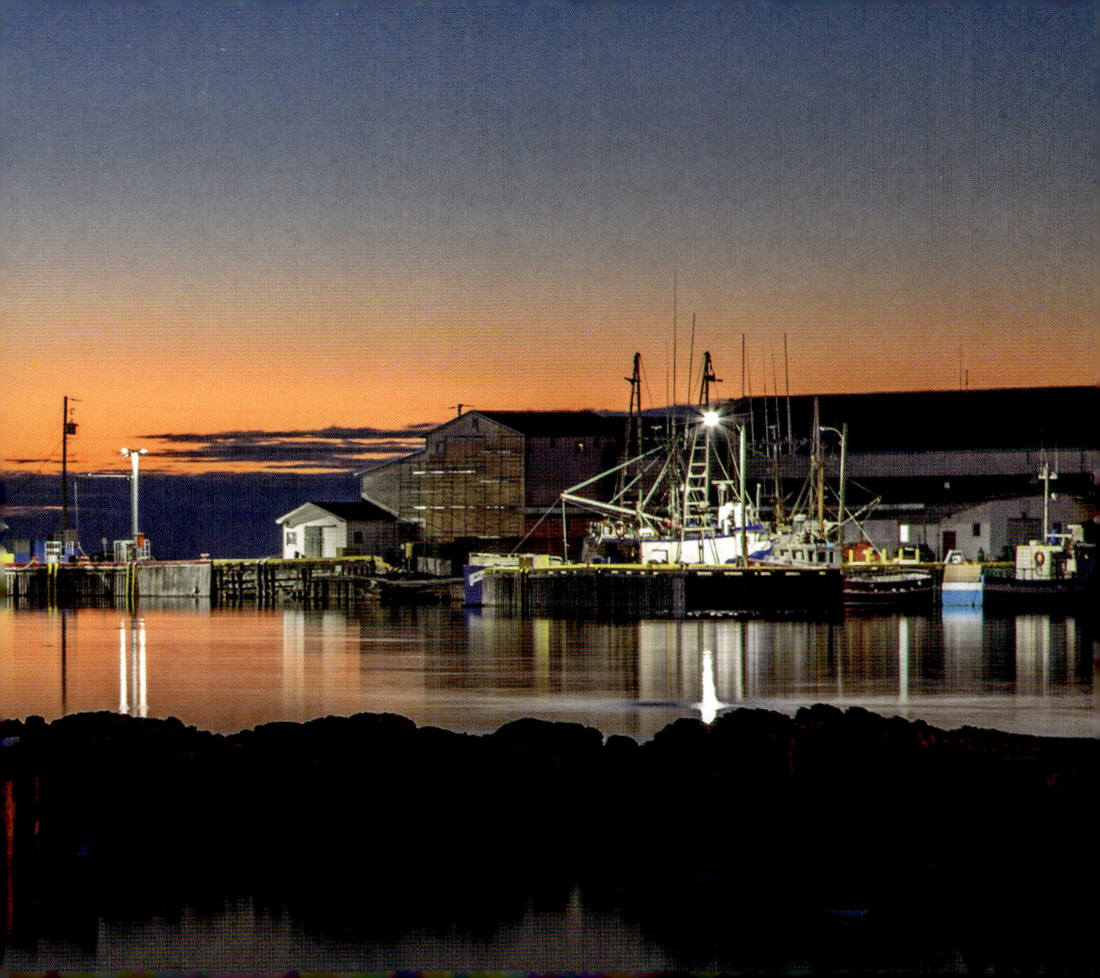

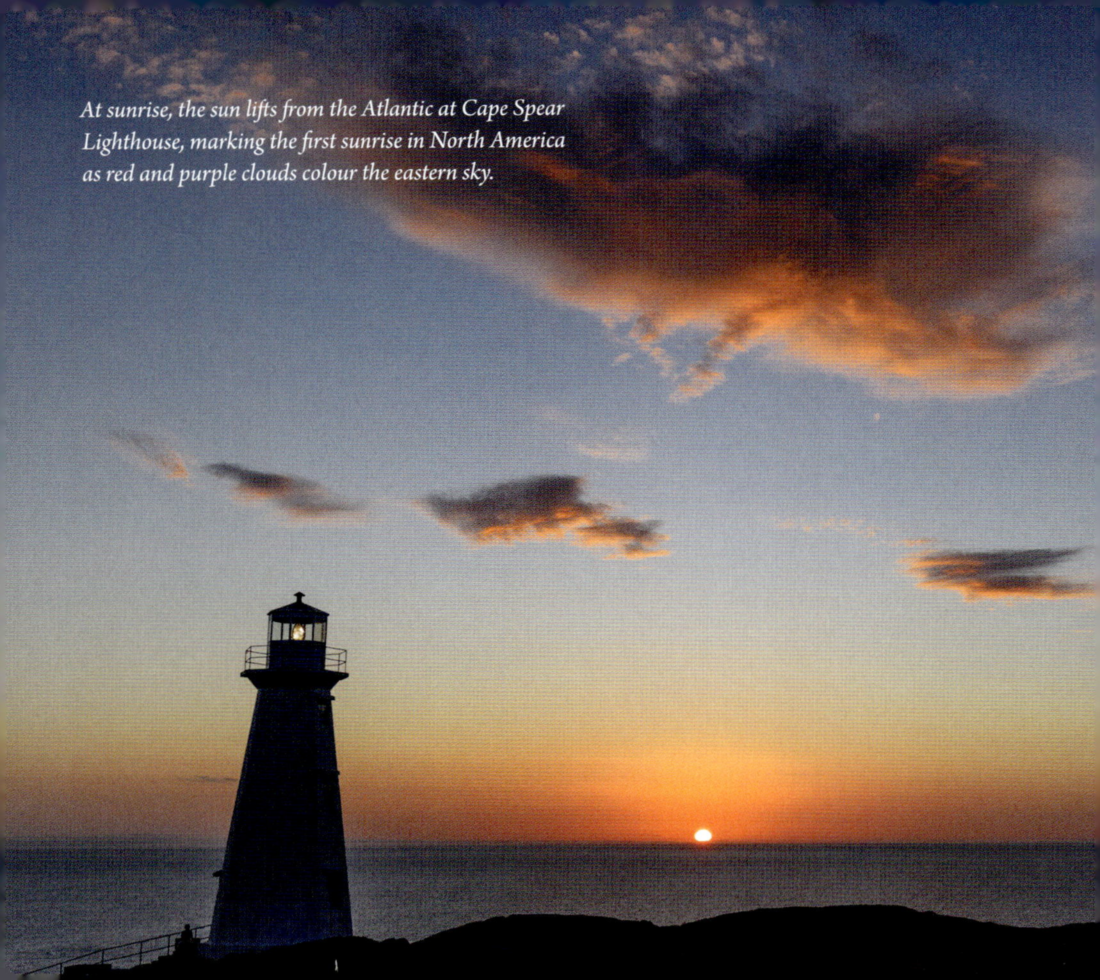

At sunrise, the sun lifts from the Atlantic at Cape Spear Lighthouse, marking the first sunrise in North America as red and purple clouds colour the eastern sky.

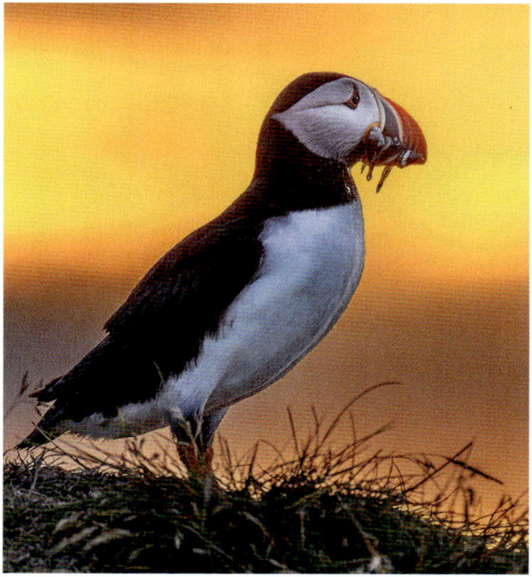

At sunrise, an Atlantic puffin perches at the edge of a cliff in Elliston, holding fish in its beak as warm orange light fills the sky behind it.

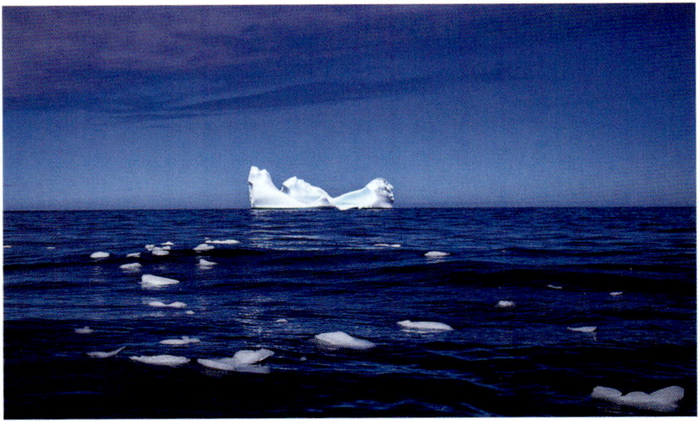

Bergy bits off Fogo Island
float away in deepest blue ocean,
as a luminous iceberg in the distance
reflects the sky.

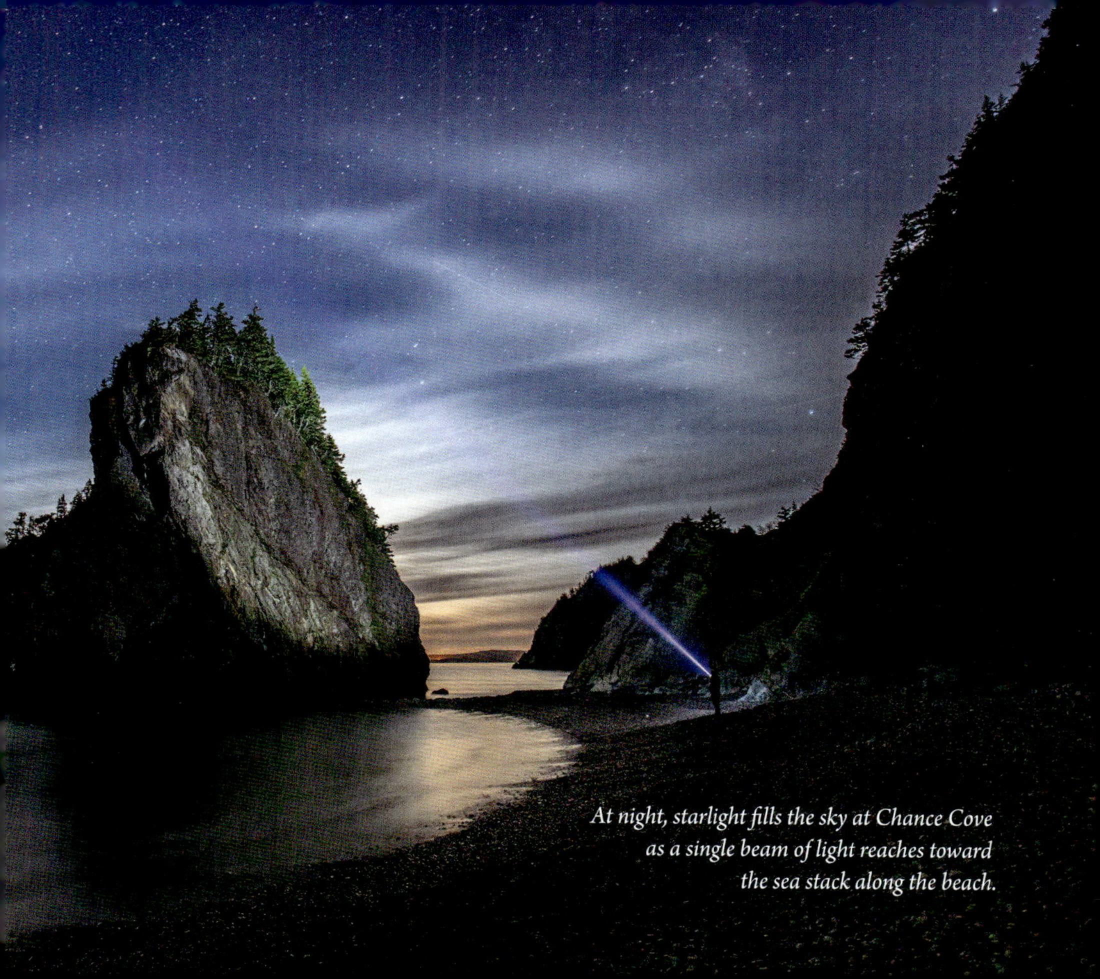

At night, starlight fills the sky at Chance Cove as a single beam of light reaches toward the sea stack along the beach.

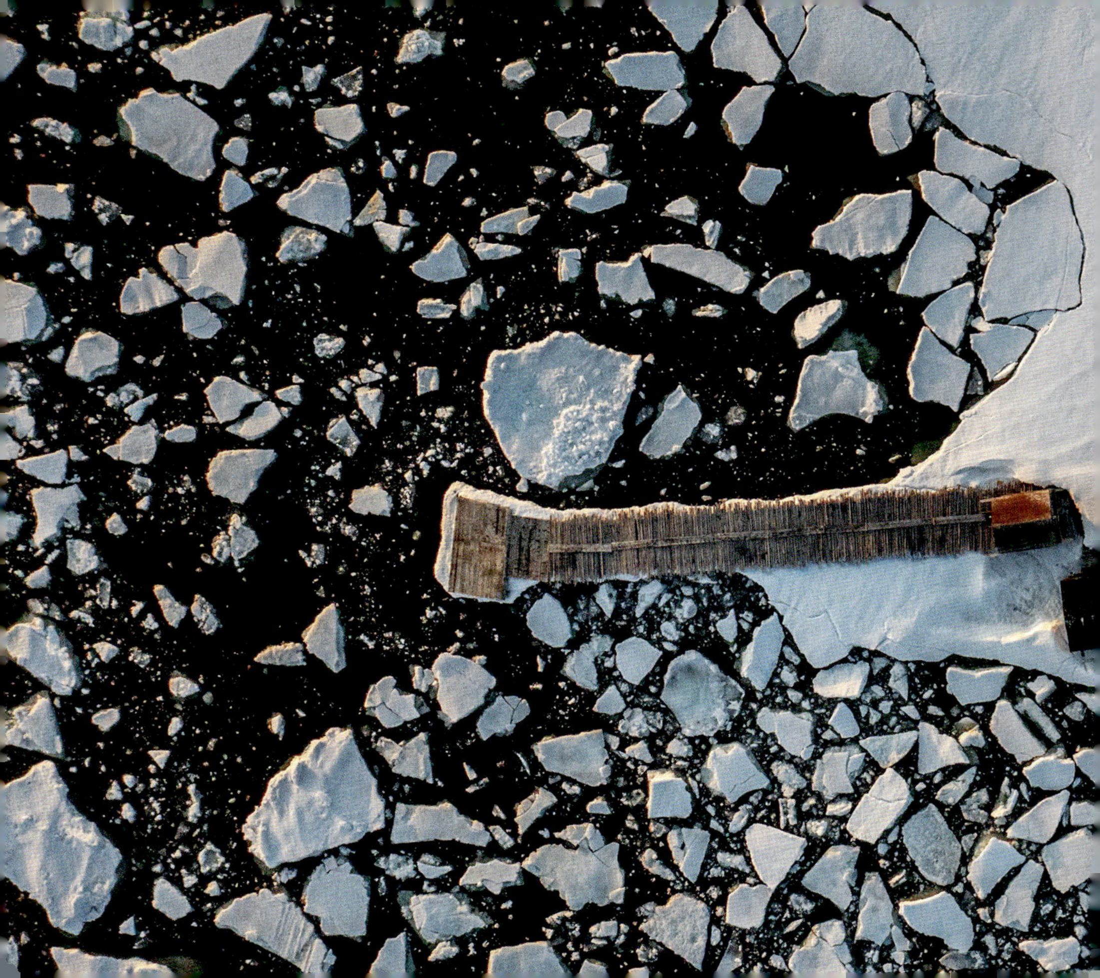

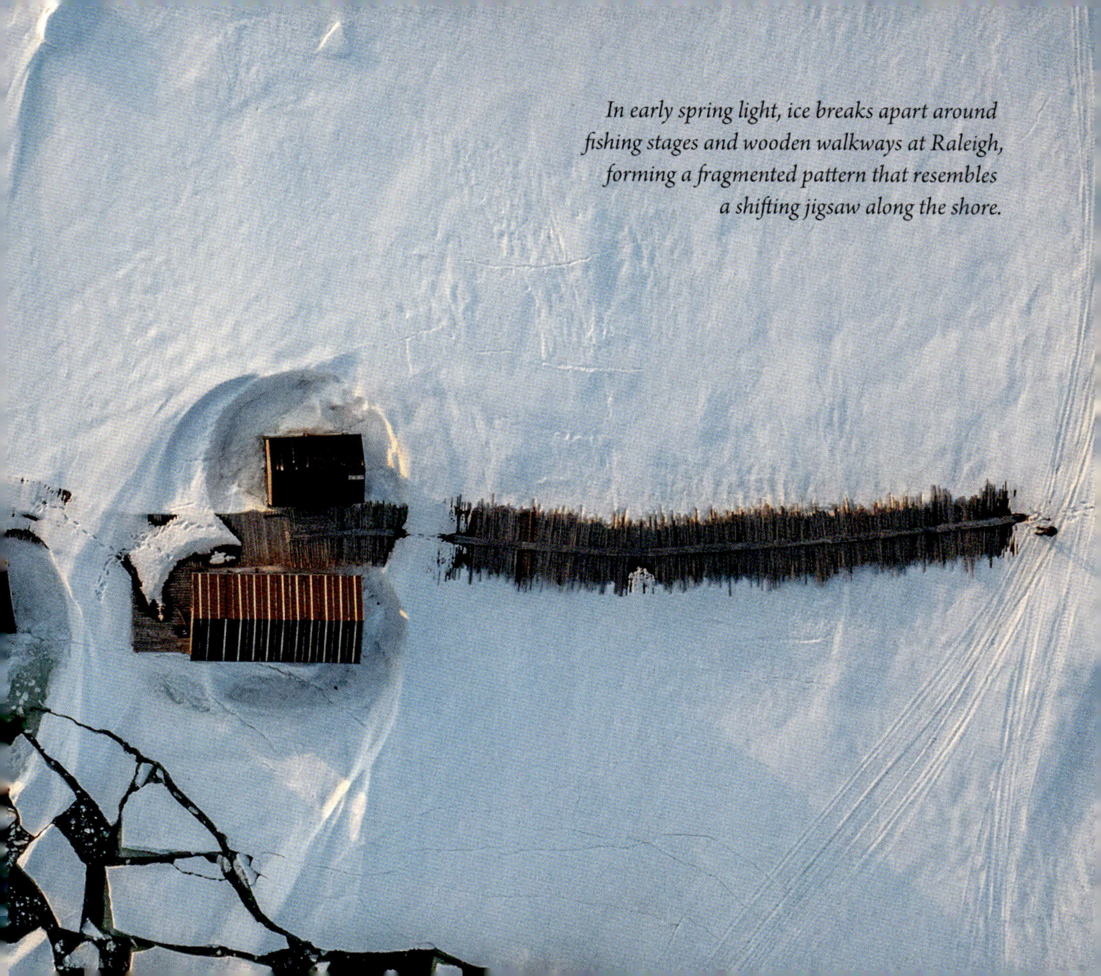

In early spring light, ice breaks apart around fishing stages and wooden walkways at Raleigh, forming a fragmented pattern that resembles a shifting jigsaw along the shore.

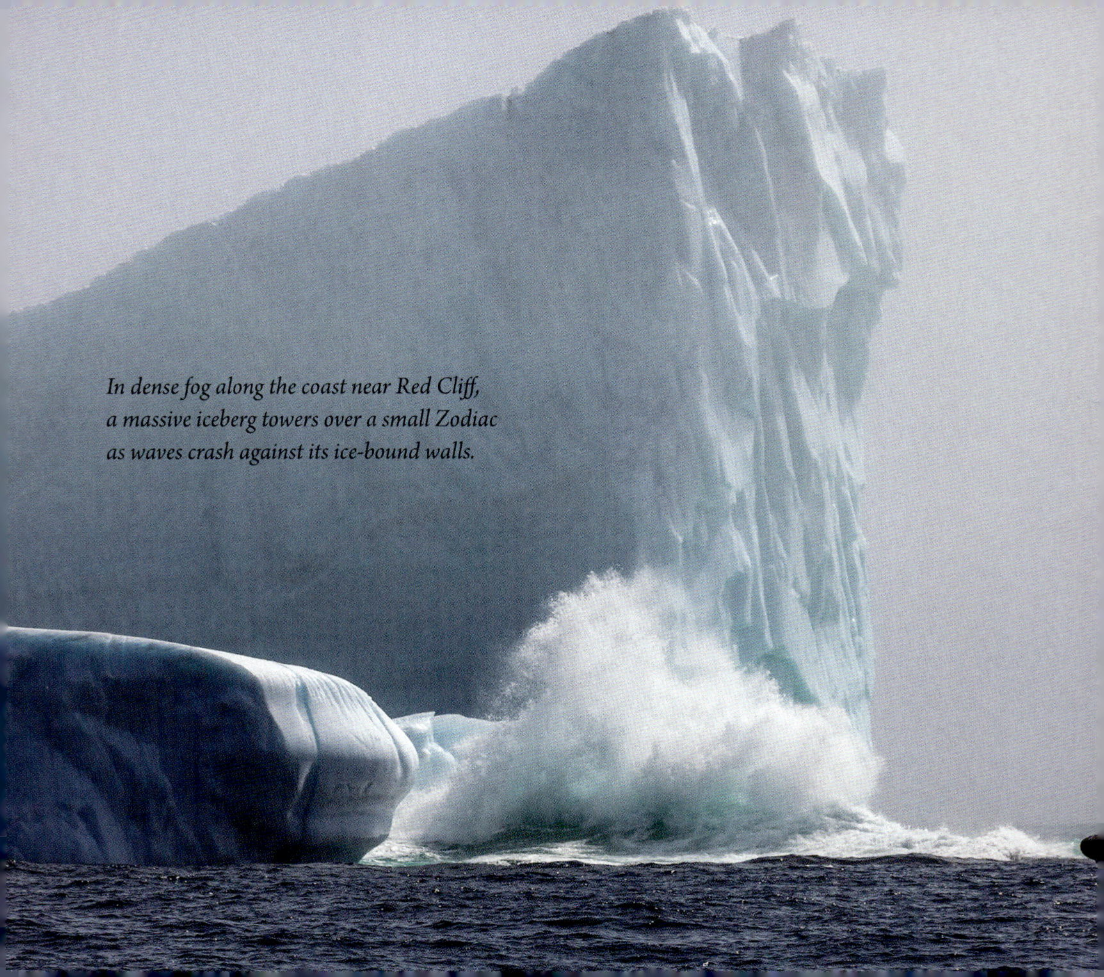

In dense fog along the coast near Red Cliff, a massive iceberg towers over a small Zodiac as waves crash against its ice-bound walls.

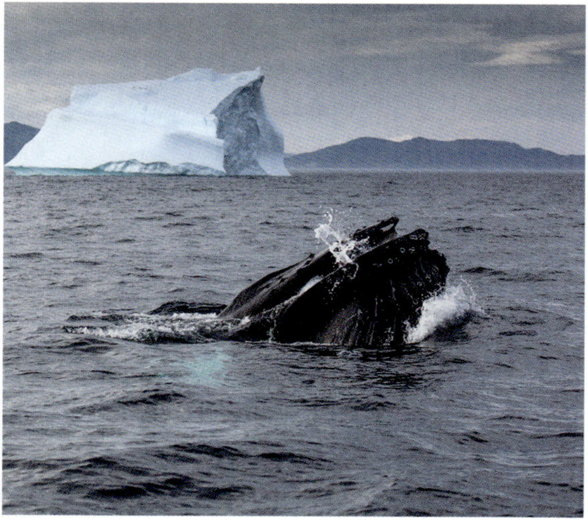

In a grey evening along the coast of Trinity Bay, a humpback whale surfaces with a mouthful of capelin as water spills free and a towering iceberg looms in the background.

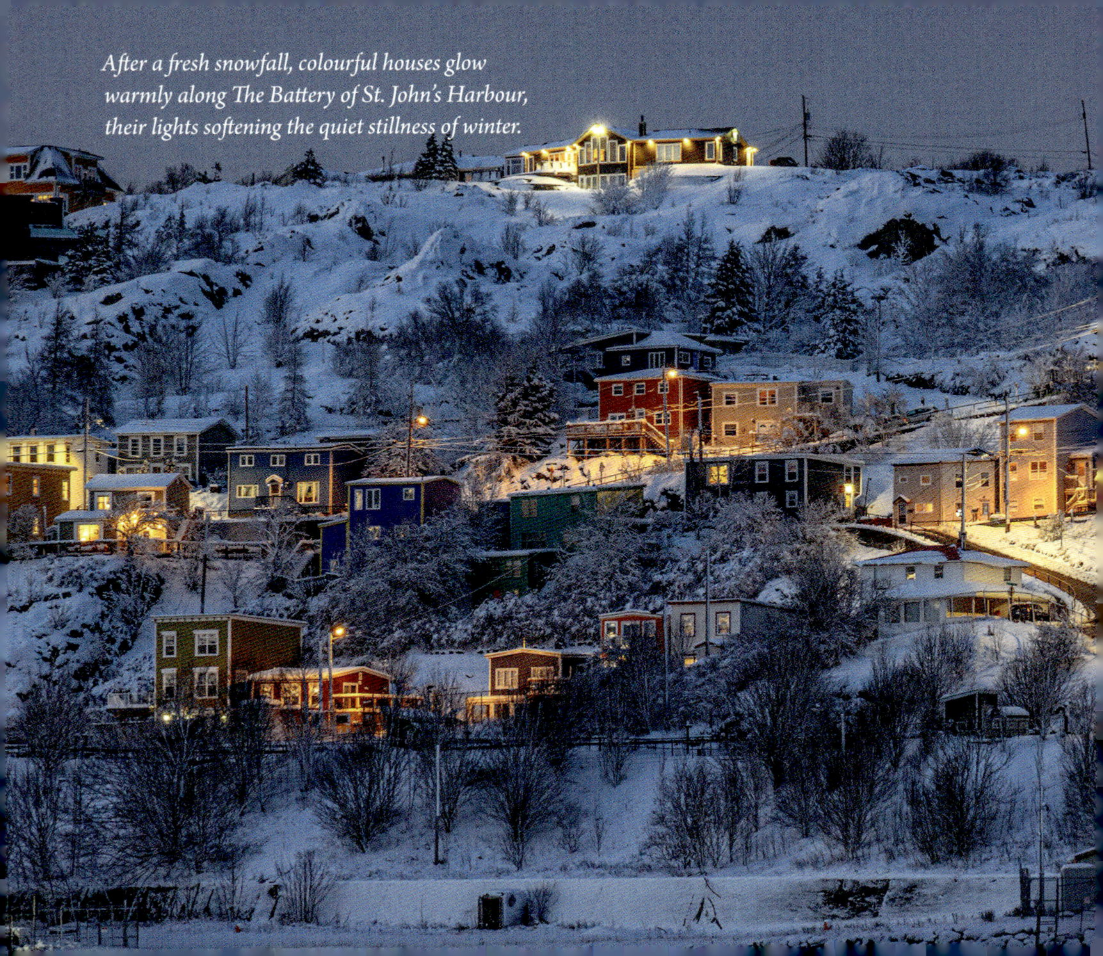

After a fresh snowfall, colourful houses glow warmly along The Battery of St. John's Harbour, their lights softening the quiet stillness of winter.

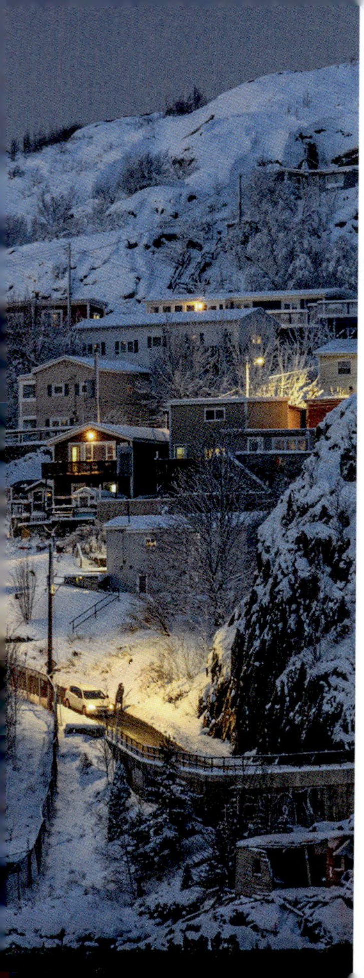

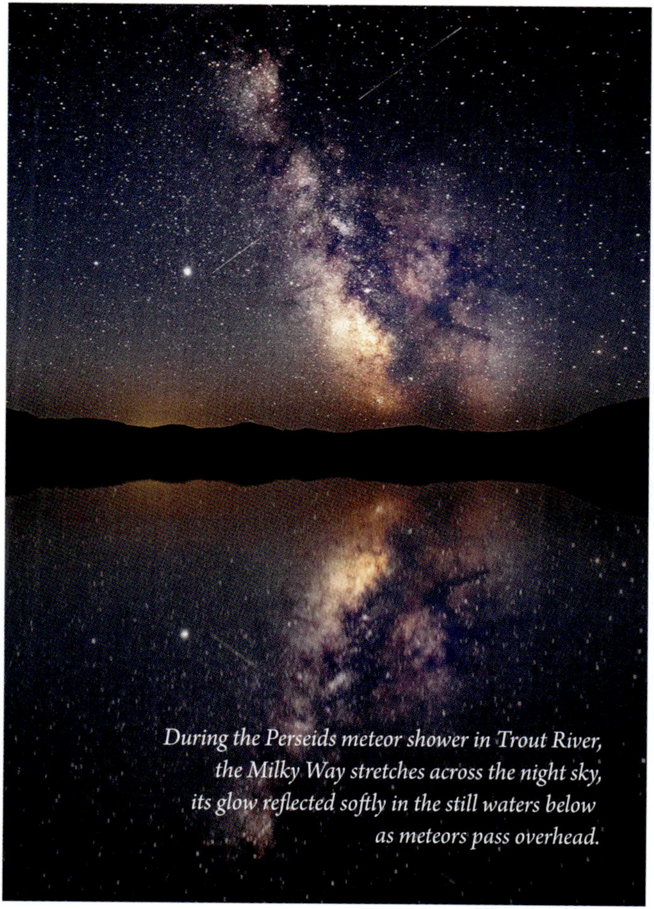

During the Perseids meteor shower in Trout River, the Milky Way stretches across the night sky, its glow reflected softly in the still waters below as meteors pass overhead.

(right) In autumn light, a fallen tree rests across a glistening marsh in Gros Morne National Park, as dramatic clouds drift above tall grasses and distant hills glow with golden colour.

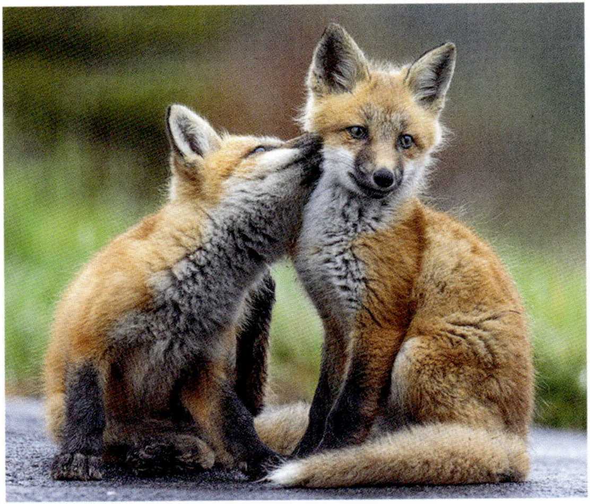

(above) In soft light, two young red fox kits rest together in Bonavista, their fresh coats glowing as one leans in to gently nuzzle the other.

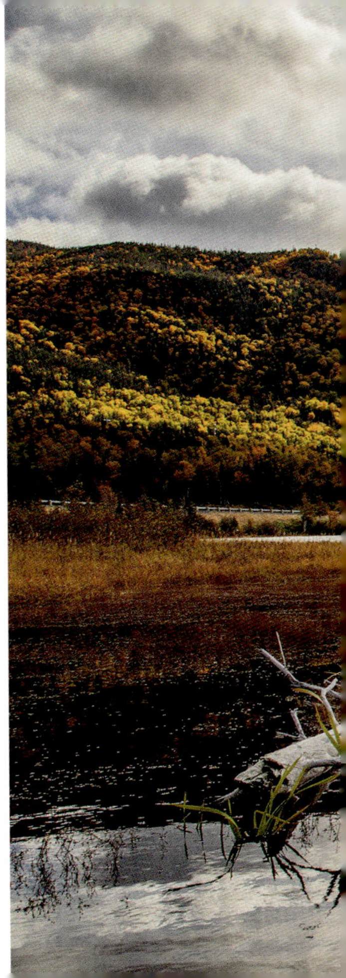

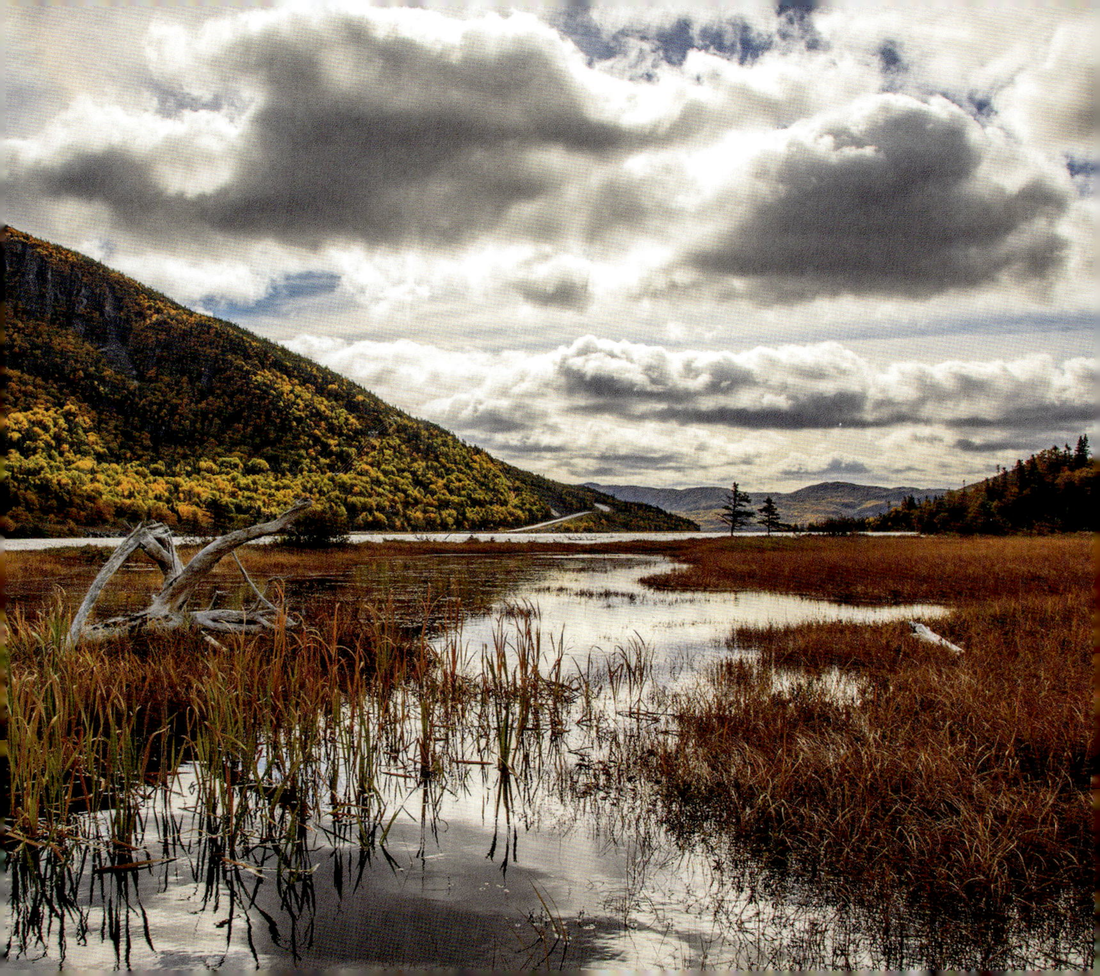

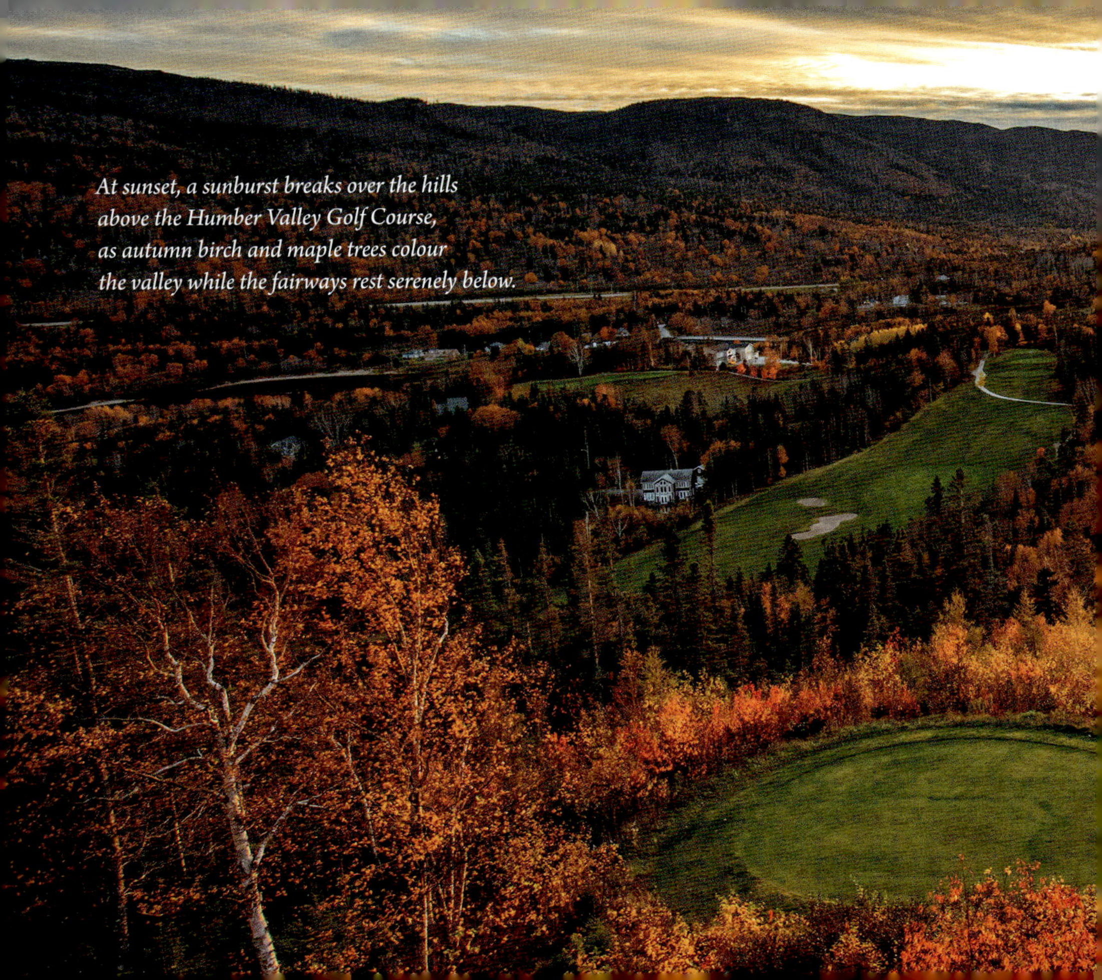

At sunset, a sunburst breaks over the hills above the Humber Valley Golf Course, as autumn birch and maple trees colour the valley while the fairways rest serenely below.

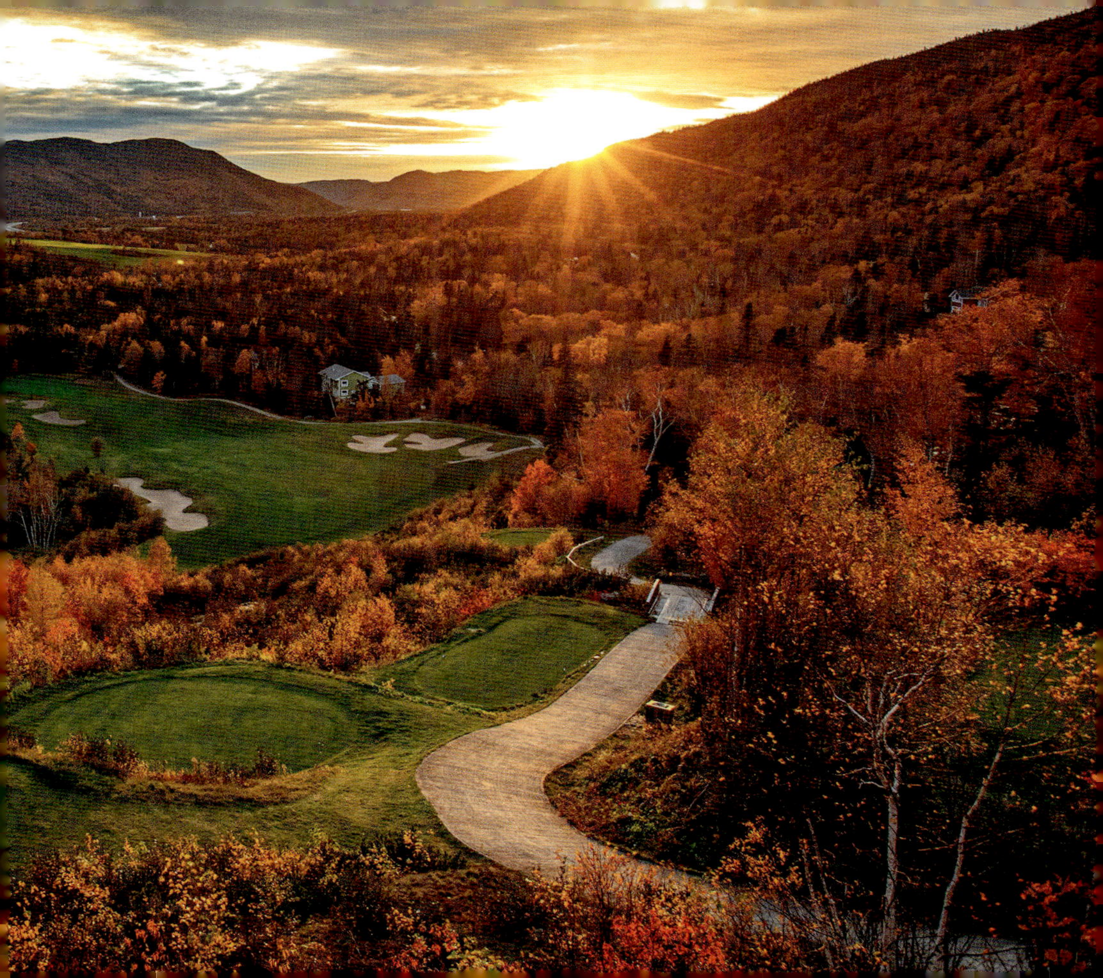

(right) On an overcast autumn day, a rusted fragment of a red vehicle rests in a field near Gillams, as birch trees and distant mountains sit beneath dramatic, shifting cloud.

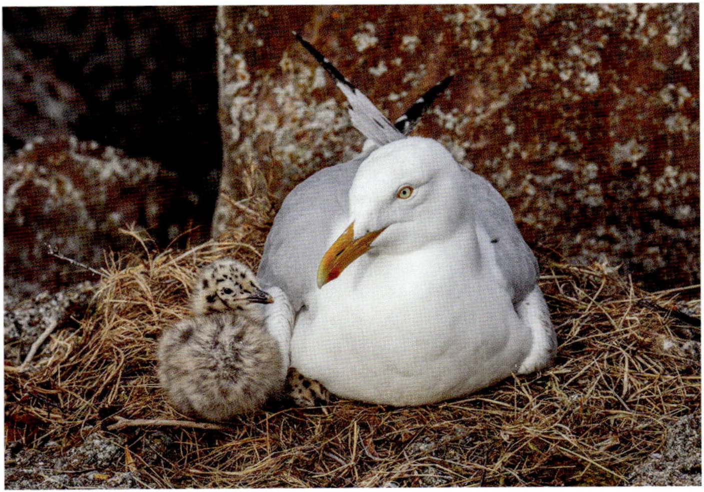

(above) In gentle light, two seabird chicks rest on the grass near St. John's, one peeking from beneath its parent while the other watches calmly from beside them.

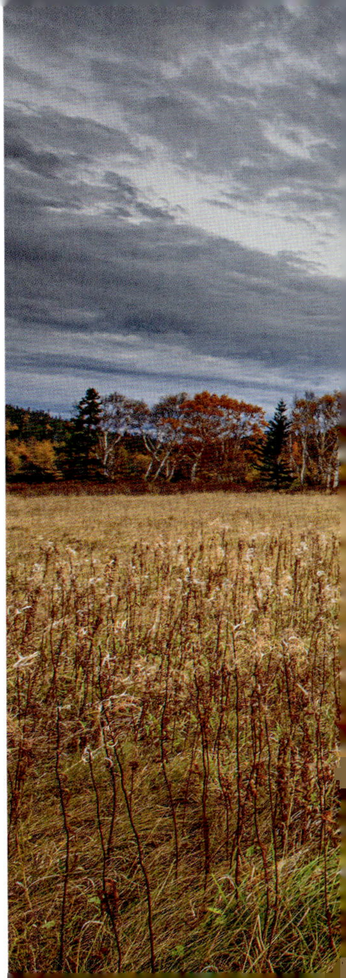

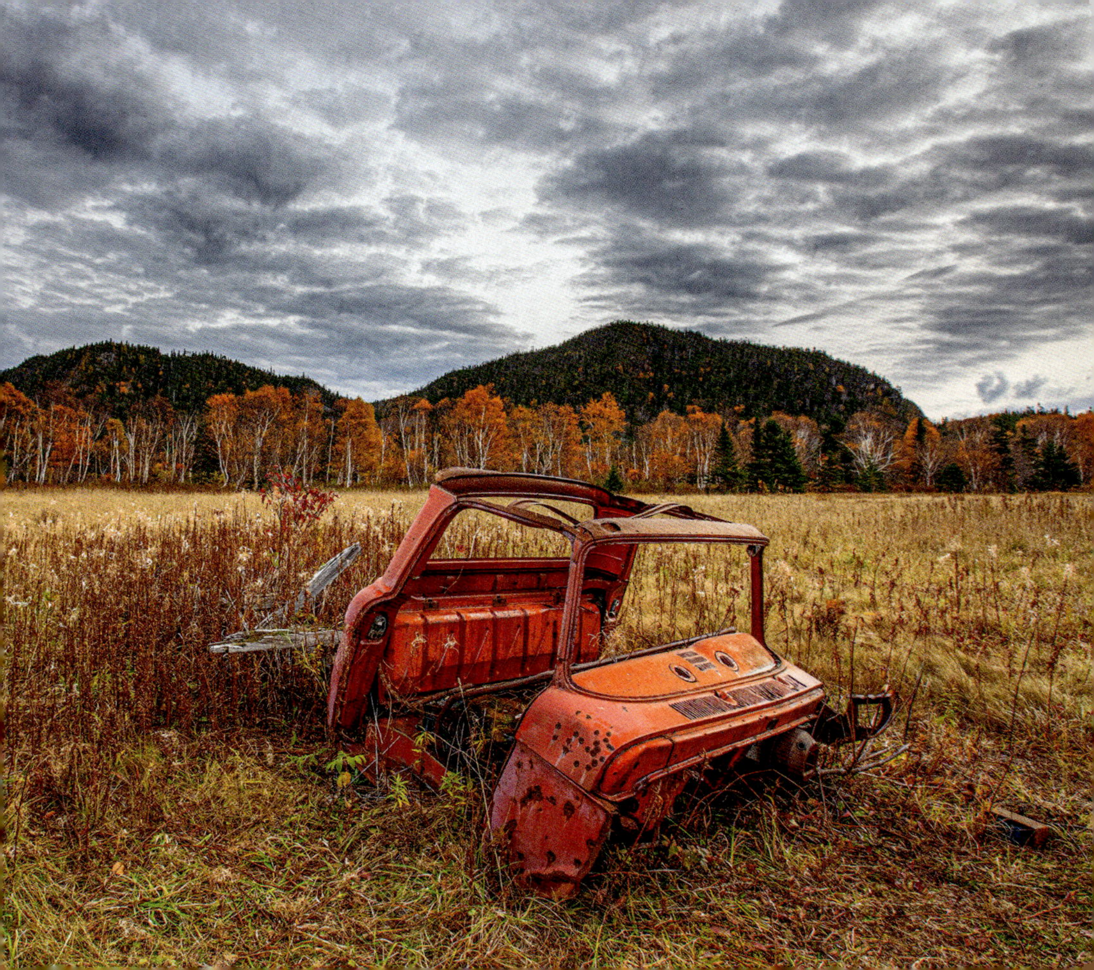

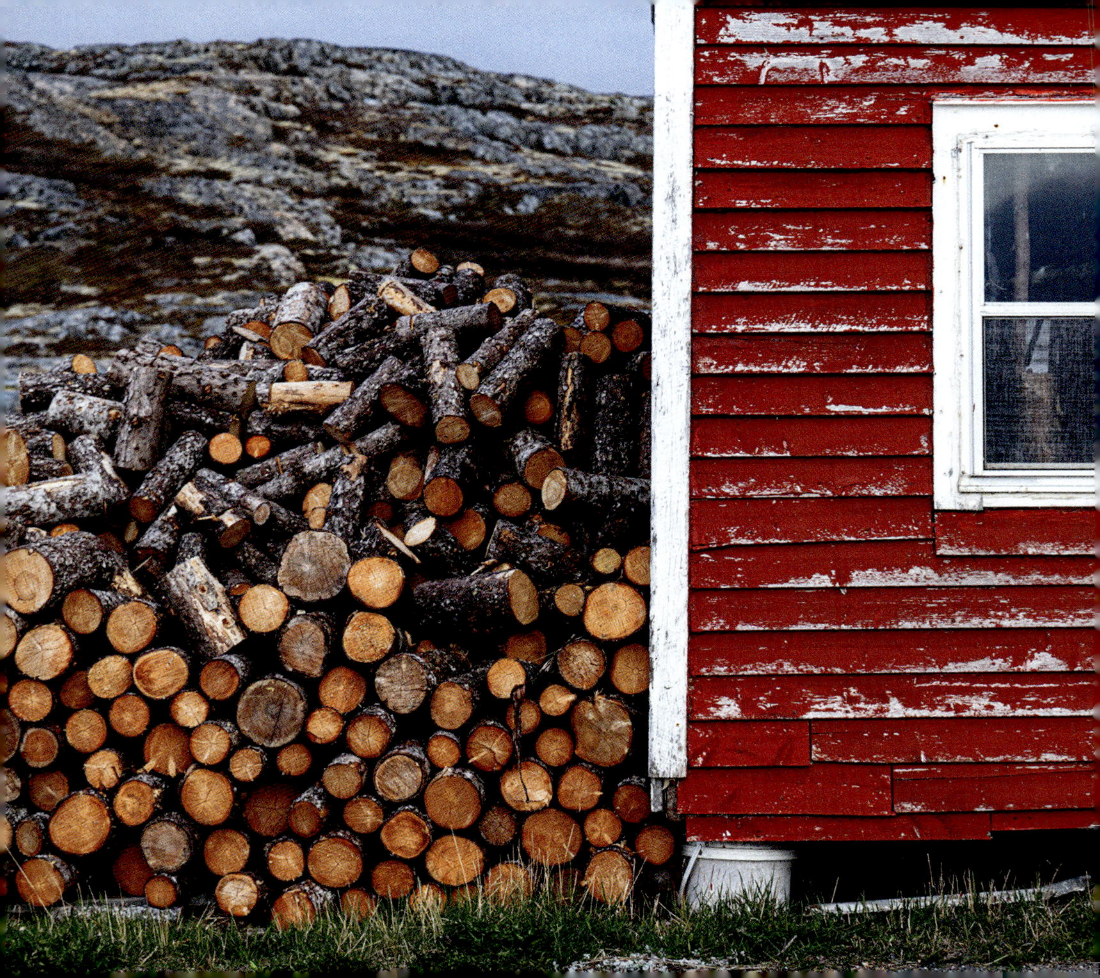

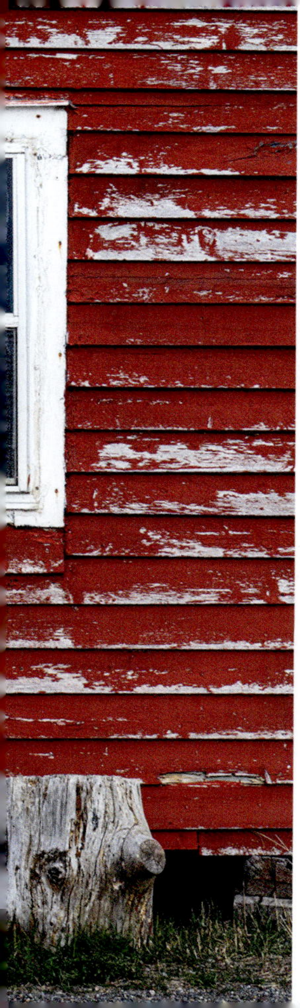

(left) In soft coastal light, a weathered red shed stands in Fogo Island, its peeling boards and small window edged by a rough pile of firewood set out to dry.

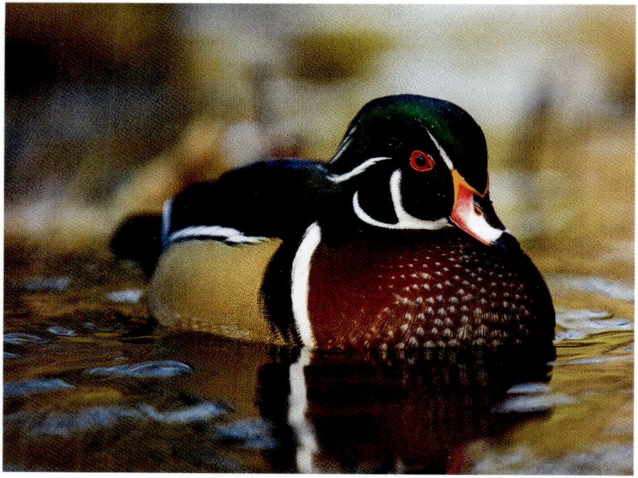

(above) In autumn light, a male wood duck drifts through Bowring Park, its colourful feathers mirrored in water tinted yellow by fallen leaves.

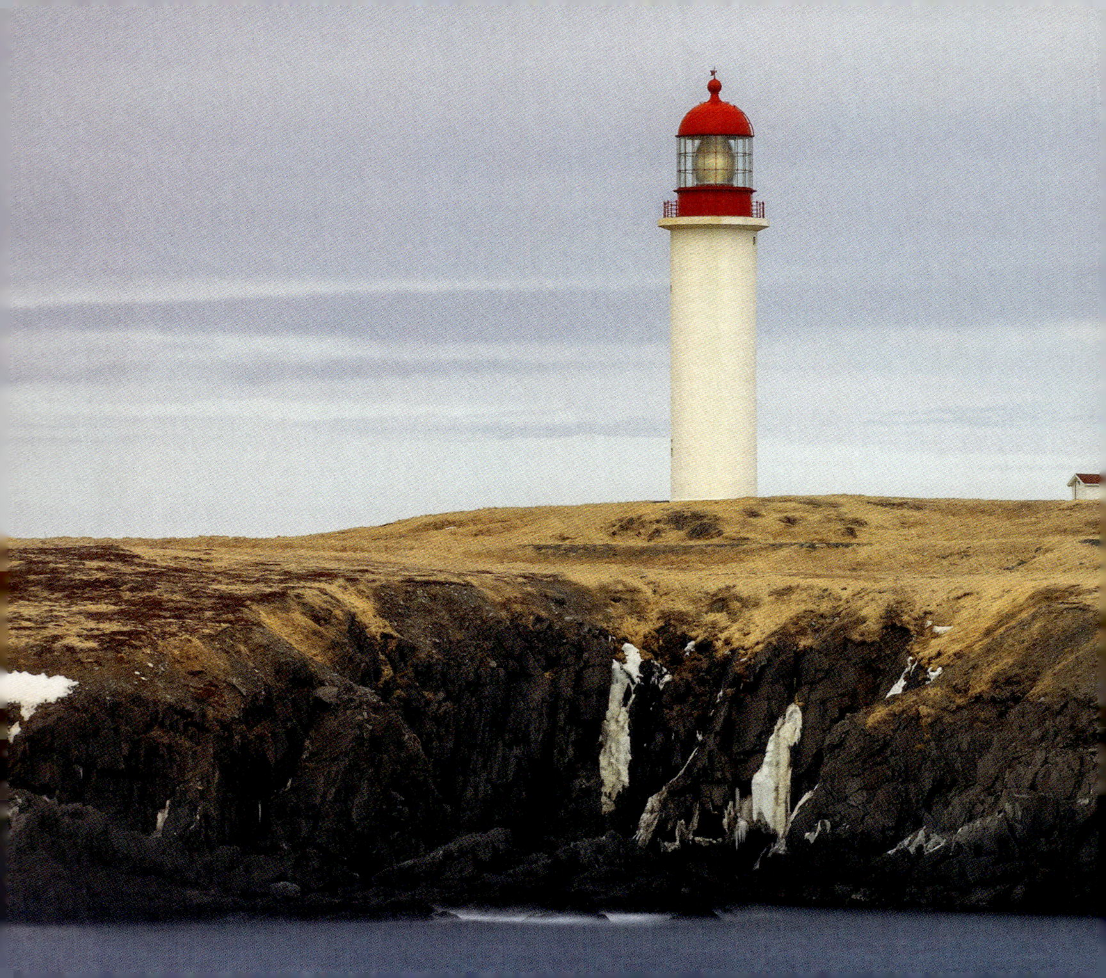

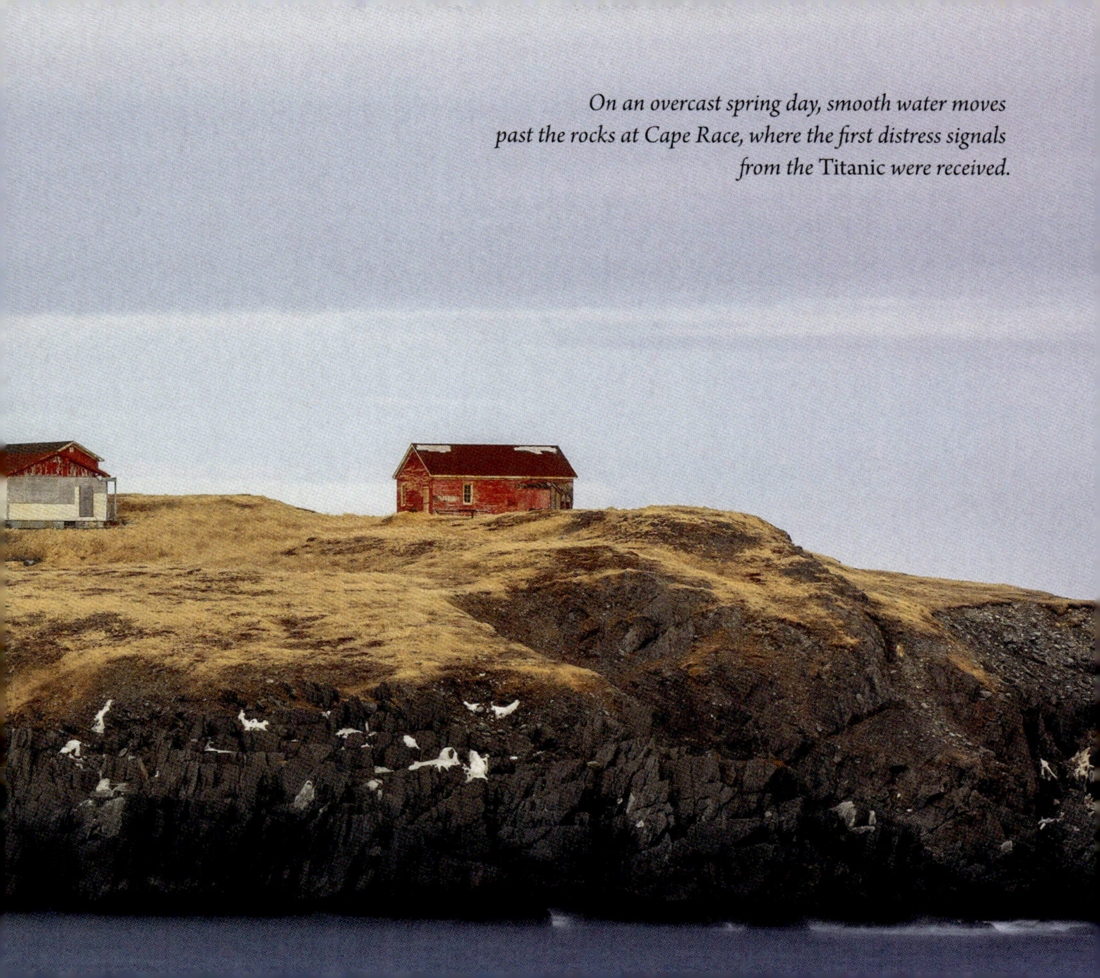

On an overcast spring day, smooth water moves past the rocks at Cape Race, where the first distress signals from the Titanic *were received.*

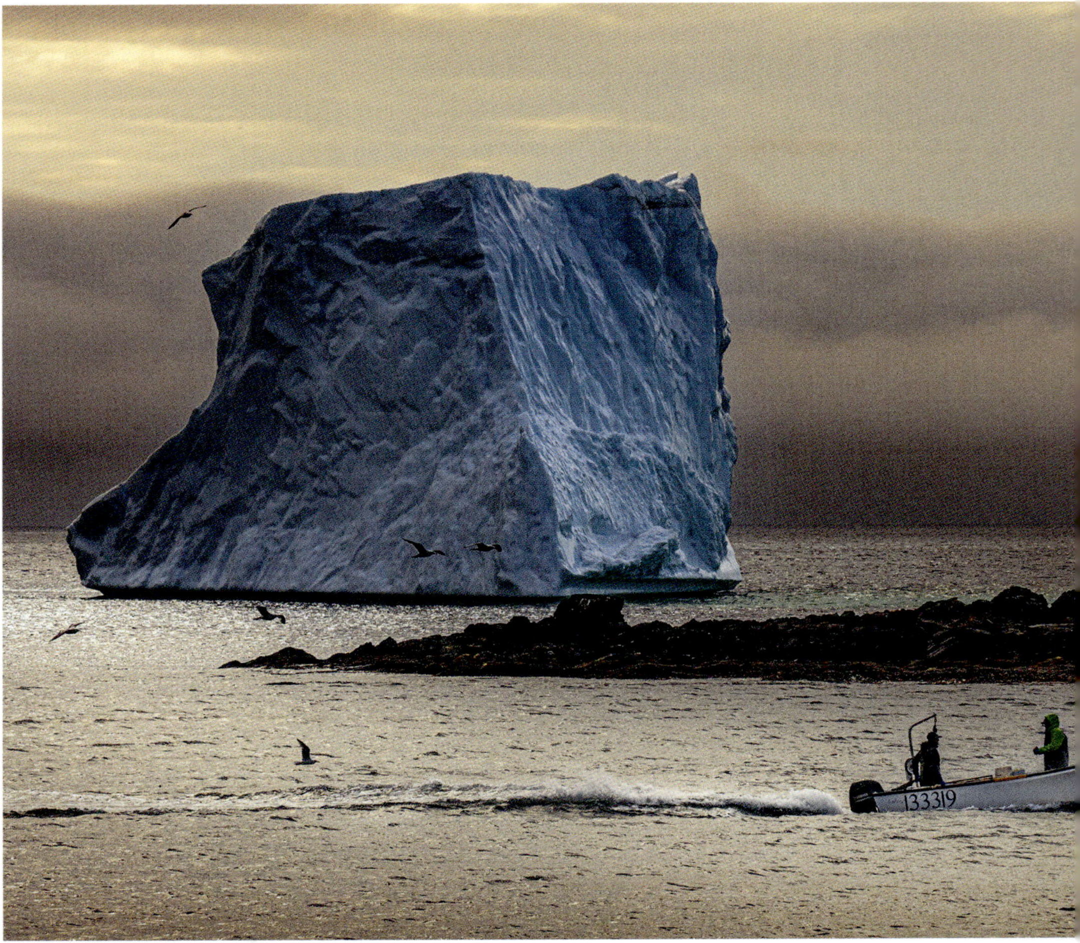
133319

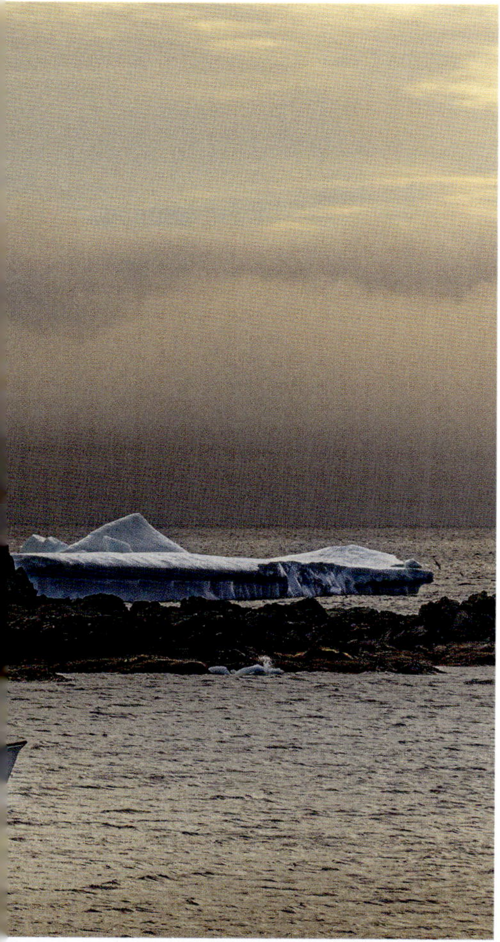

In heavy light at Twillingate, a lobster boat presses on beneath circling gulls as a towering iceberg shadows the scene, capturing the quiet danger faced by those who work the cold North Atlantic.

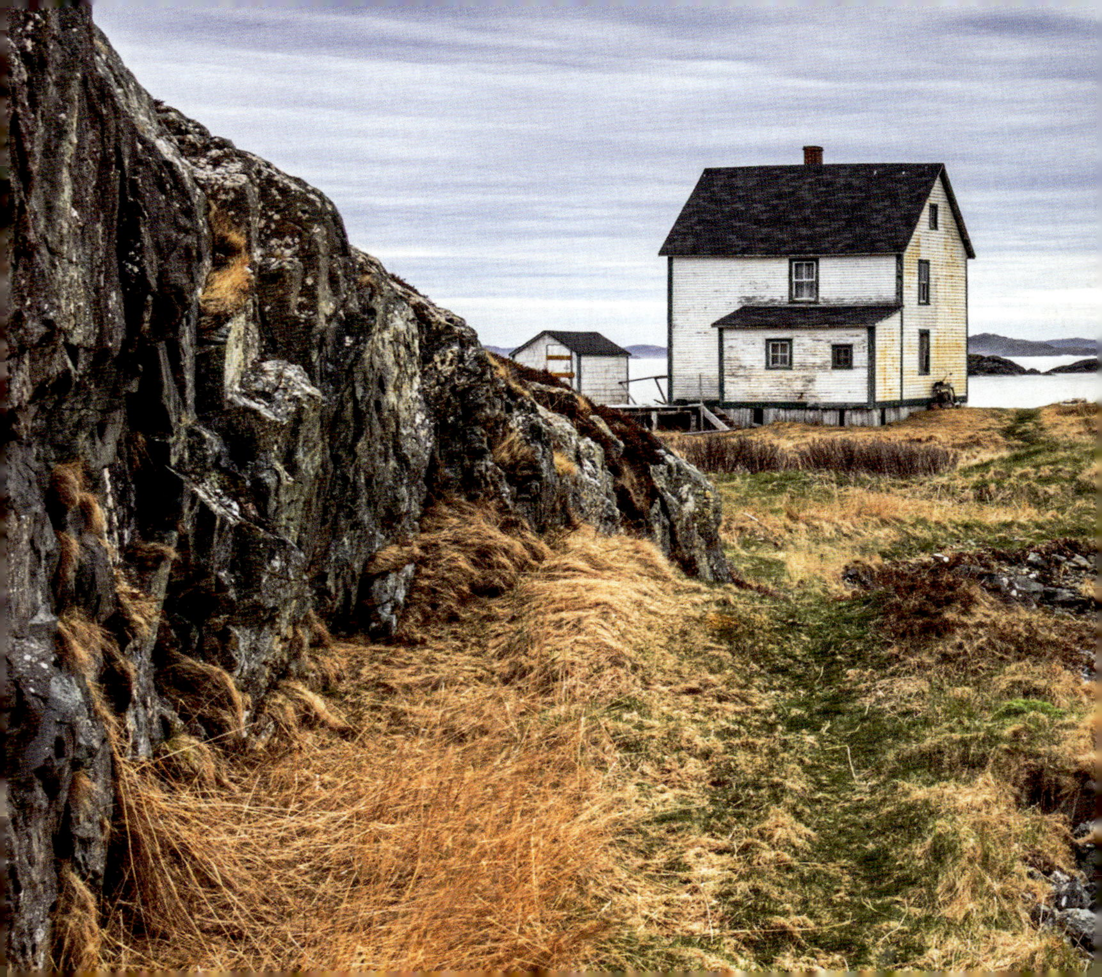

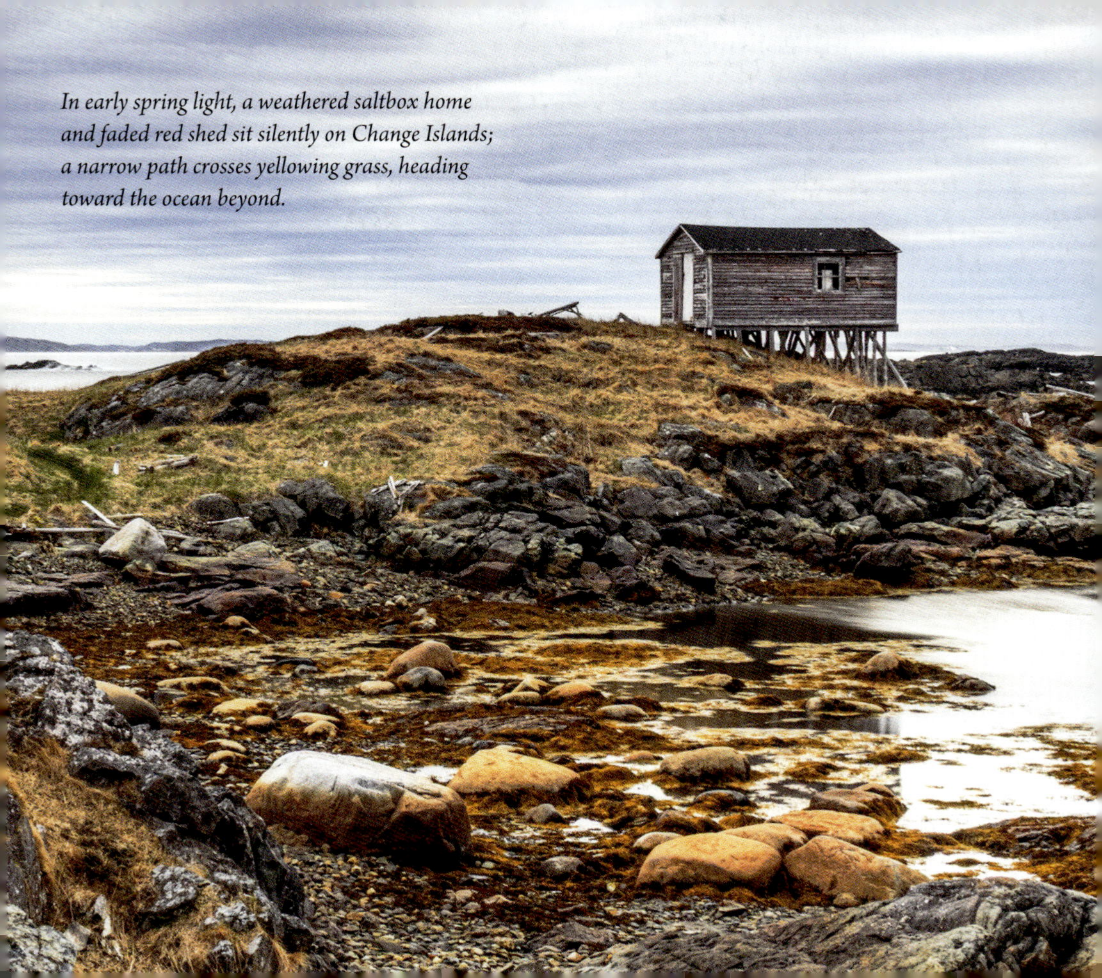

In early spring light, a weathered saltbox home and faded red shed sit silently on Change Islands; a narrow path crosses yellowing grass, heading toward the ocean beyond.

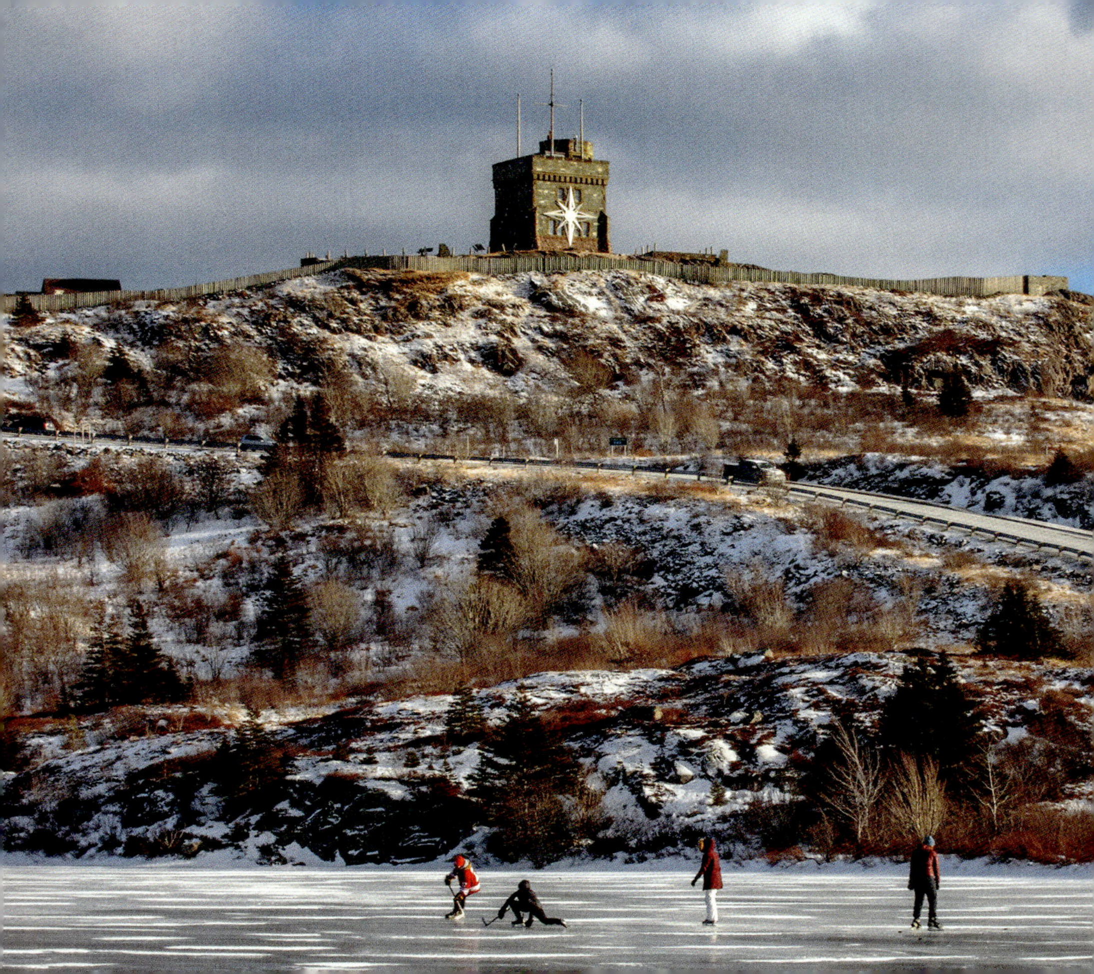

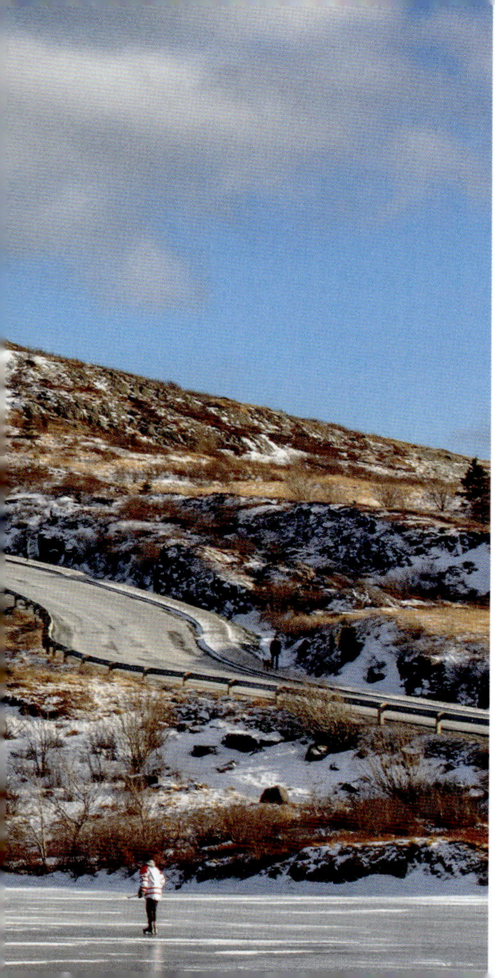

In early winter light, skaters and hockey players gather on George's Pond at Signal Hill, as Cabot Tower rises in the background above the frozen ice.

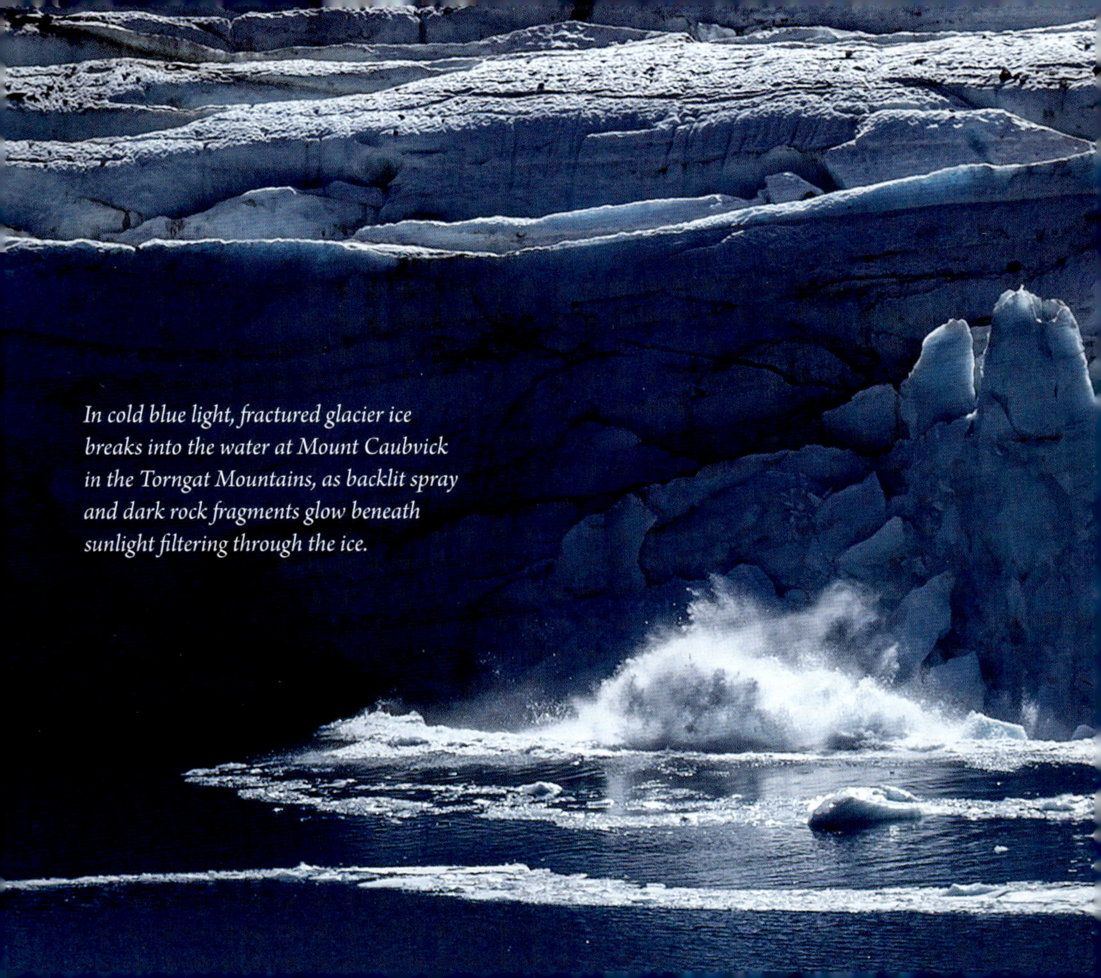

In cold blue light, fractured glacier ice breaks into the water at Mount Caubvick in the Torngat Mountains, as backlit spray and dark rock fragments glow beneath sunlight filtering through the ice.

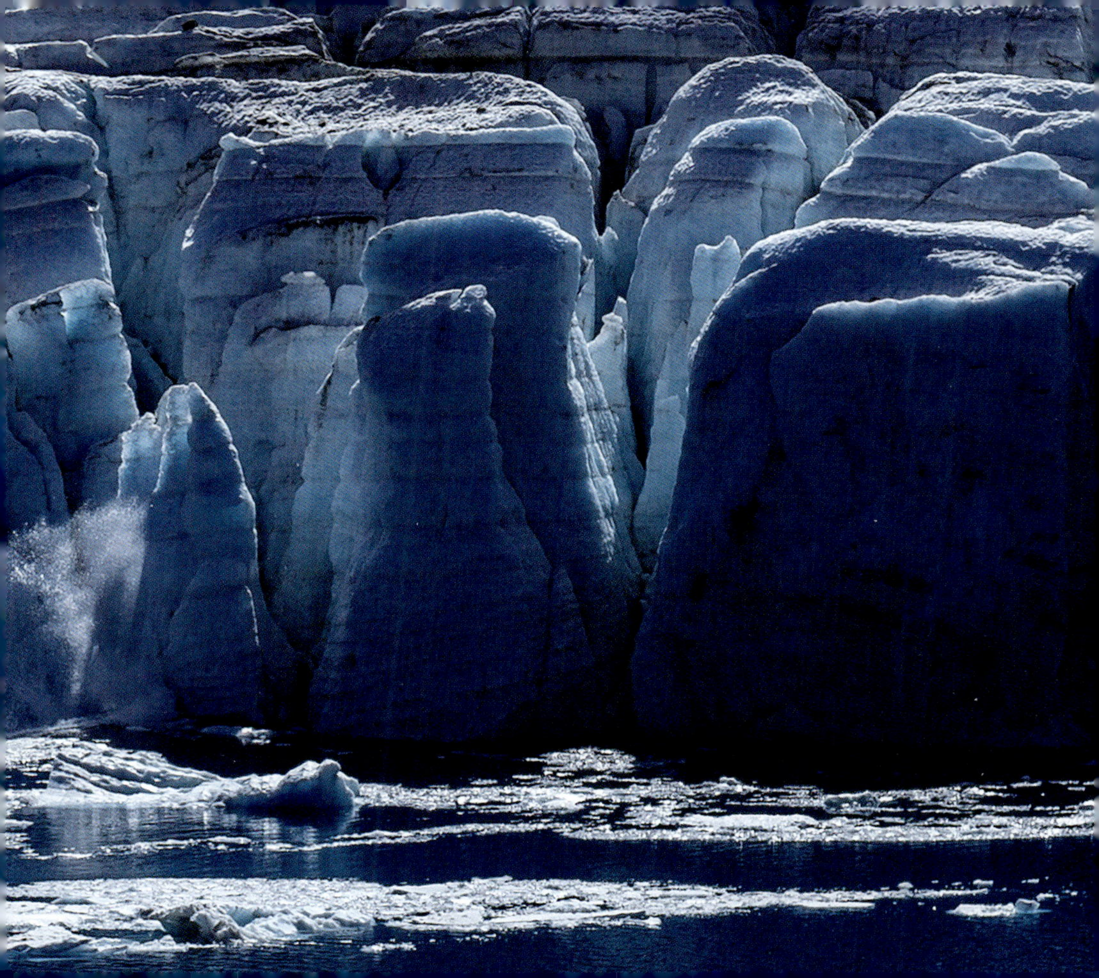

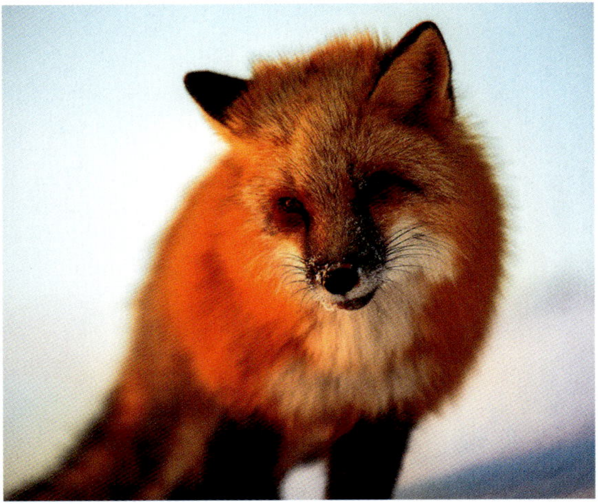

In early morning light, a red fox stands alert in St. John's, warm sunlight catching its fur as sharp eyes and whiskers hold focus, a faint trace of blood on its nose from a recent hunt in the snow.

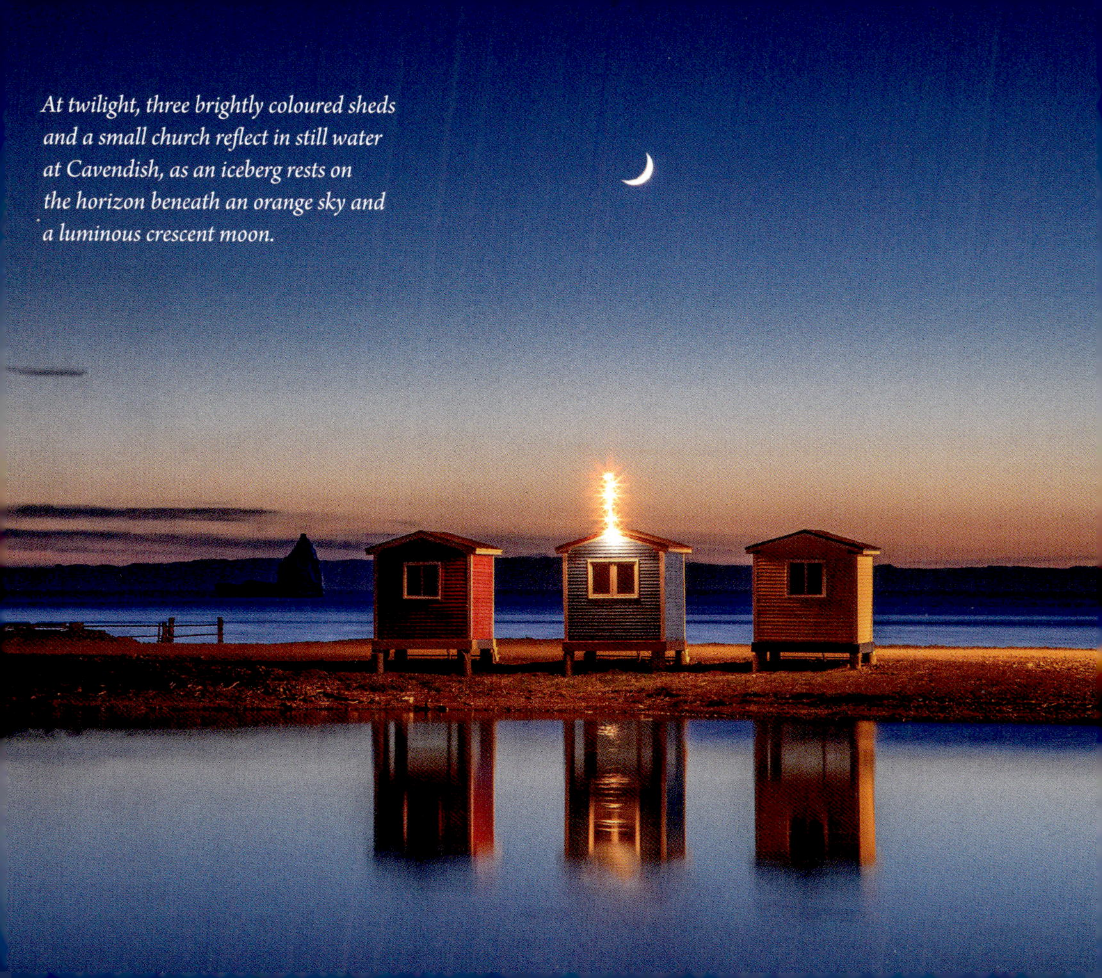

At twilight, three brightly coloured sheds and a small church reflect in still water at Cavendish, as an iceberg rests on the horizon beneath an orange sky and a luminous crescent moon.

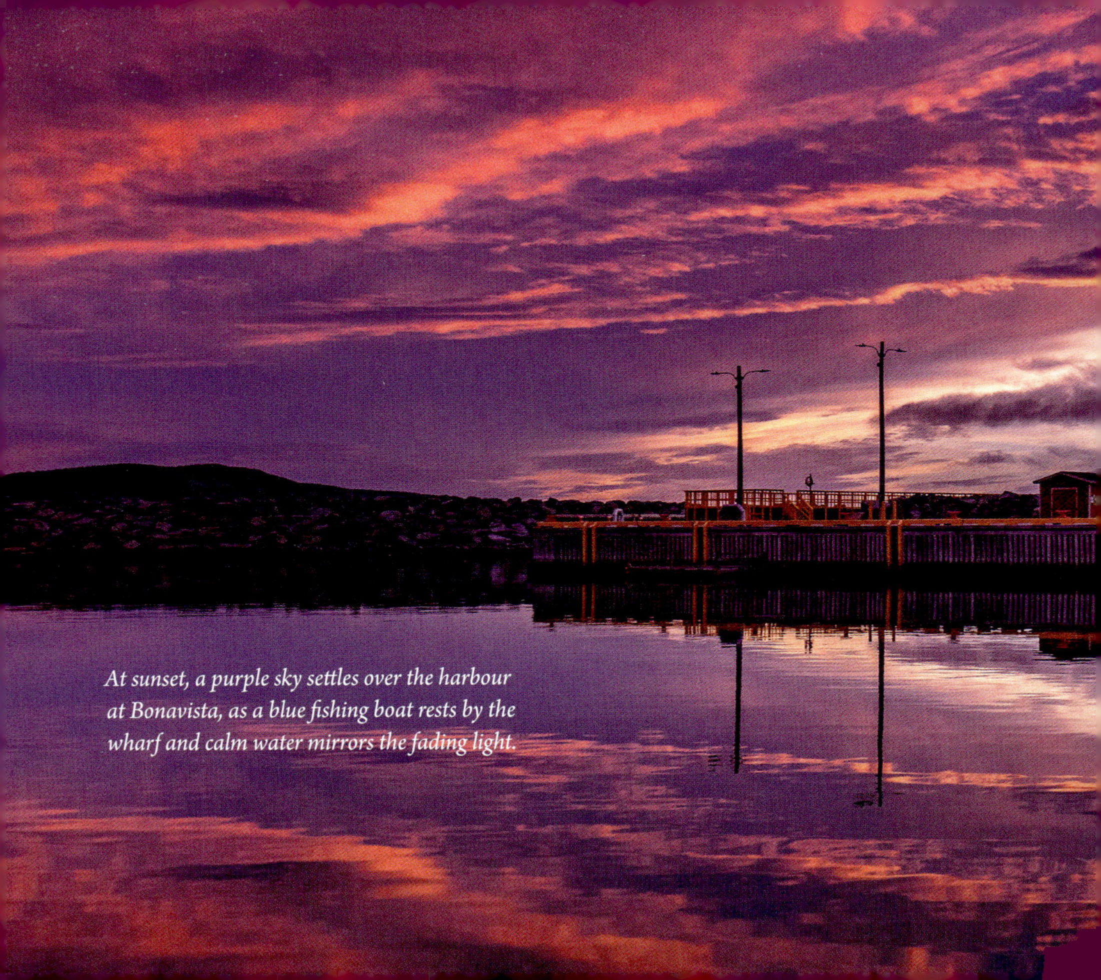

At sunset, a purple sky settles over the harbour at Bonavista, as a blue fishing boat rests by the wharf and calm water mirrors the fading light.

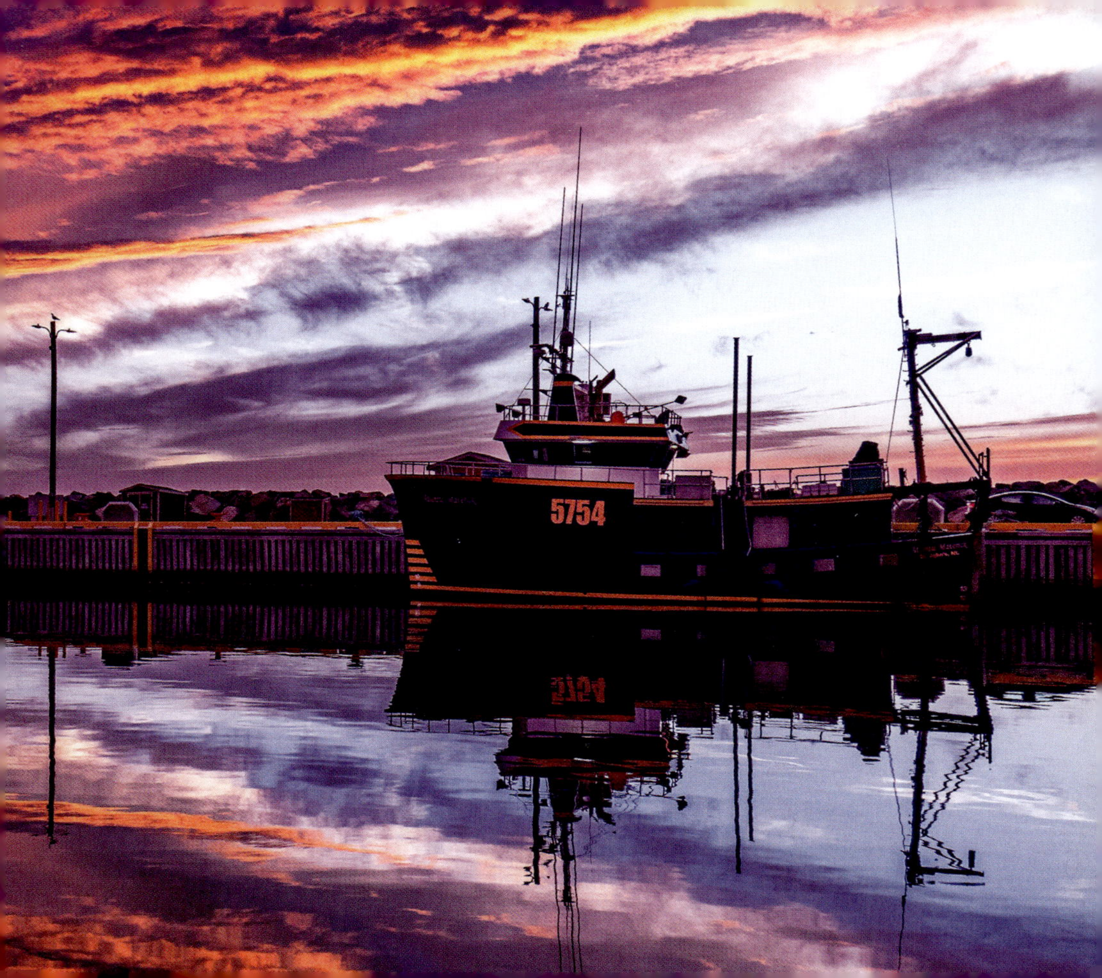
5754

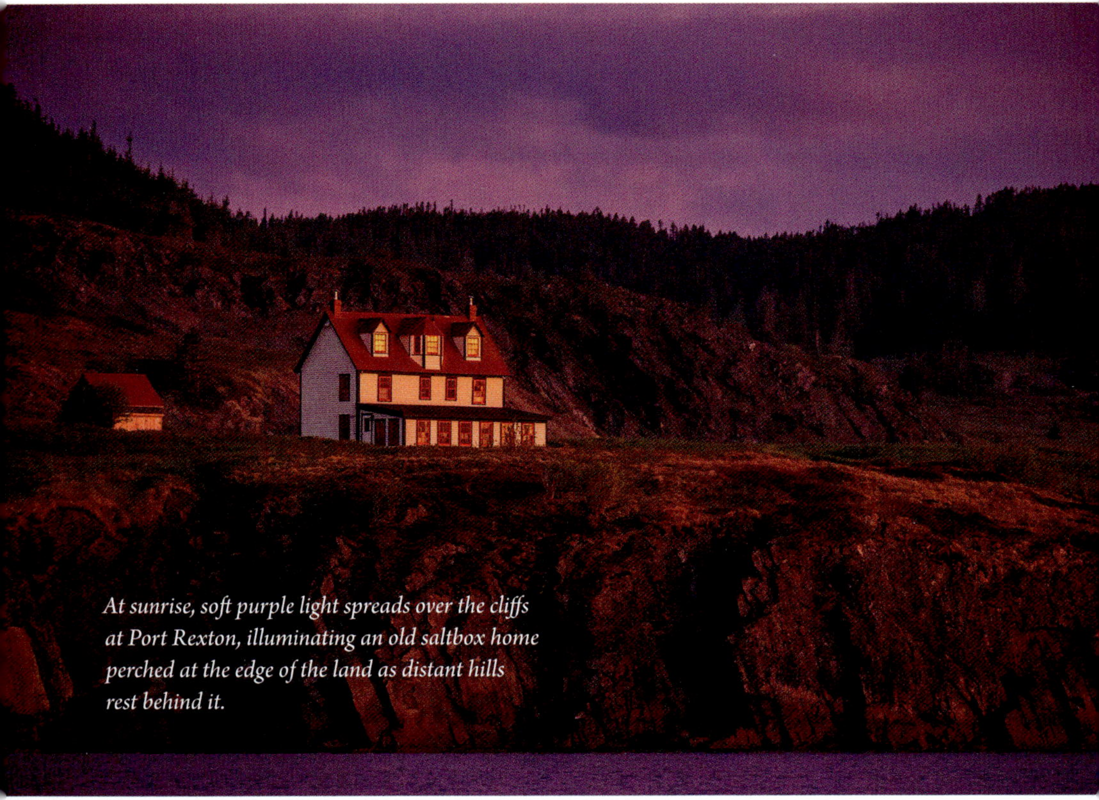

At sunrise, soft purple light spreads over the cliffs at Port Rexton, illuminating an old saltbox home perched at the edge of the land as distant hills rest behind it.

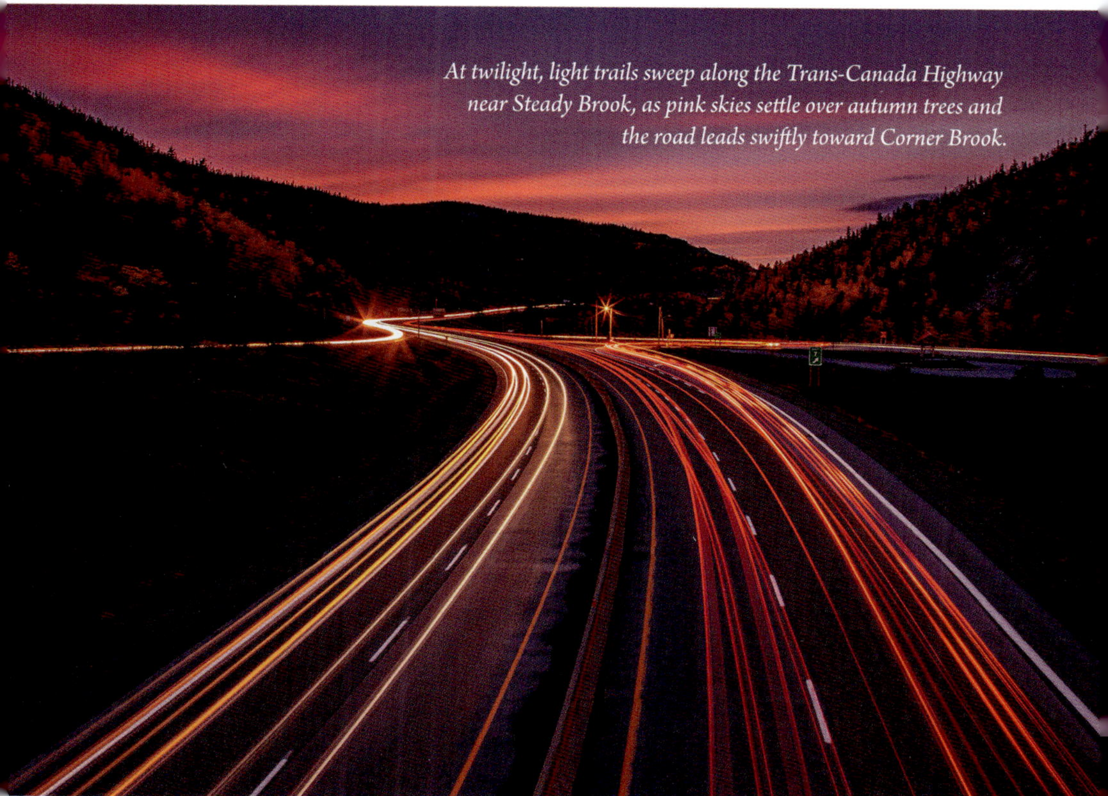

At twilight, light trails sweep along the Trans-Canada Highway near Steady Brook, as pink skies settle over autumn trees and the road leads swiftly toward Corner Brook.

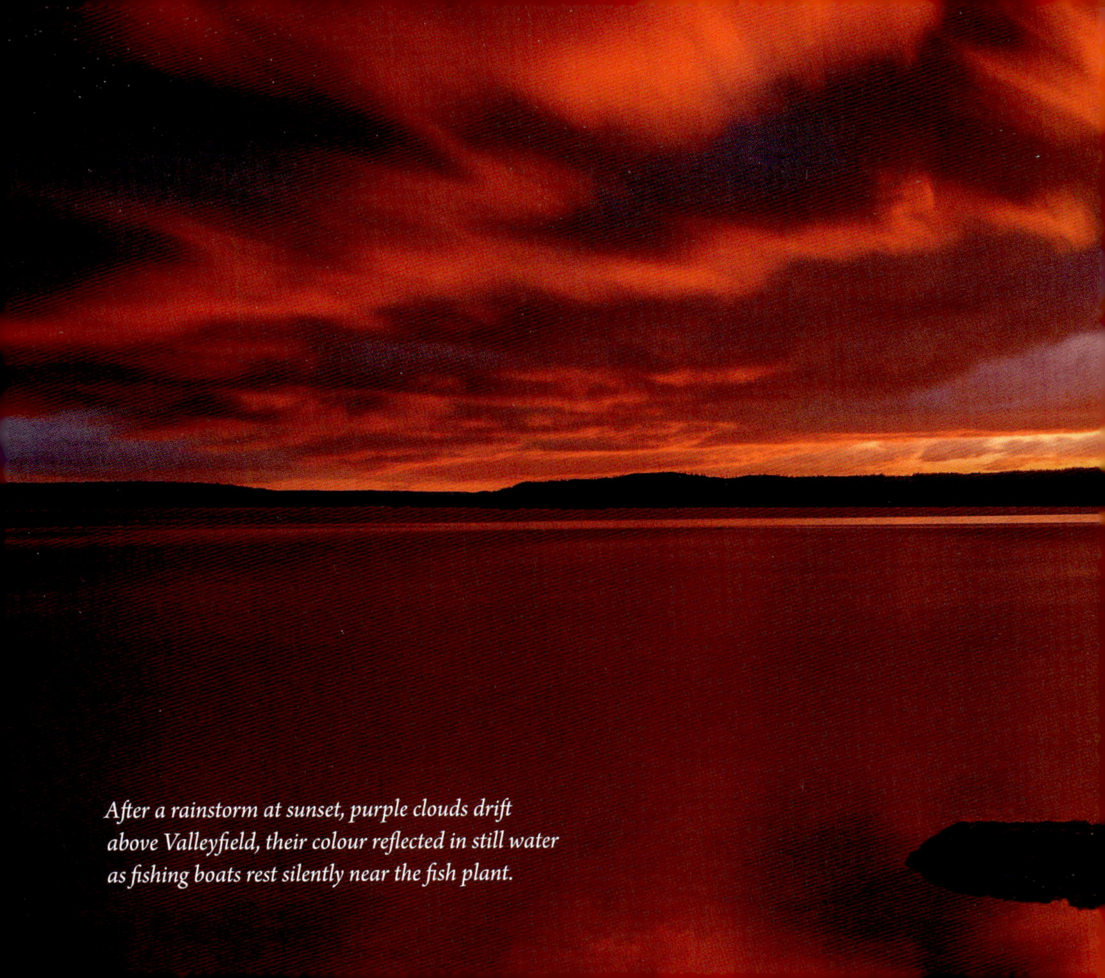

After a rainstorm at sunset, purple clouds drift above Valleyfield, their colour reflected in still water as fishing boats rest silently near the fish plant.

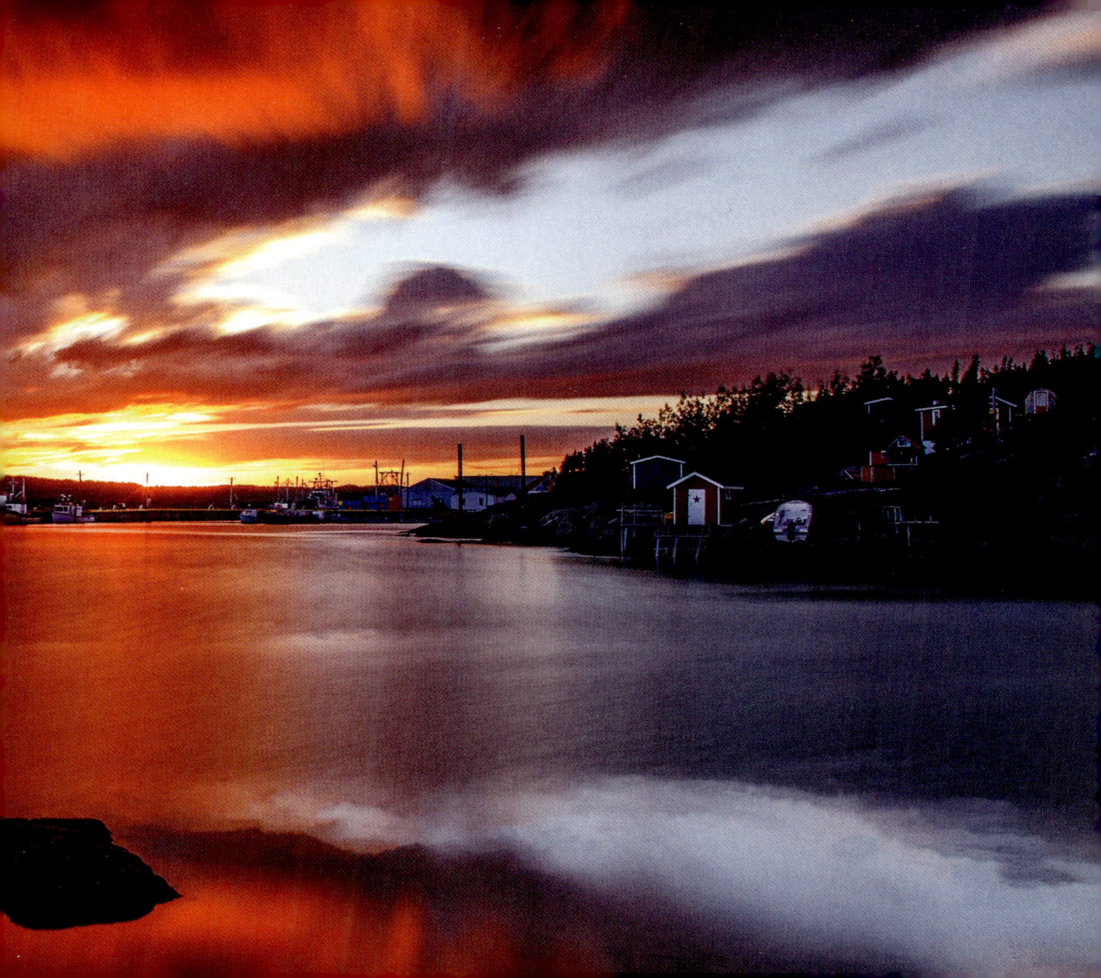

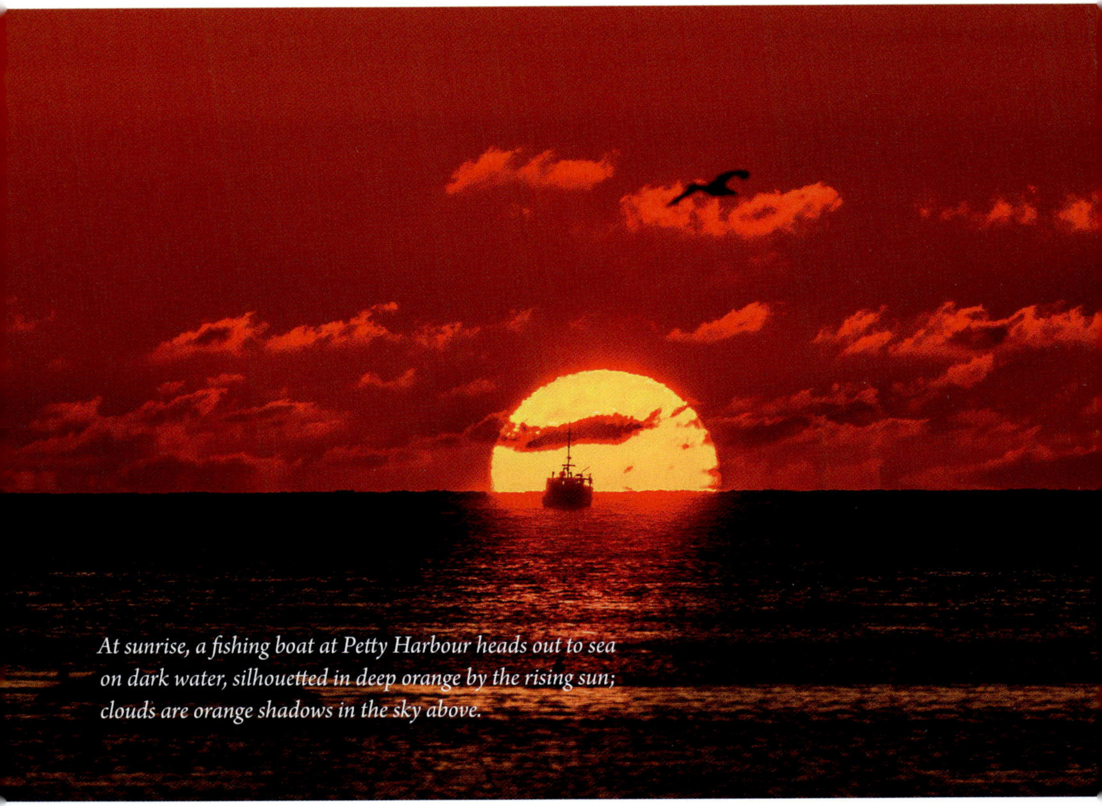

At sunrise, a fishing boat at Petty Harbour heads out to sea on dark water, silhouetted in deep orange by the rising sun; clouds are orange shadows in the sky above.

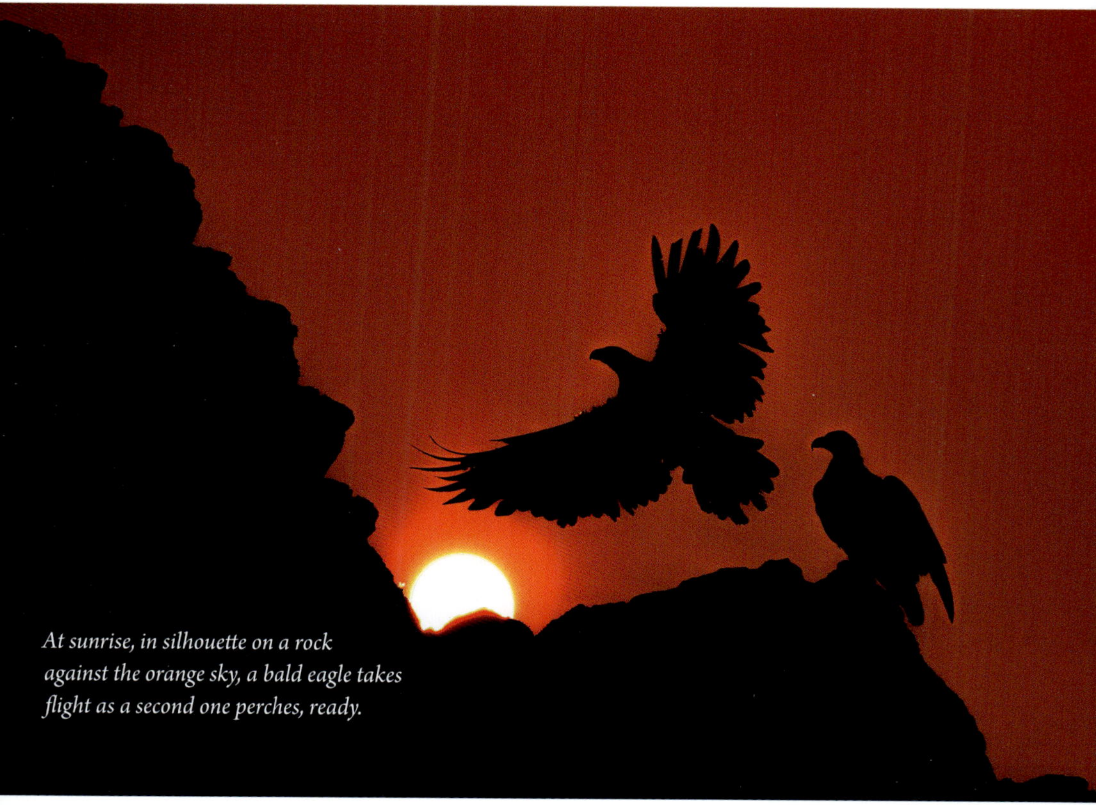

At sunrise, in silhouette on a rock against the orange sky, a bald eagle takes flight as a second one perches, ready.

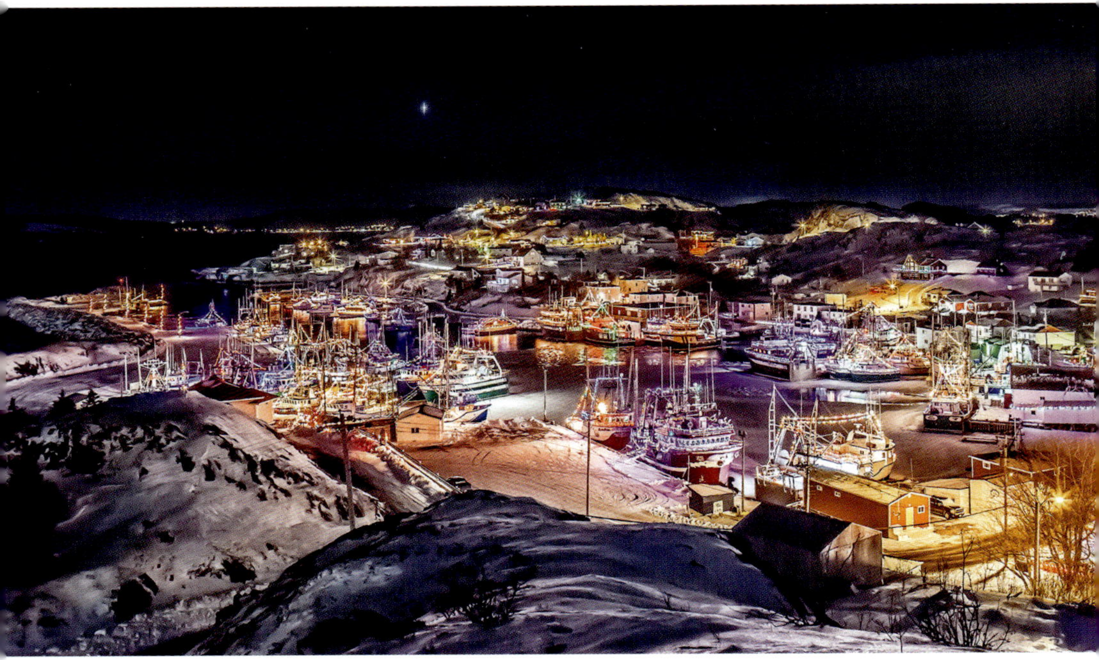

On a winter night, the harbour at Port de Grave glows during the annual Christmas boat lighting; snow lines the shore and a lone star shines in the sky above the decorated vessels.

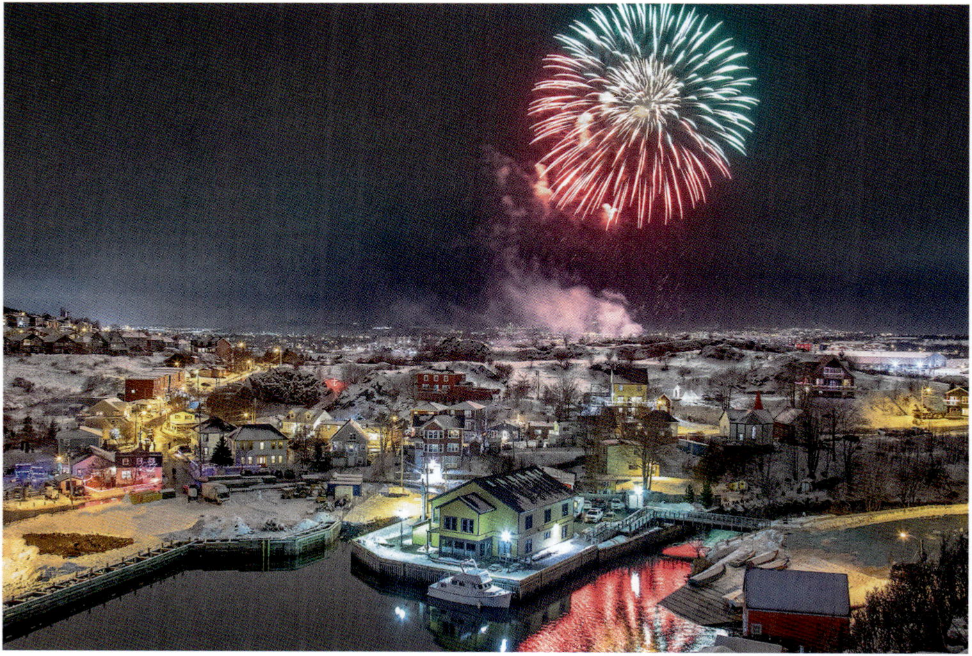

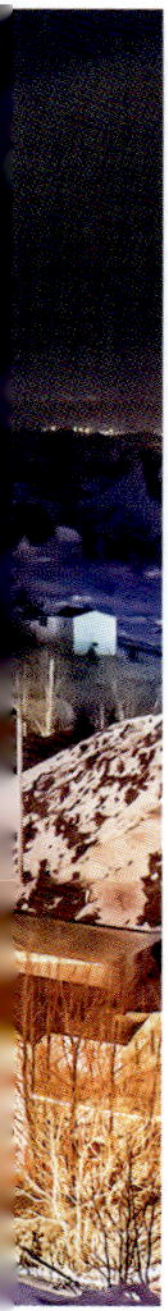

On New Year's Eve, fireworks light the sky over Quidi Vidi, as fresh snow blankets the harbour and bursts of colour reflect softly in the water below.

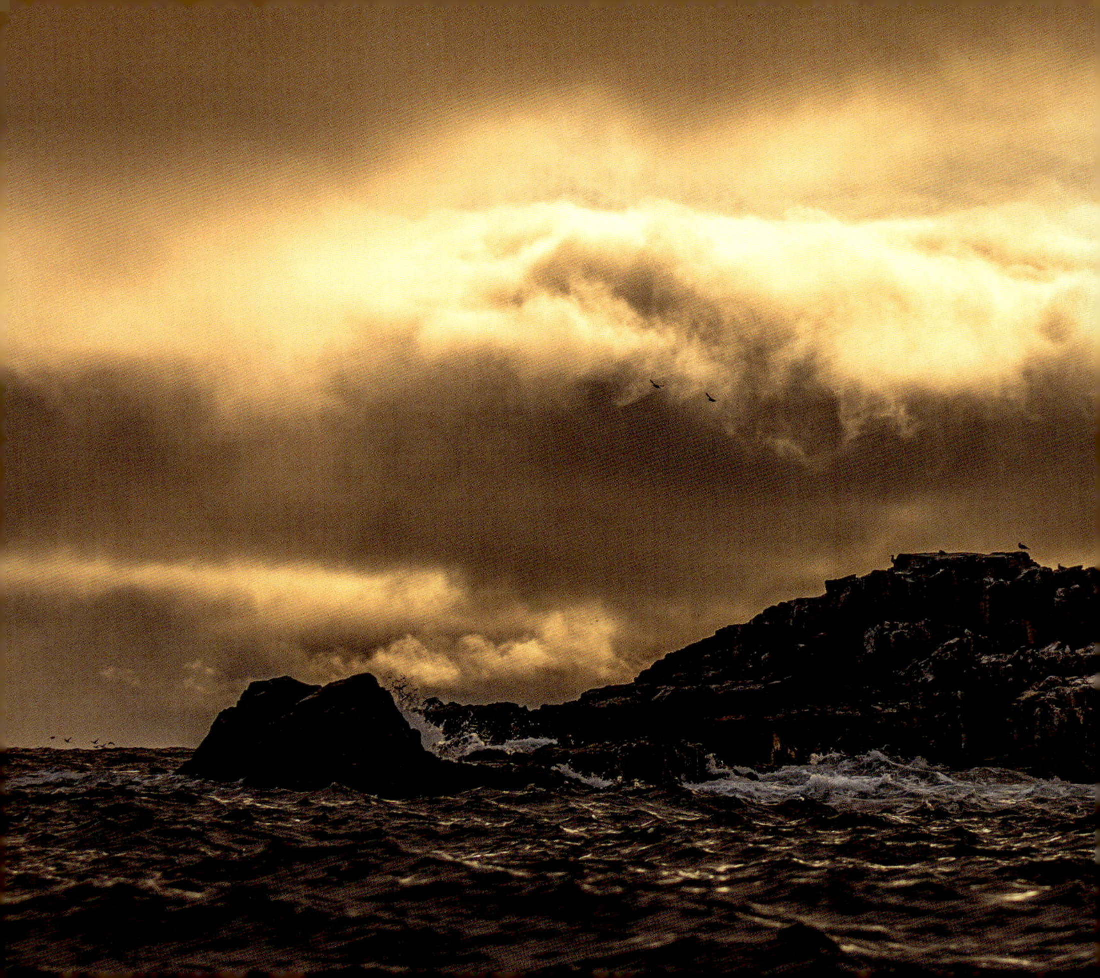

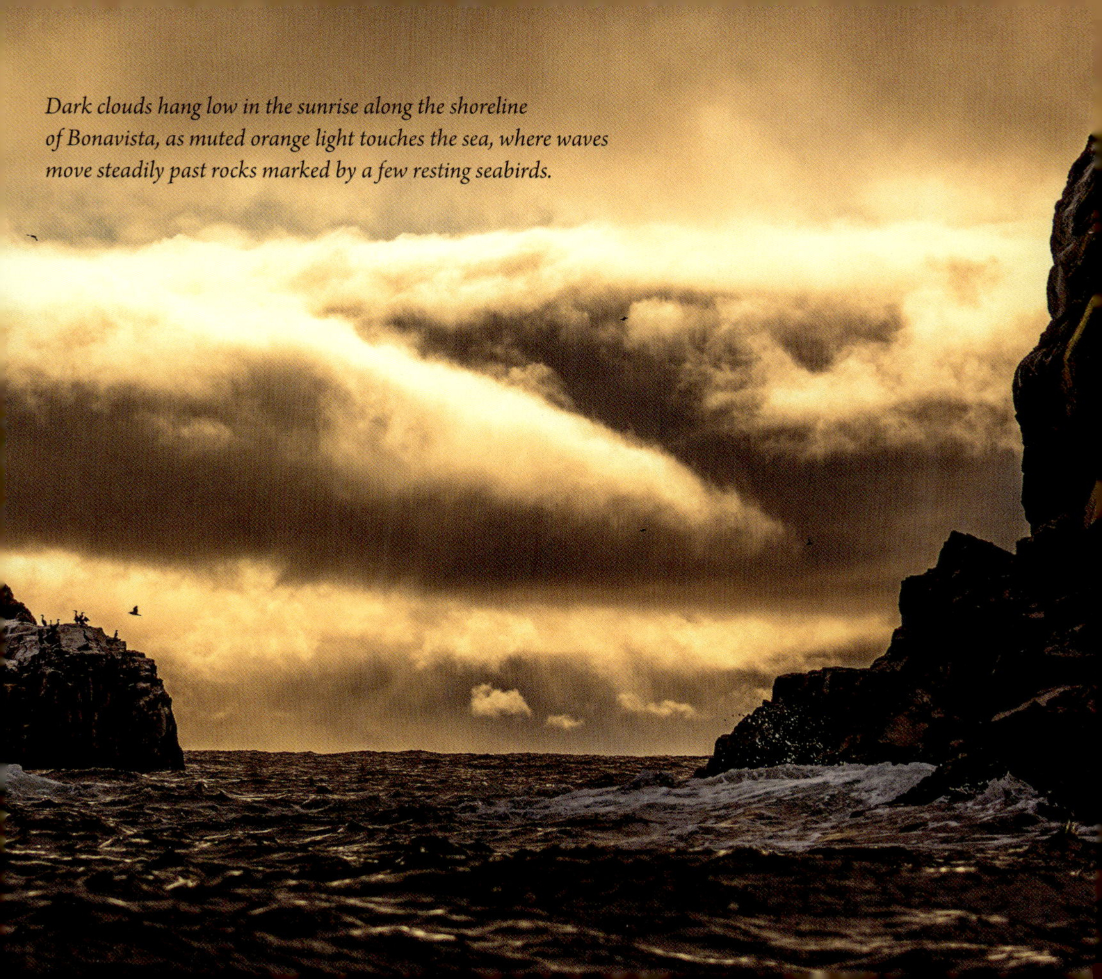

Dark clouds hang low in the sunrise along the shoreline of Bonavista, as muted orange light touches the sea, where waves move steadily past rocks marked by a few resting seabirds.

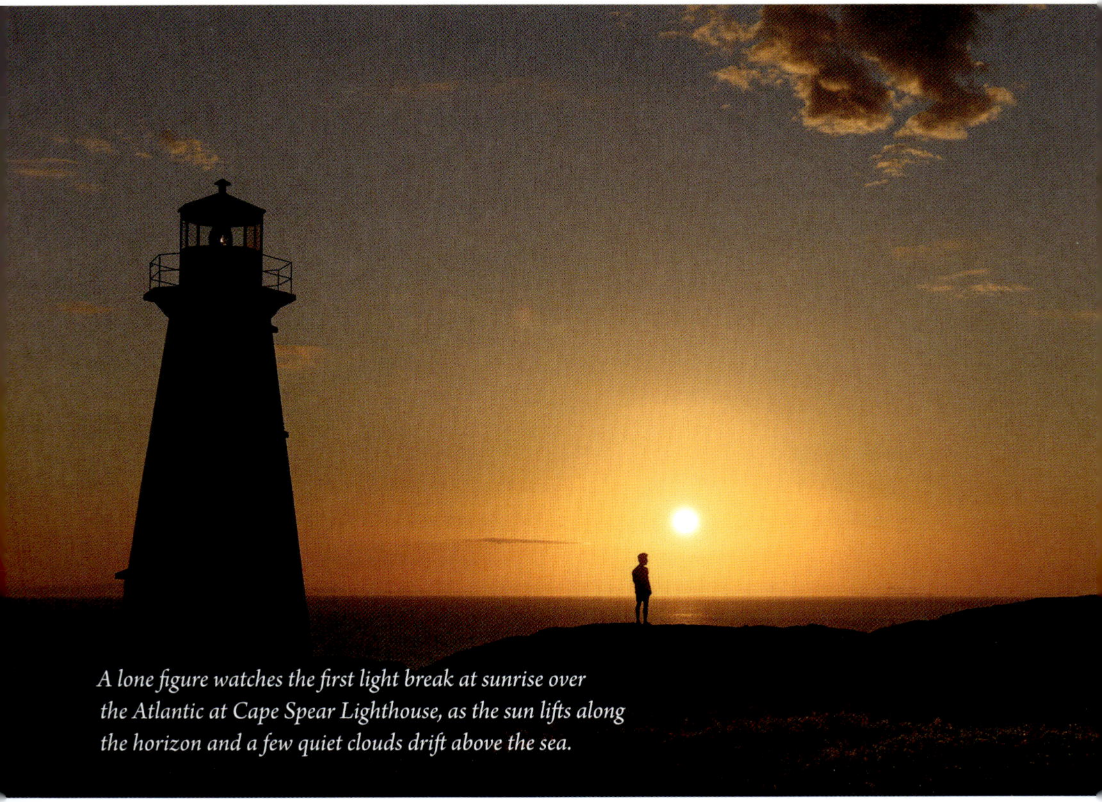

A lone figure watches the first light break at sunrise over the Atlantic at Cape Spear Lighthouse, as the sun lifts along the horizon and a few quiet clouds drift above the sea.

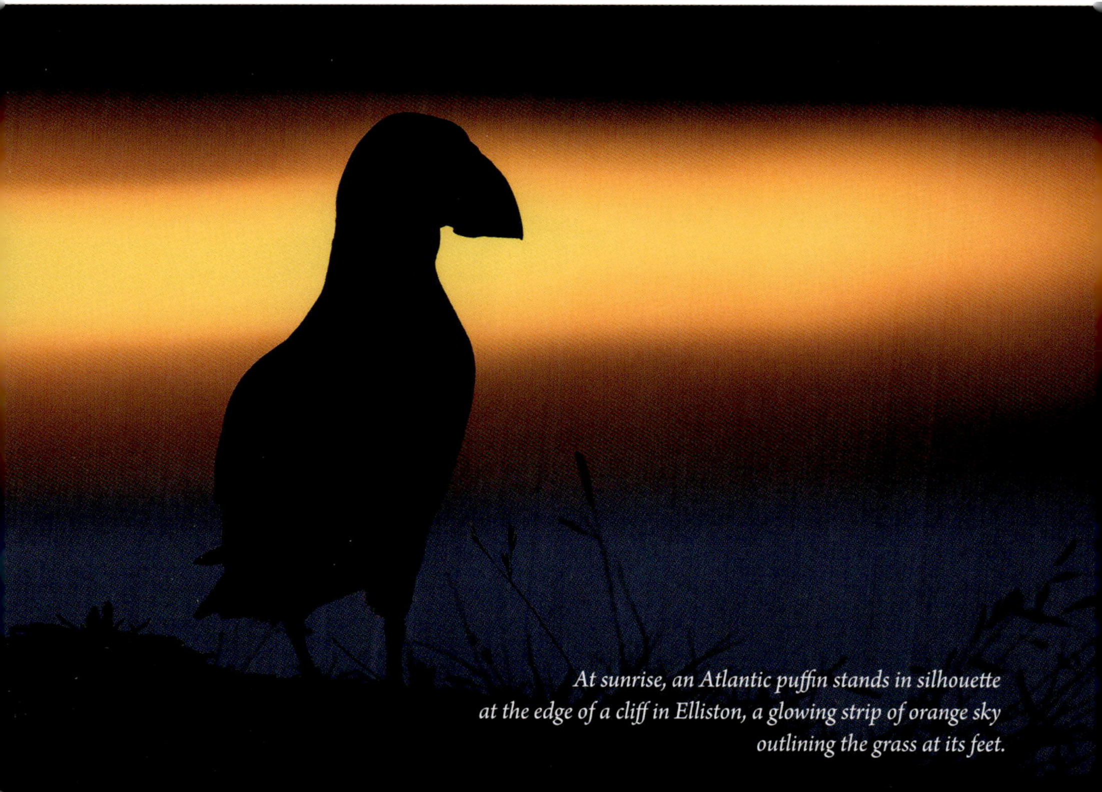

At sunrise, an Atlantic puffin stands in silhouette at the edge of a cliff in Elliston, a glowing strip of orange sky outlining the grass at its feet.

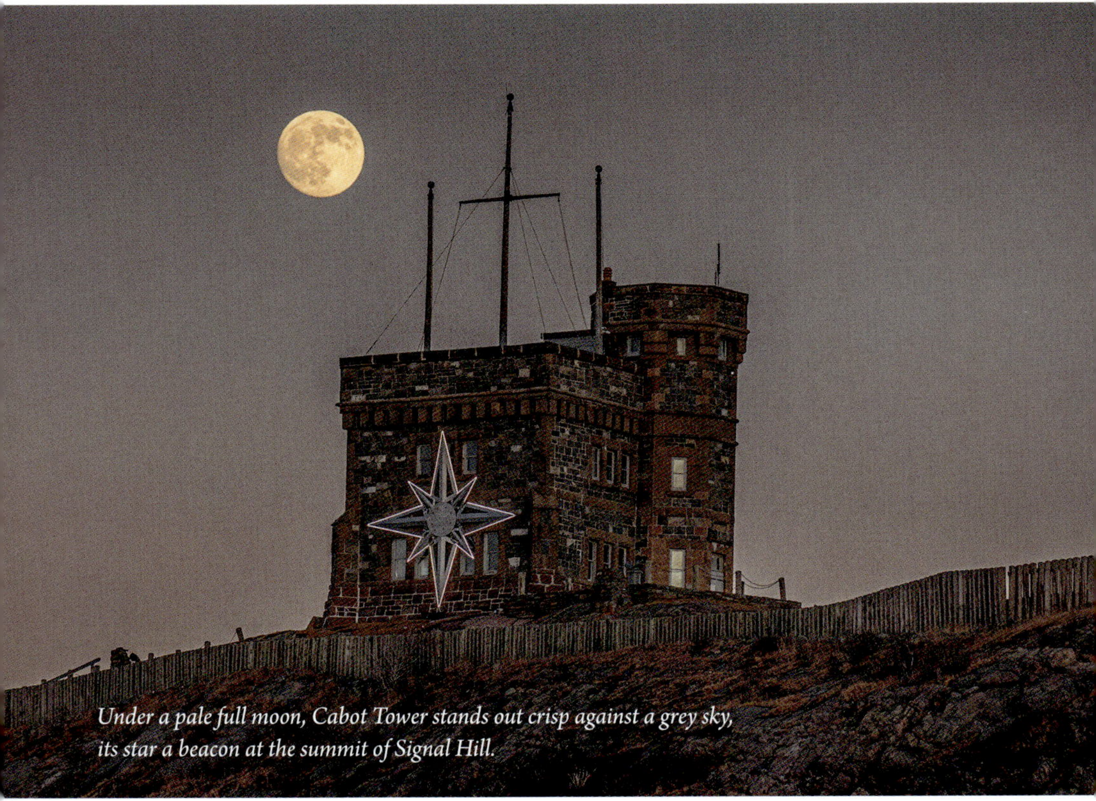

Under a pale full moon, Cabot Tower stands out crisp against a grey sky, its star a beacon at the summit of Signal Hill.

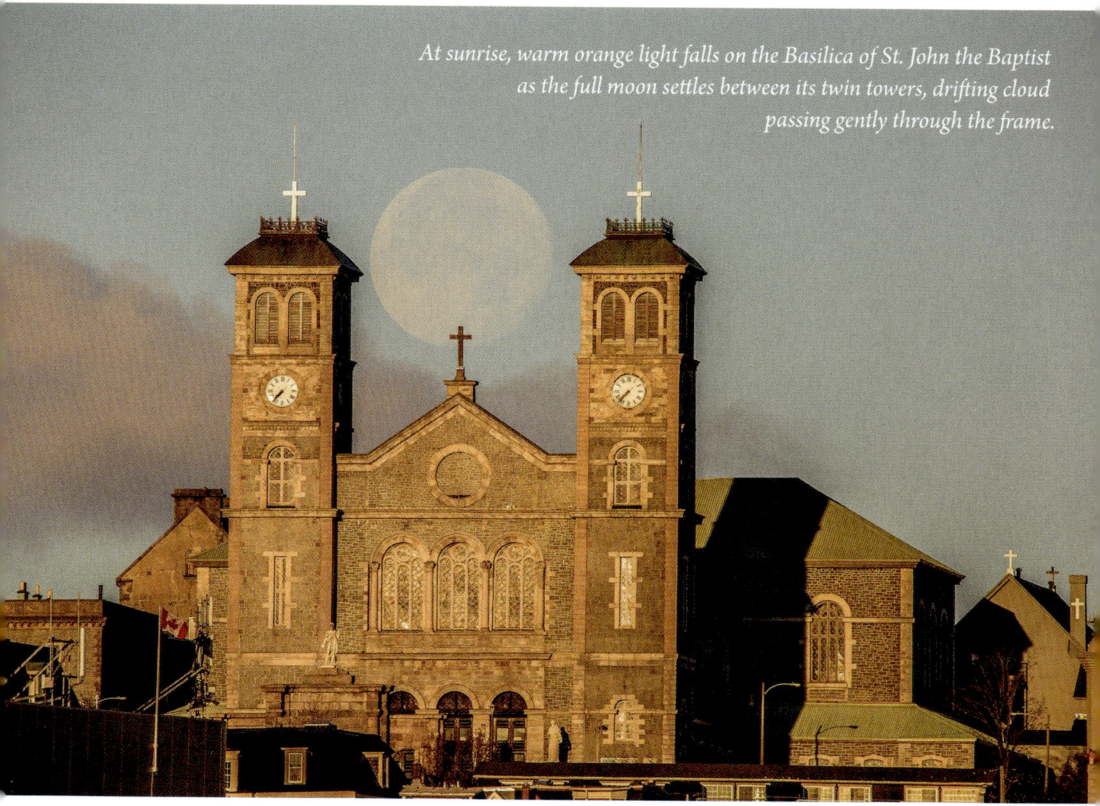

At sunrise, warm orange light falls on the Basilica of St. John the Baptist as the full moon settles between its twin towers, drifting cloud passing gently through the frame.

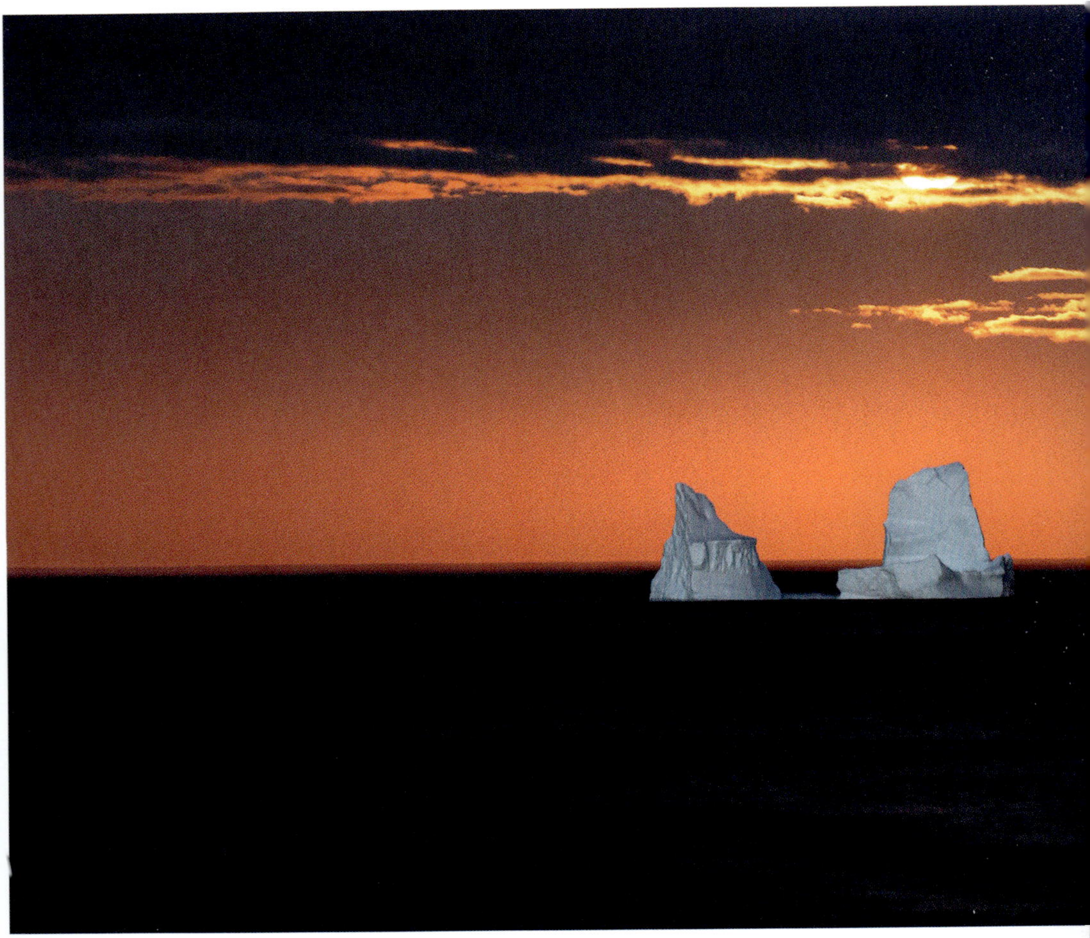

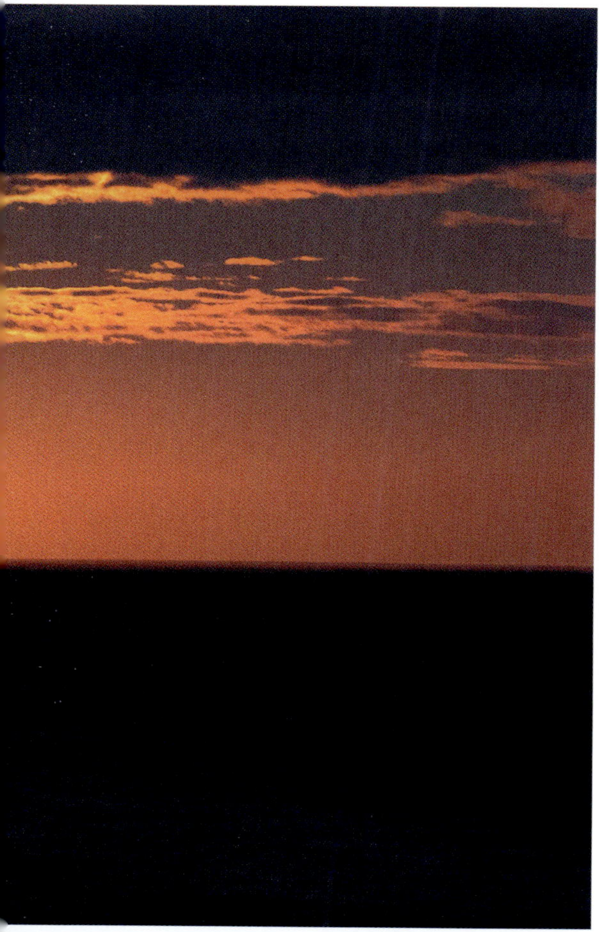

At moonrise, a two-pillared iceberg rests on the horizon near Maddox Cove, glowing softly beneath clouded moonlight as dark blue water stretches in the foreground.

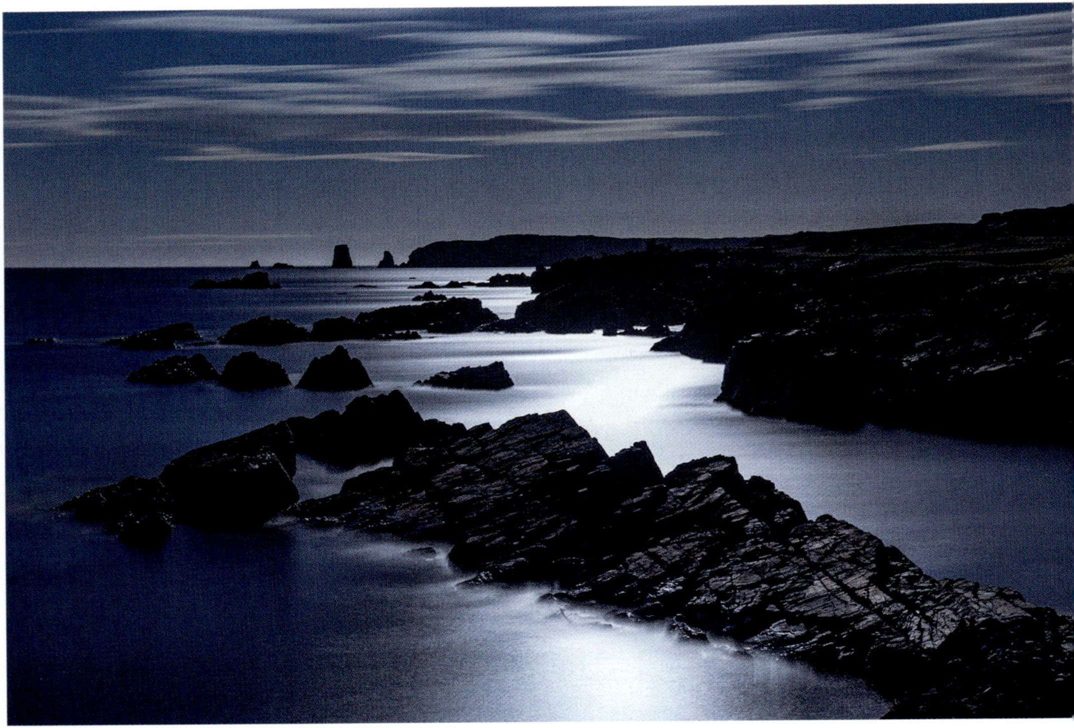

At night, moonlight spills across the coastline of Dungeon Provincial Park, where dark sea stacks rise from blue water and lead the eye toward the distant horizon.

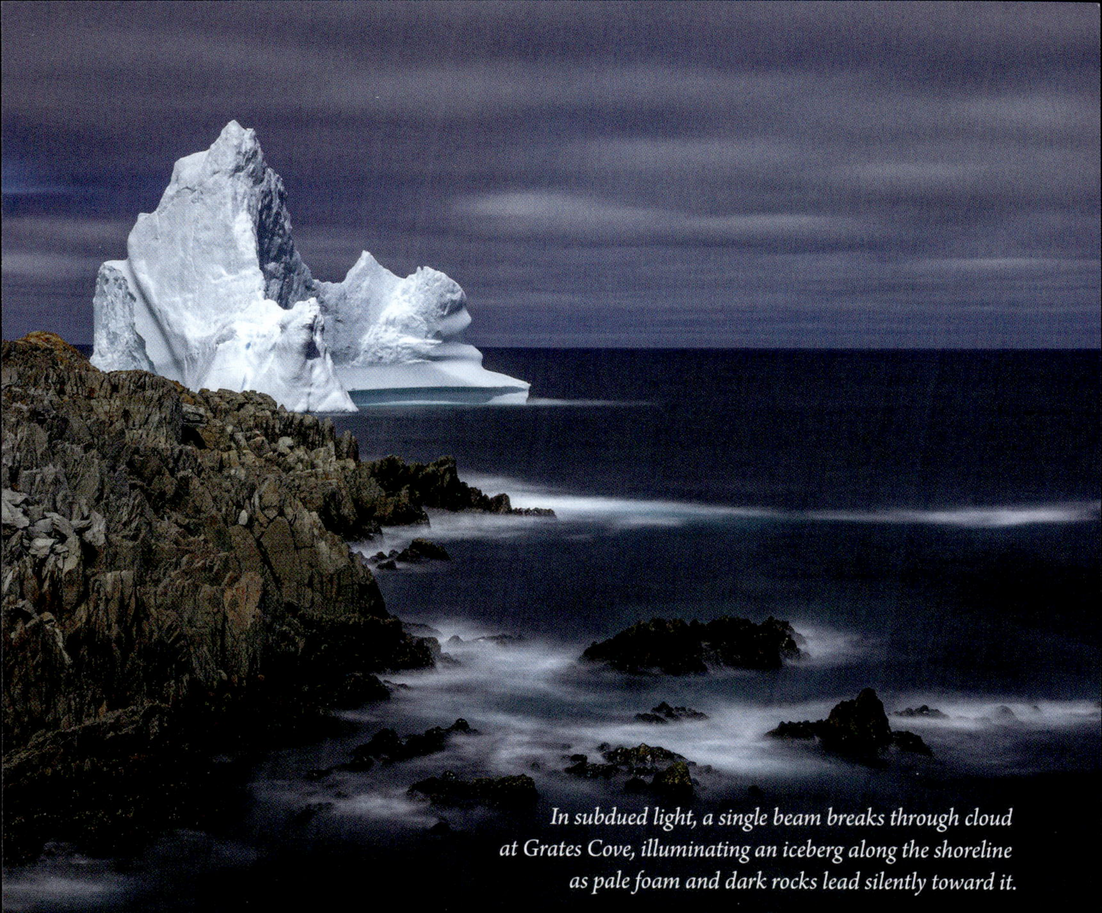

In subdued light, a single beam breaks through cloud at Grates Cove, illuminating an iceberg along the shoreline as pale foam and dark rocks lead silently toward it.

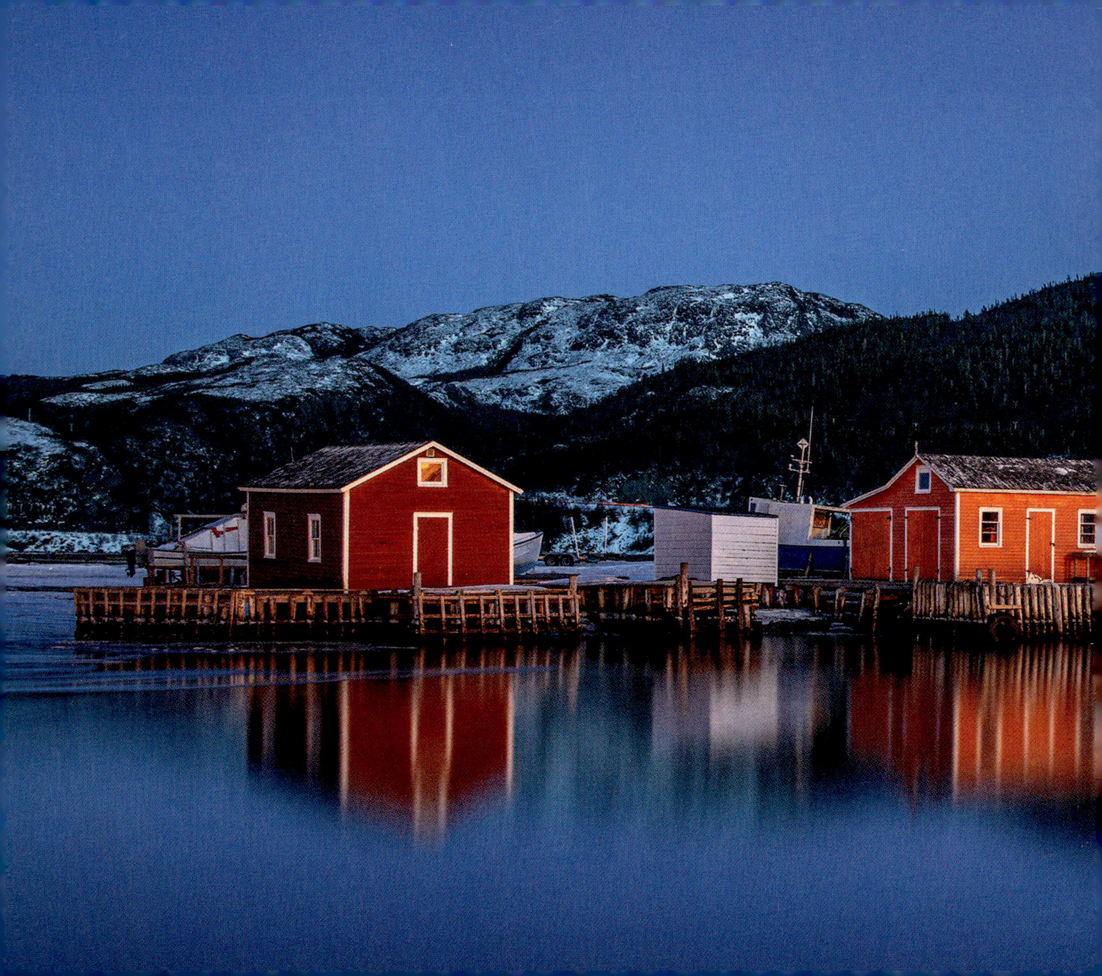

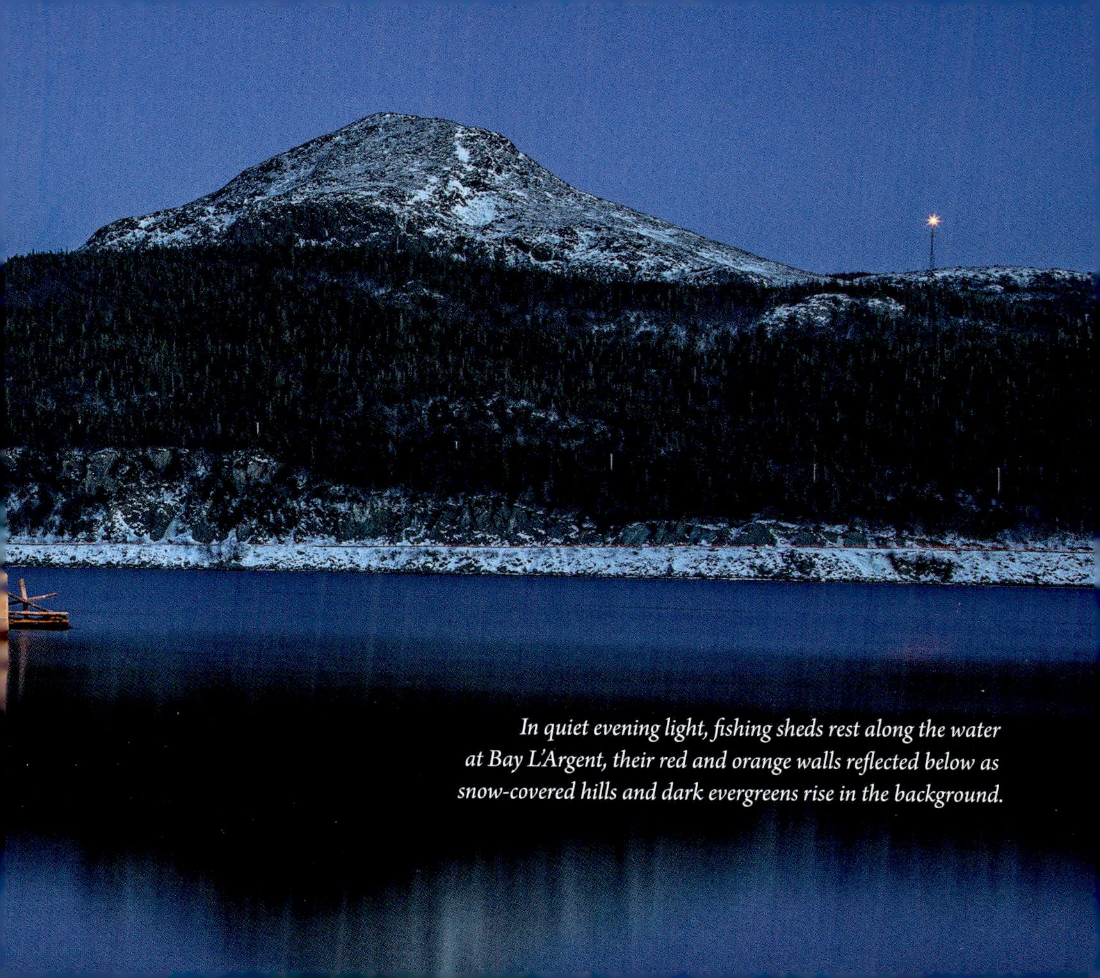

In quiet evening light, fishing sheds rest along the water at Bay L'Argent, their red and orange walls reflected below as snow-covered hills and dark evergreens rise in the background.

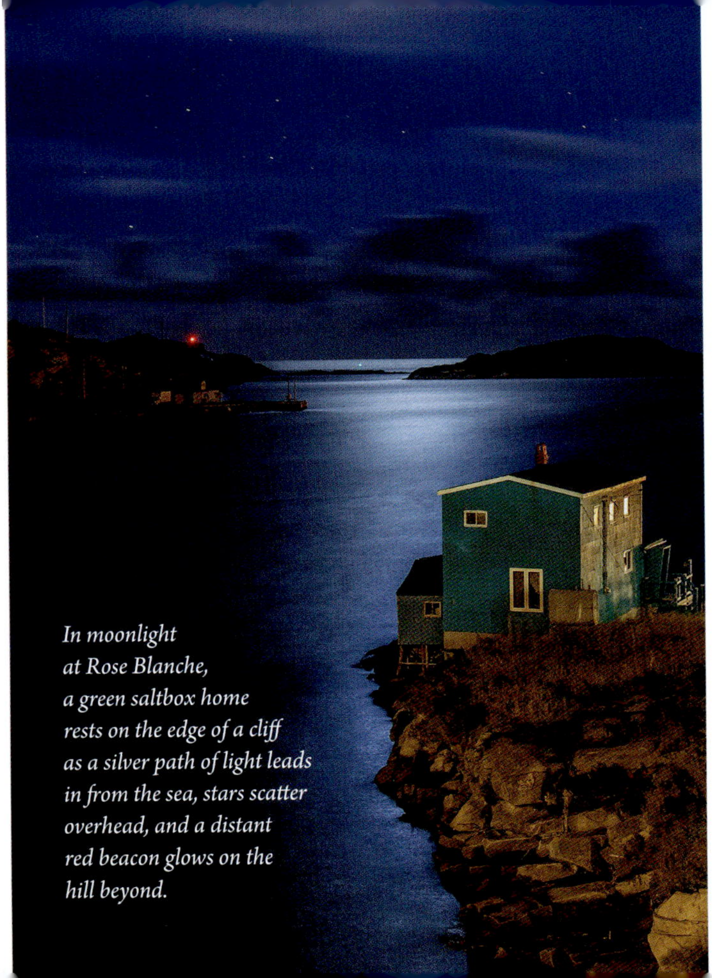

In moonlight
at Rose Blanche,
a green saltbox home
rests on the edge of a cliff
as a silver path of light leads
in from the sea, stars scatter
overhead, and a distant
red beacon glows on the
hill beyond.

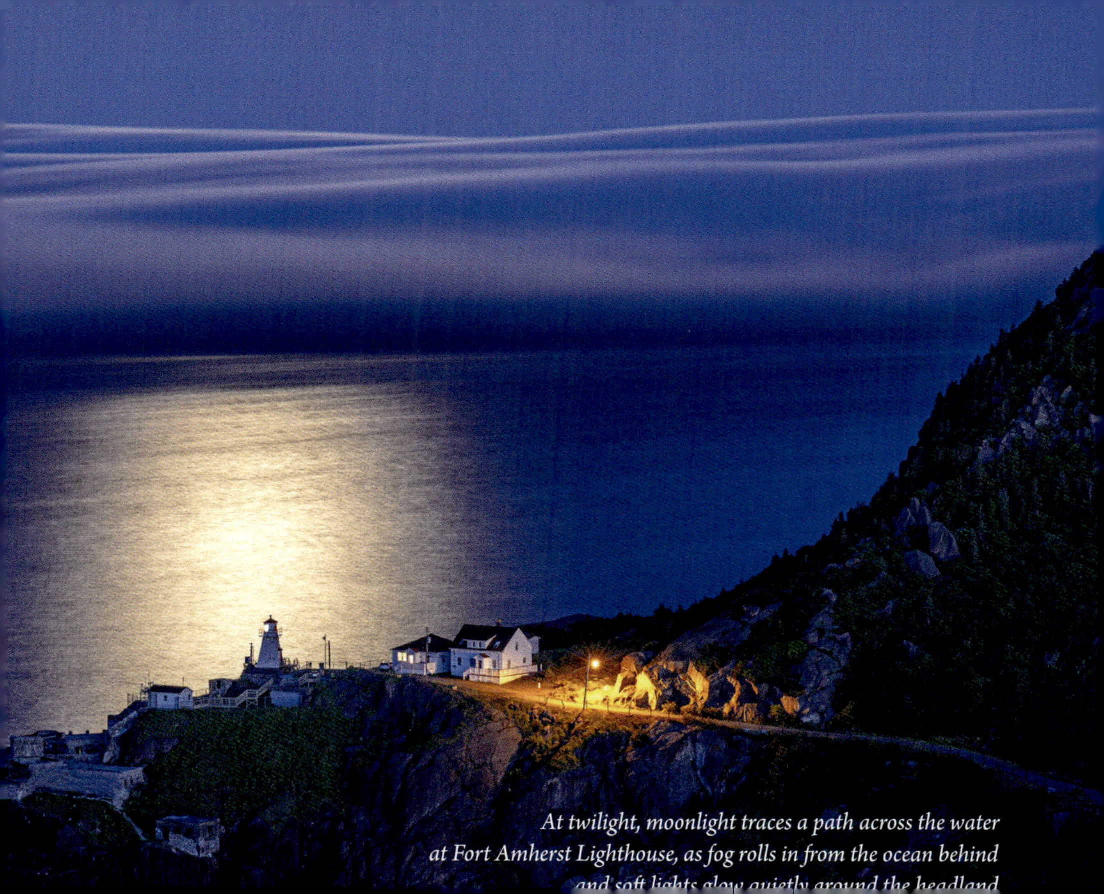

At twilight, moonlight traces a path across the water at Fort Amherst Lighthouse, as fog rolls in from the ocean behind and soft lights glow quietly around the headland

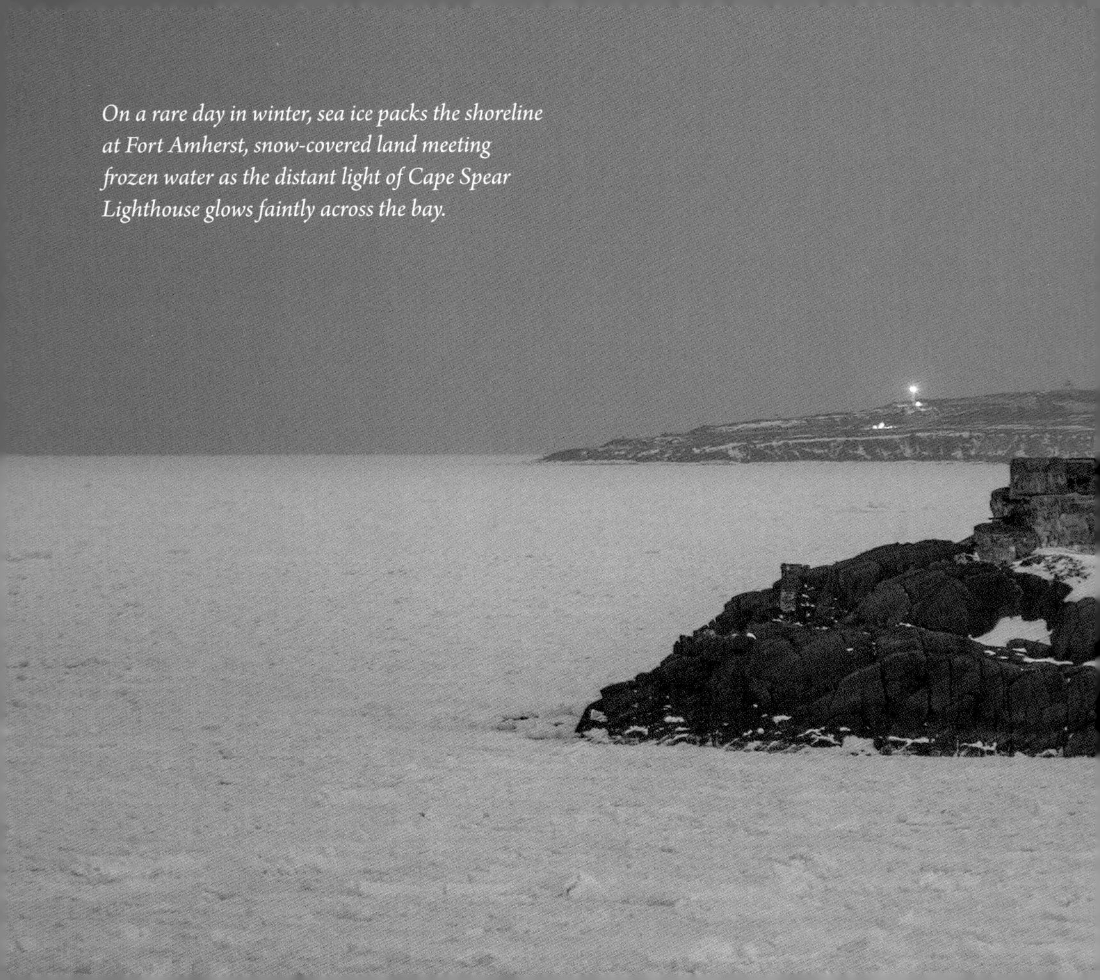

On a rare day in winter, sea ice packs the shoreline at Fort Amherst, snow-covered land meeting frozen water as the distant light of Cape Spear Lighthouse glows faintly across the bay.

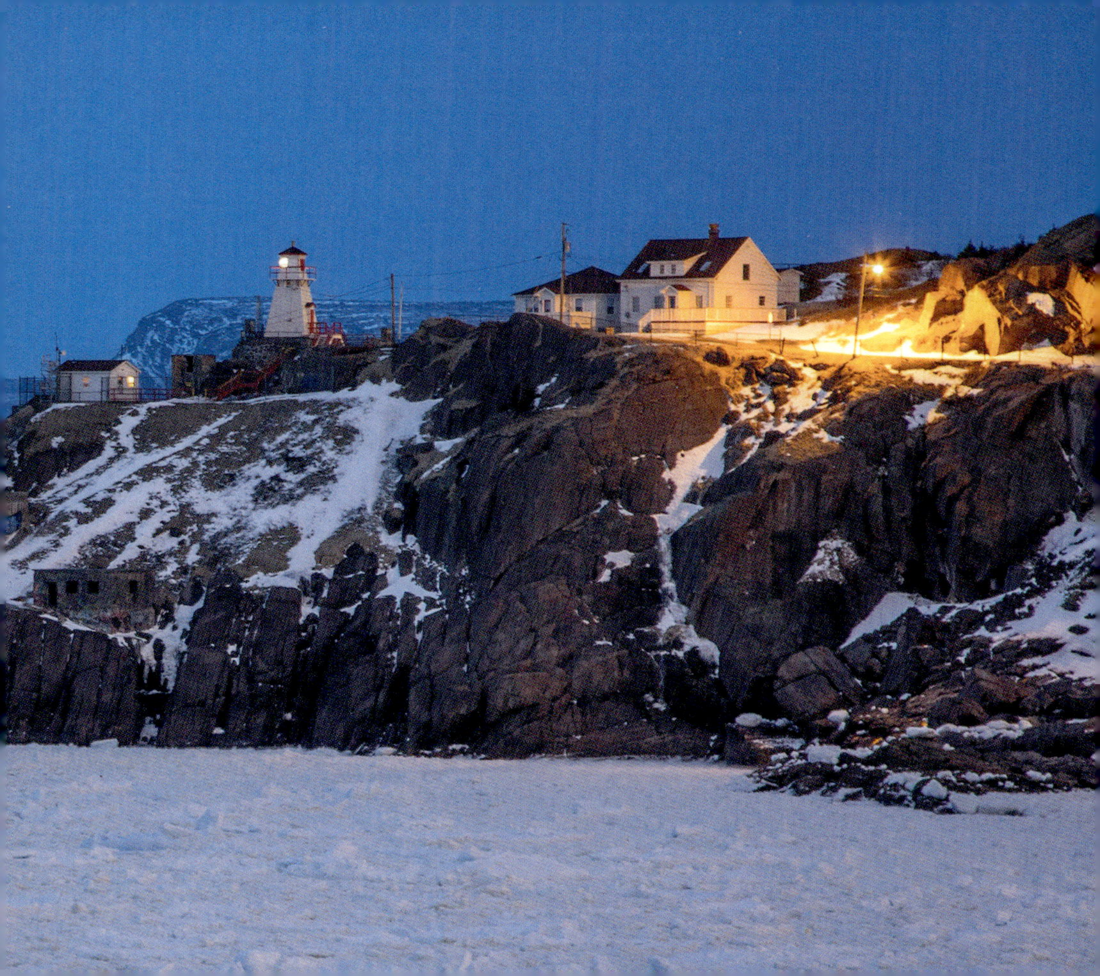

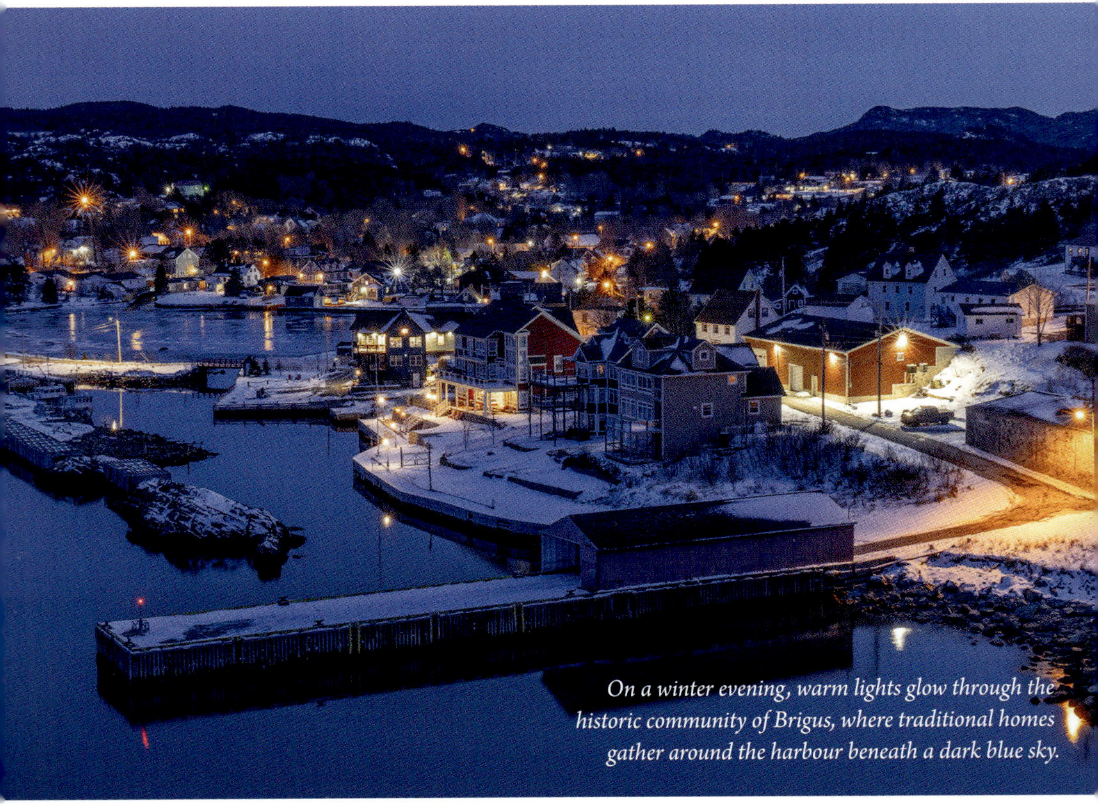

On a winter evening, warm lights glow through the historic community of Brigus, where traditional homes gather around the harbour beneath a dark blue sky.

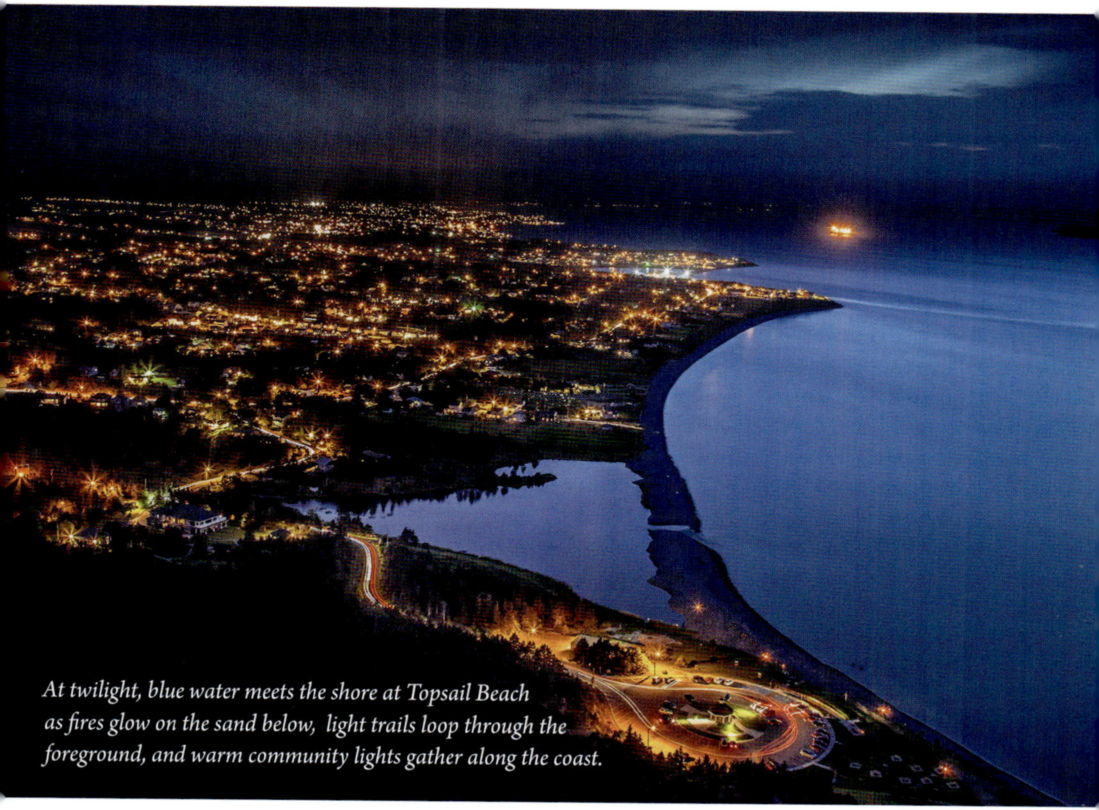

At twilight, blue water meets the shore at Topsail Beach as fires glow on the sand below, light trails loop through the foreground, and warm community lights gather along the coast.

At first light, traditional salt fish lie drying on the ground in Tilting, their forms captured in black and white, reflecting generations of practice beneath the rising sun.

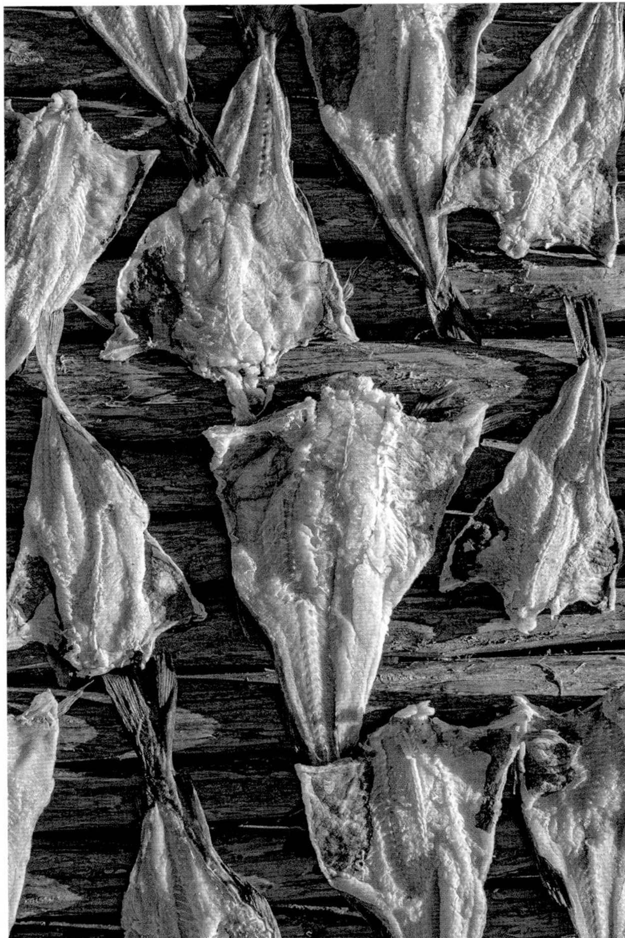

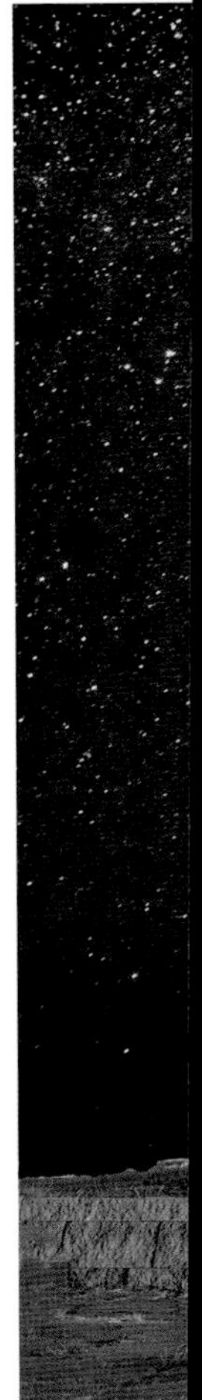

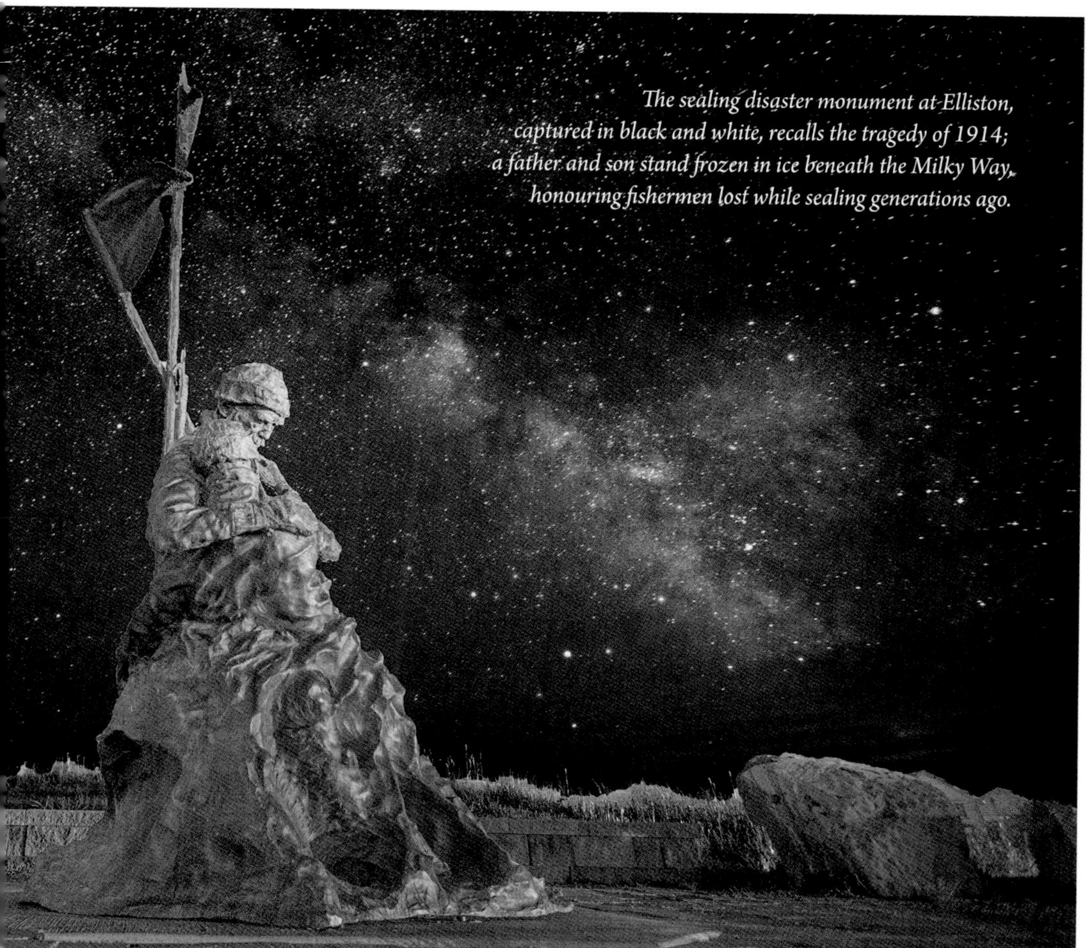

The sealing disaster monument at Elliston, captured in black and white, recalls the tragedy of 1914; a father and son stand frozen in ice beneath the Milky Way, honouring fishermen lost while sealing generations ago.

In black and white, a humpback whale erupts from the sea near Bonavista, frozen mid-breach as bright spray scatters against a deep, dark backdrop.

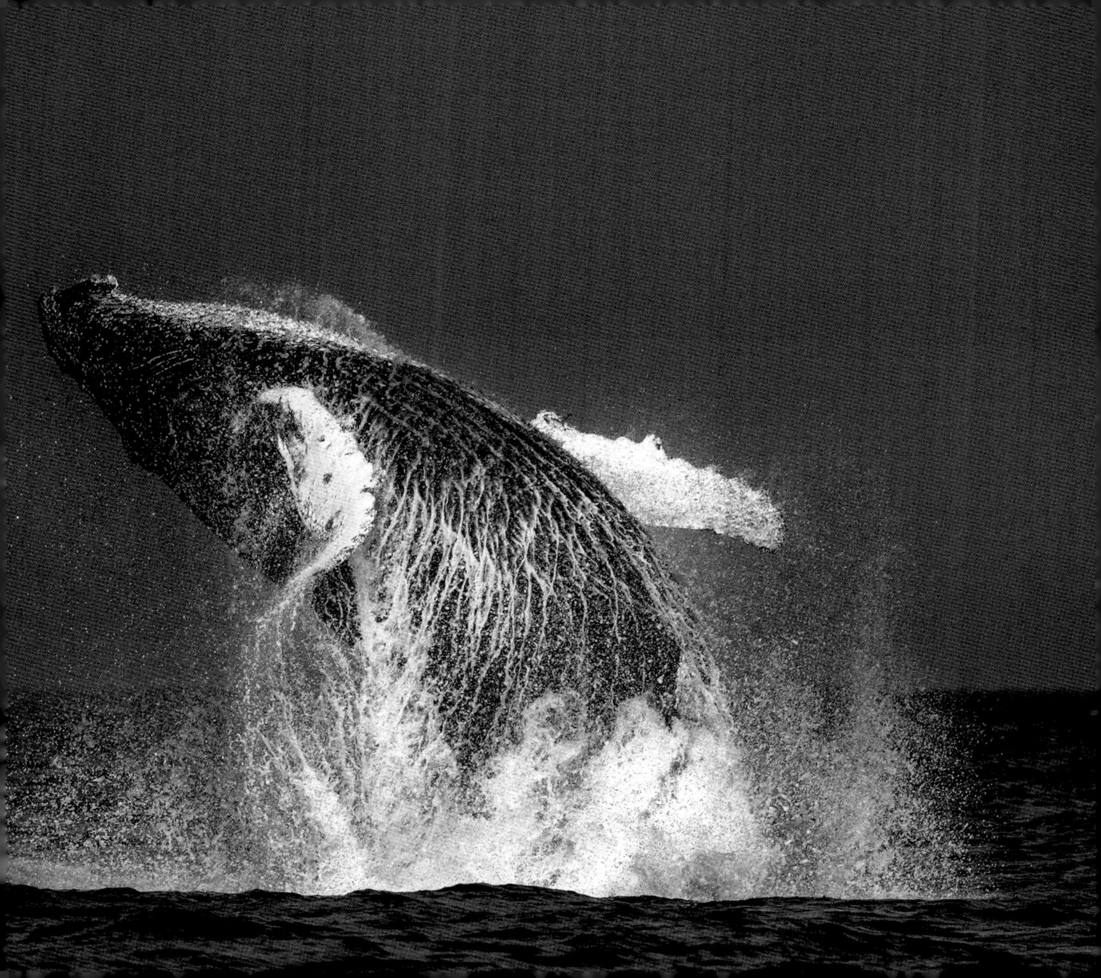

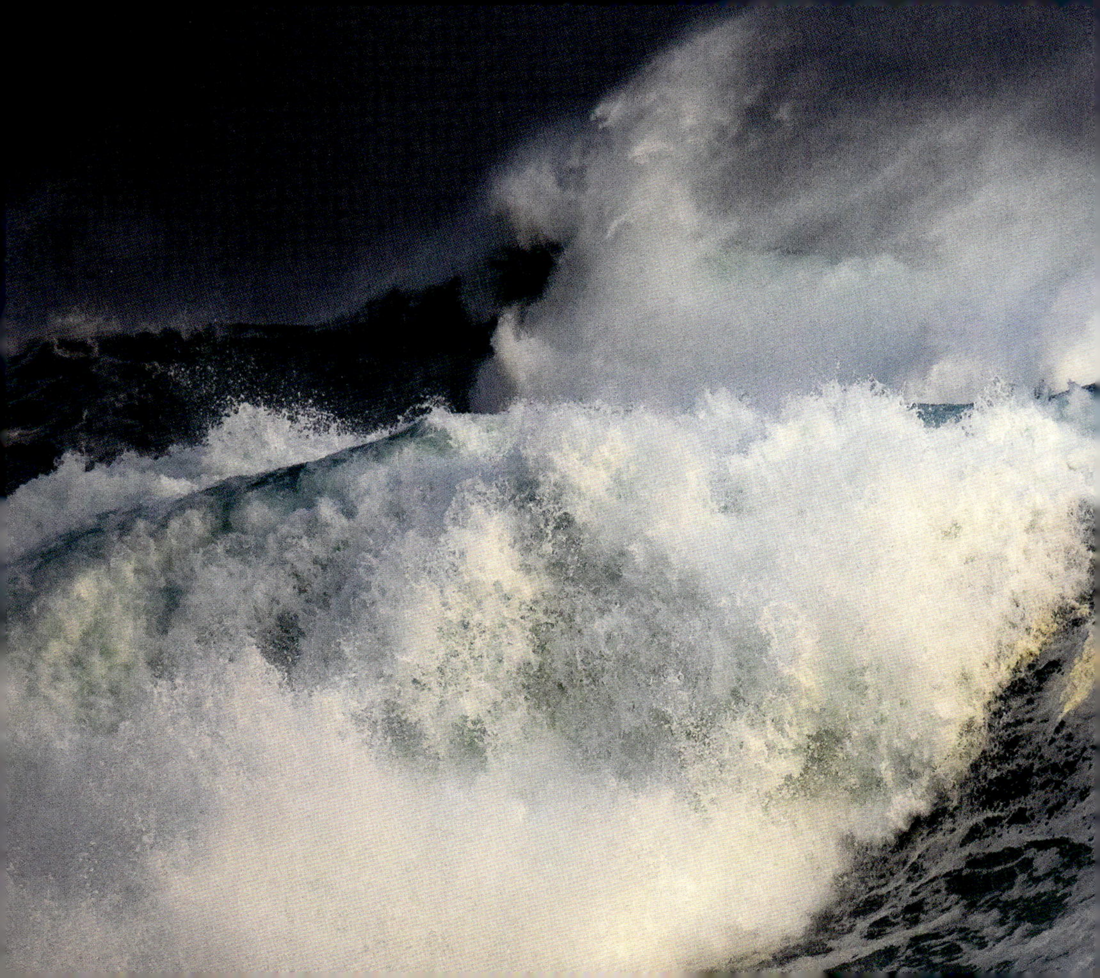

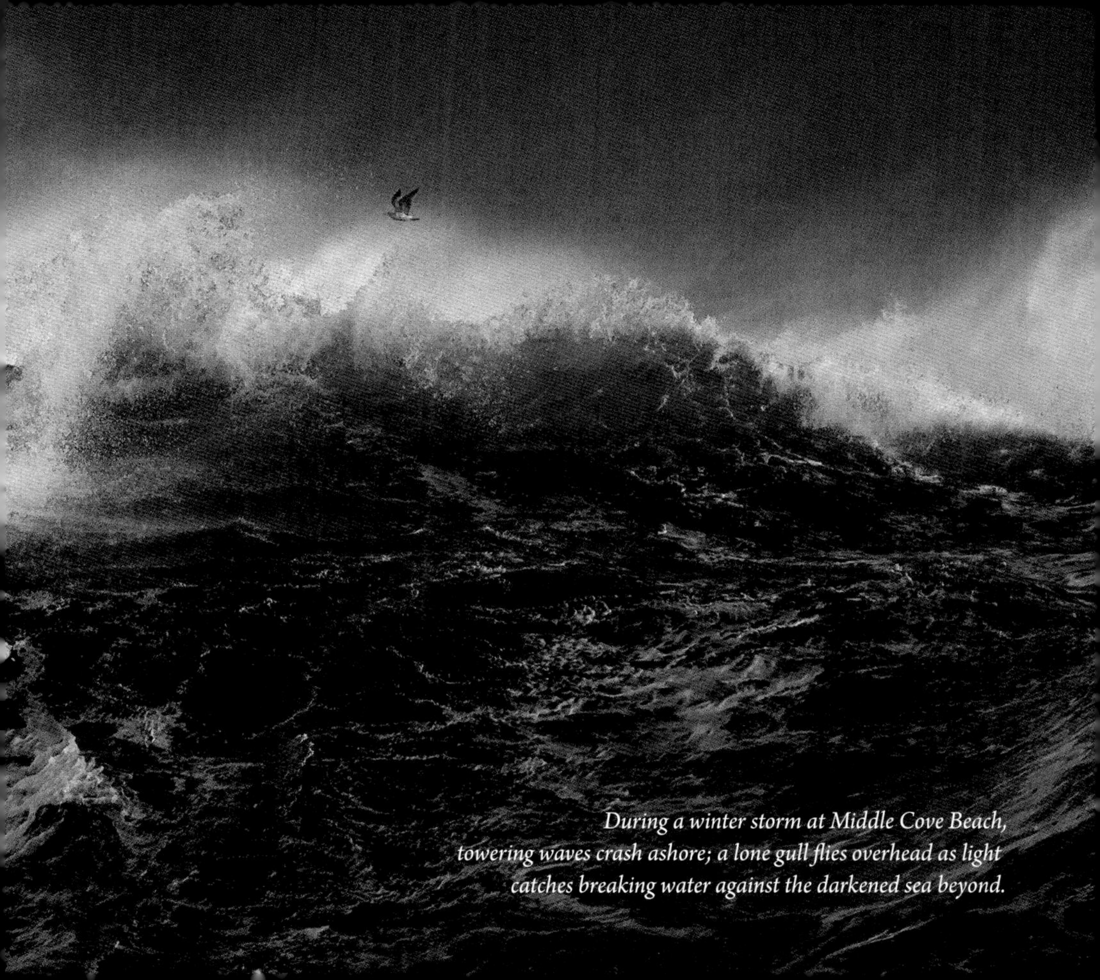

During a winter storm at Middle Cove Beach, towering waves crash ashore; a lone gull flies overhead as light catches breaking water against the darkened sea beyond.

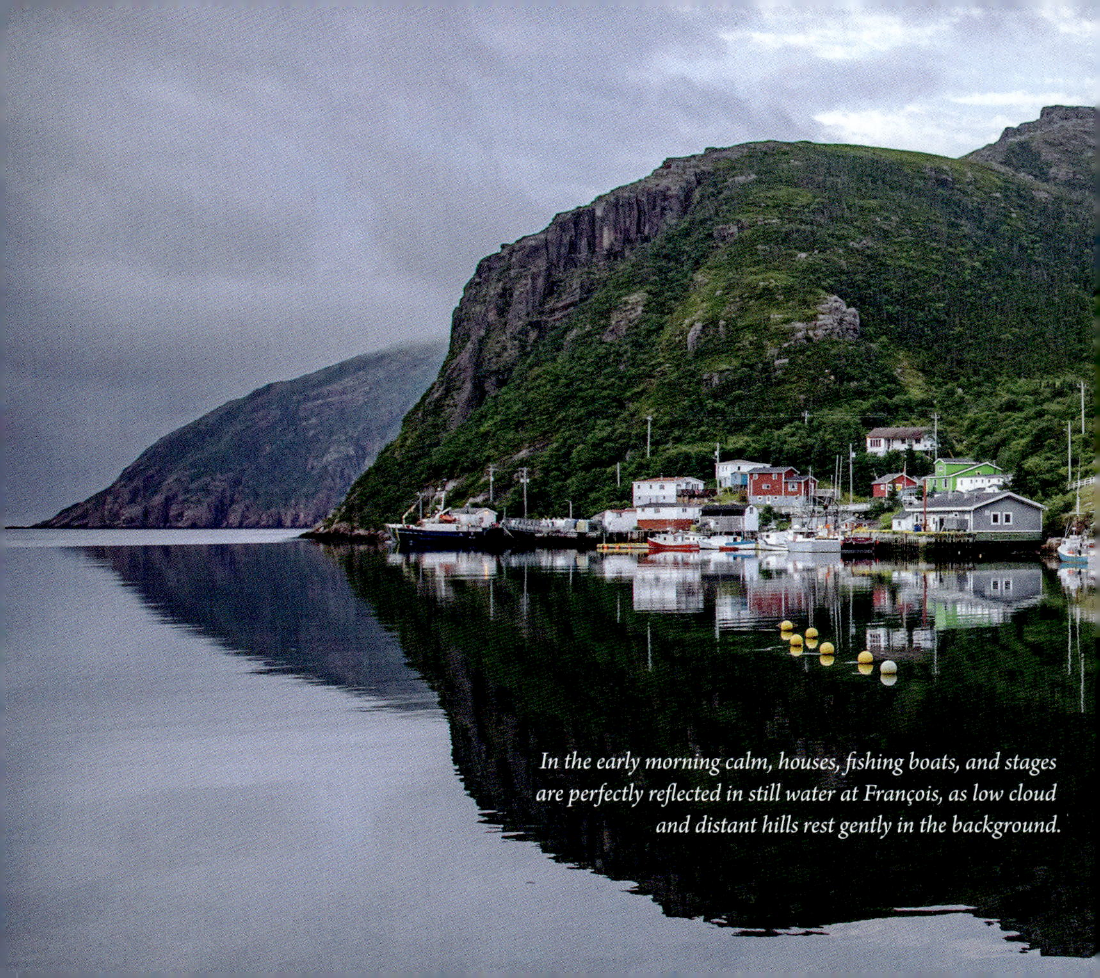

In the early morning calm, houses, fishing boats, and stages are perfectly reflected in still water at François, as low cloud and distant hills rest gently in the background.

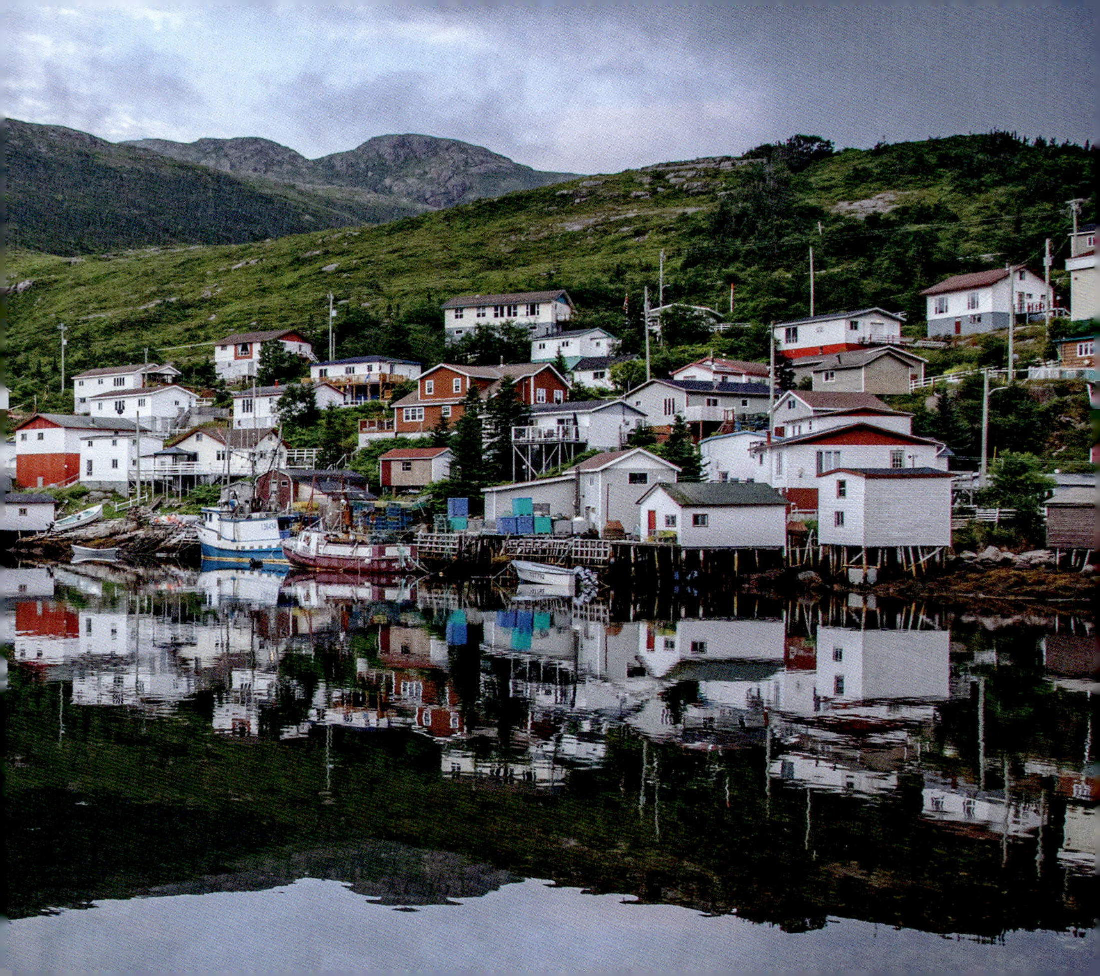

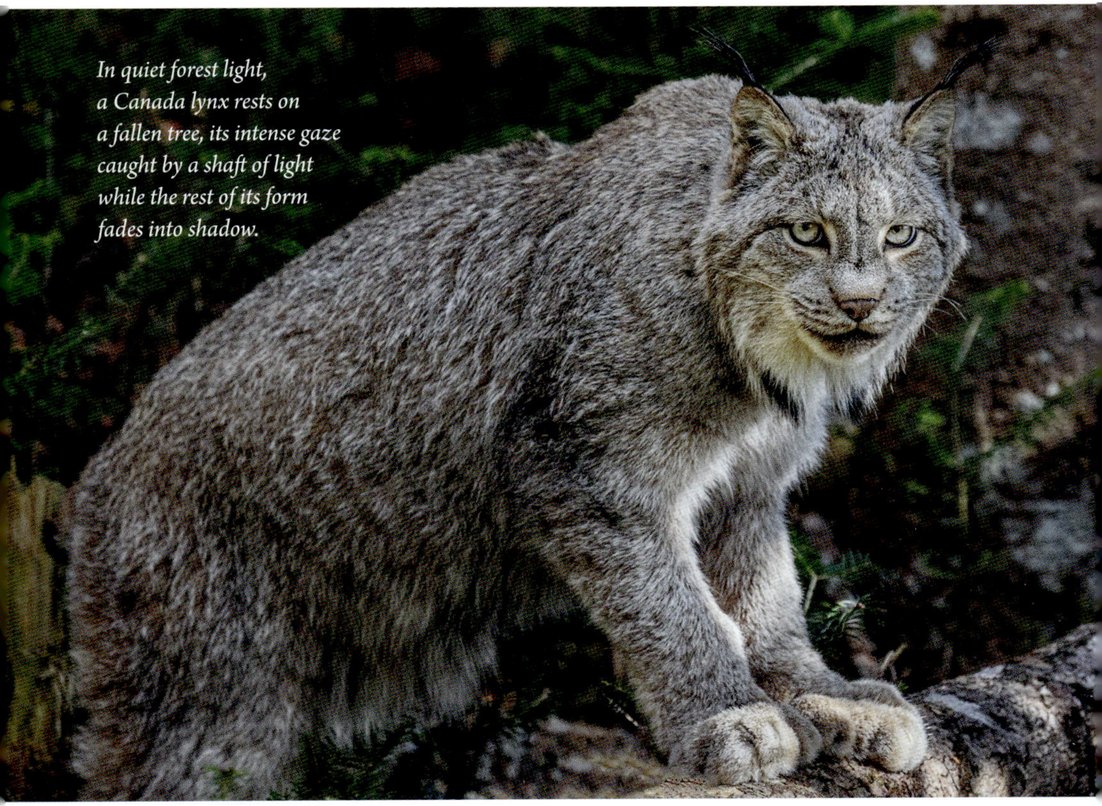
In quiet forest light,
a Canada lynx rests on
a fallen tree, its intense gaze
caught by a shaft of light
while the rest of its form
fades into shadow.

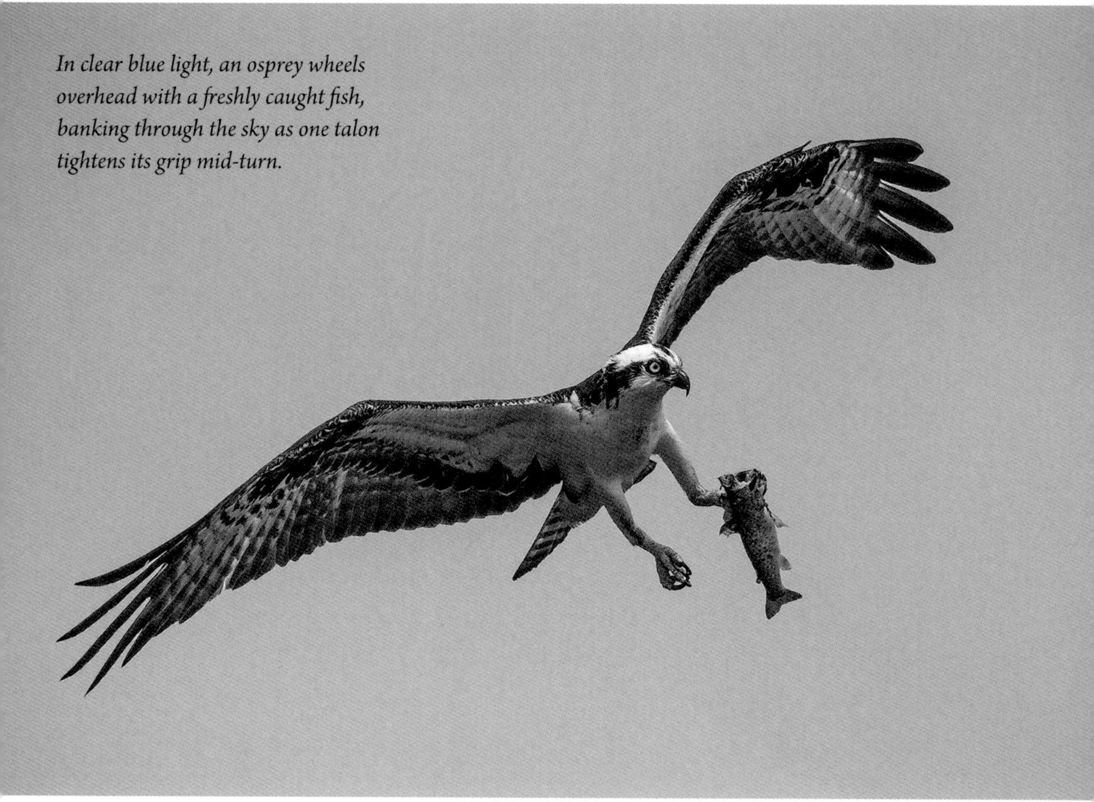

In clear blue light, an osprey wheels overhead with a freshly caught fish, banking through the sky as one talon tightens its grip mid-turn.

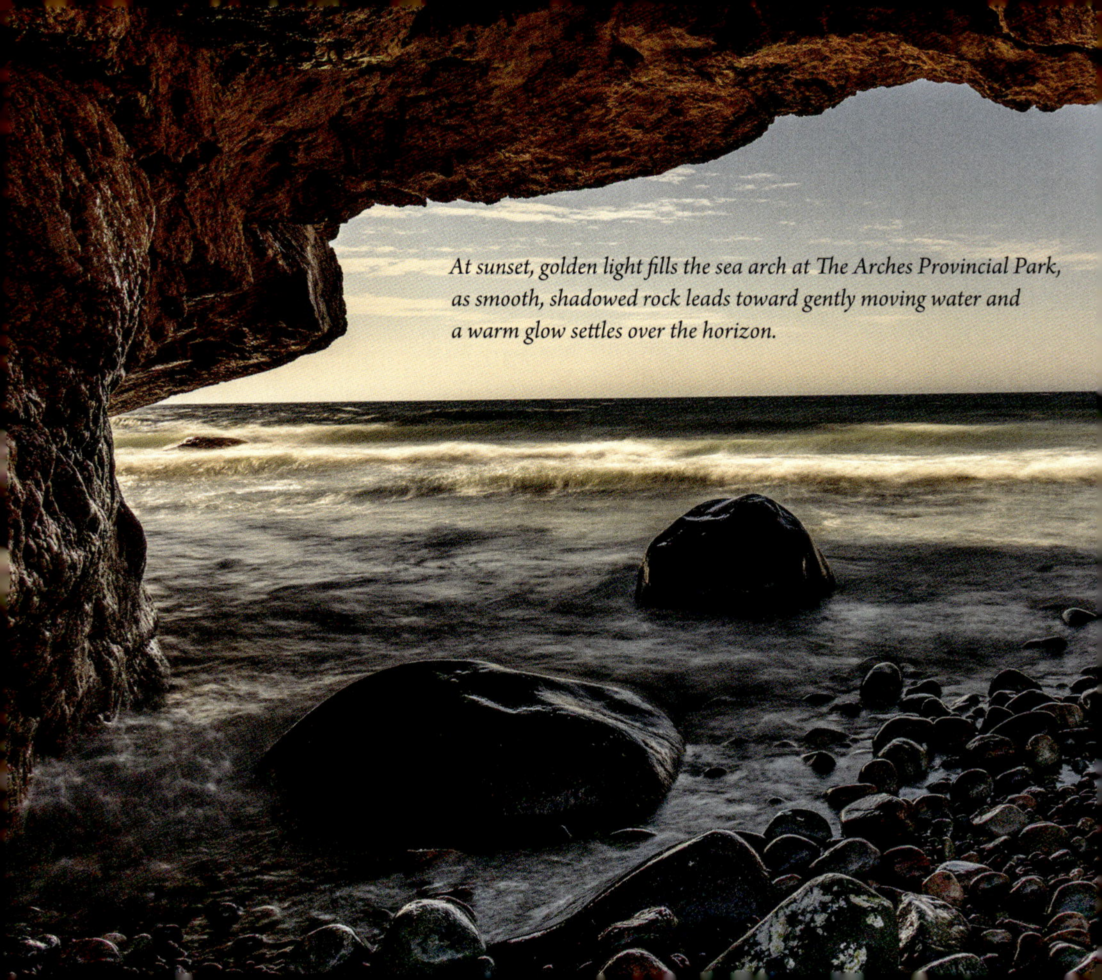

At sunset, golden light fills the sea arch at The Arches Provincial Park, as smooth, shadowed rock leads toward gently moving water and a warm glow settles over the horizon.

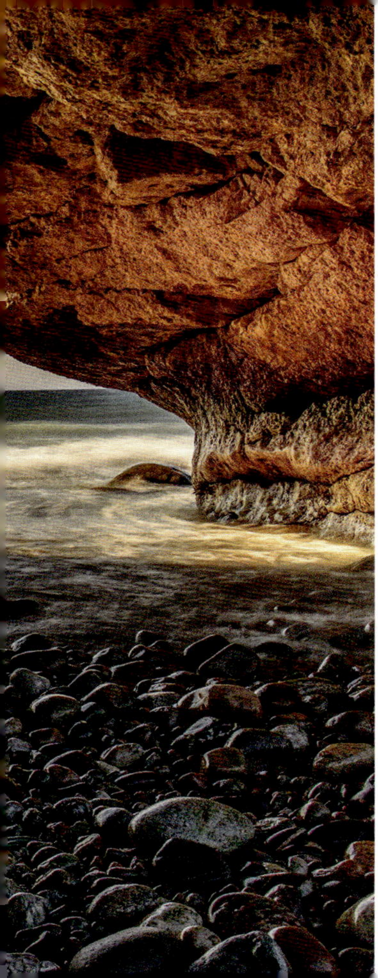

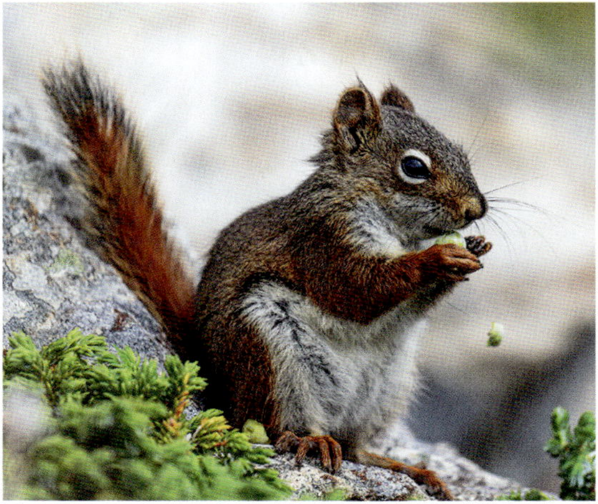

In evening light, a squirrel feeds on berries in Bonavista, caught in close focus as a single piece drops to the ground against a softly blurred background.

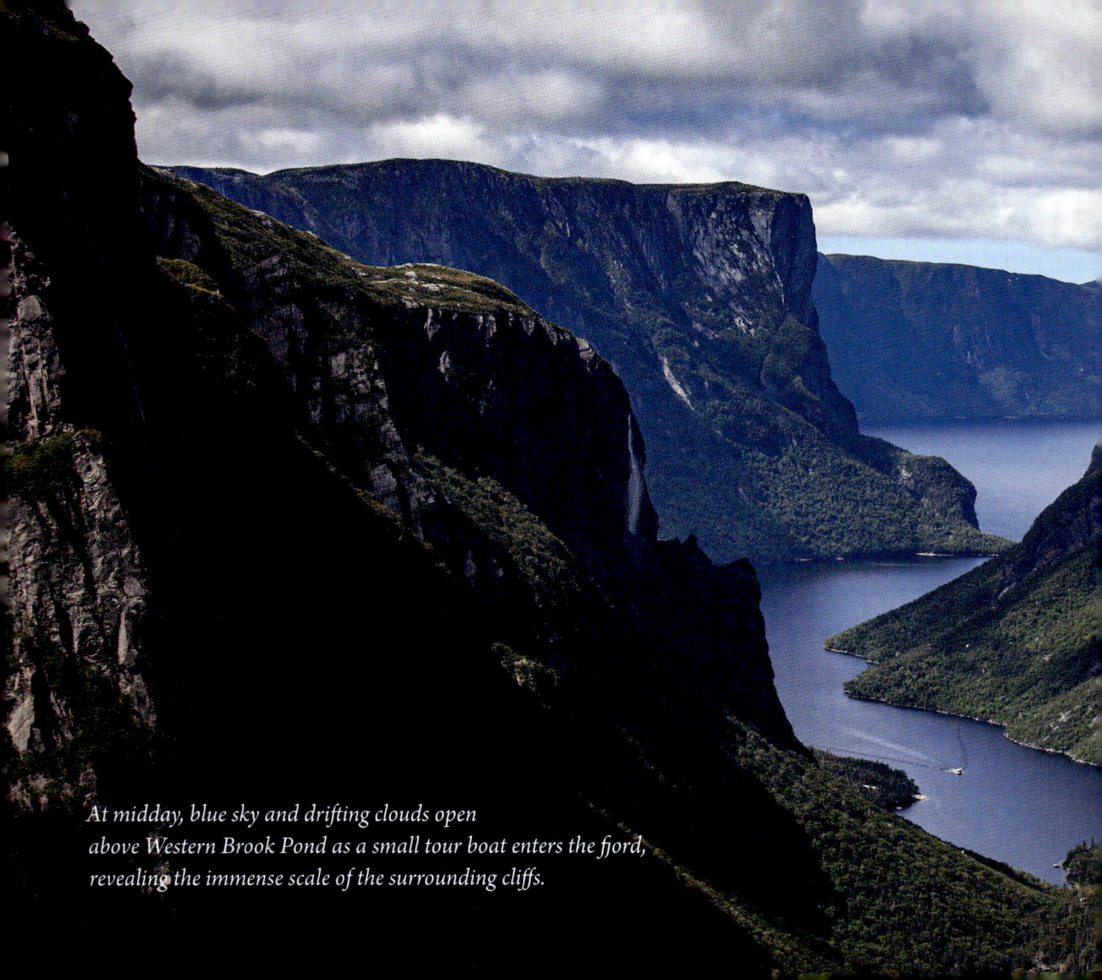

At midday, blue sky and drifting clouds open above Western Brook Pond as a small tour boat enters the fjord, revealing the immense scale of the surrounding cliffs.

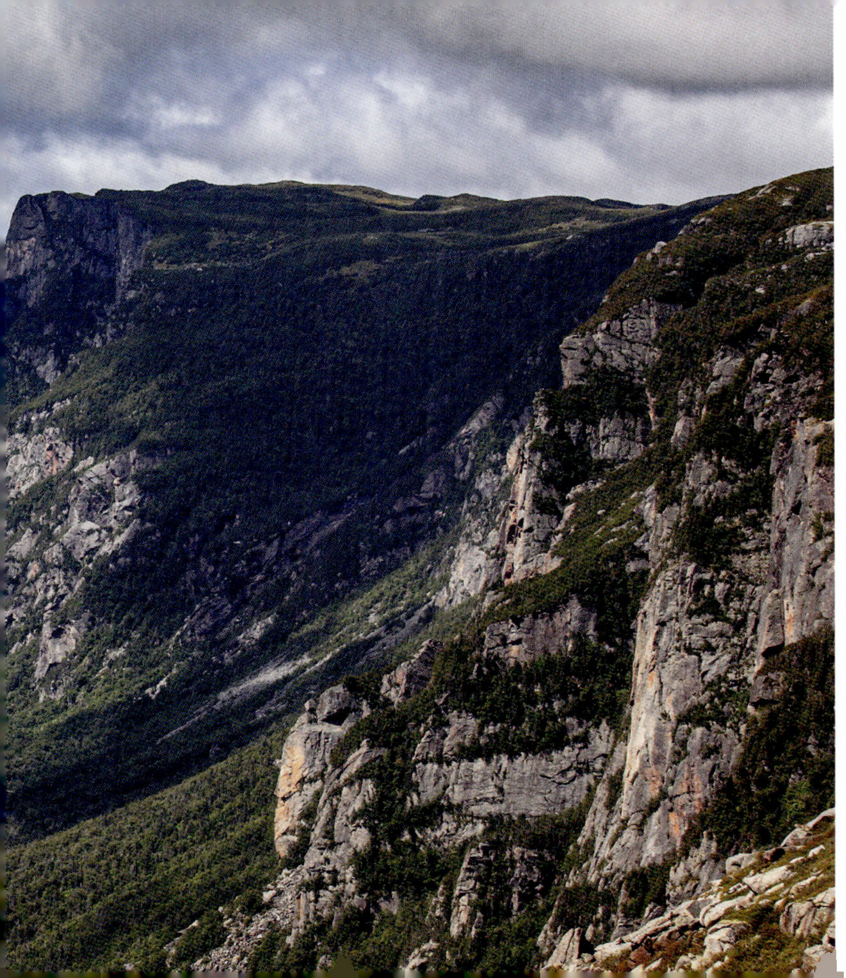

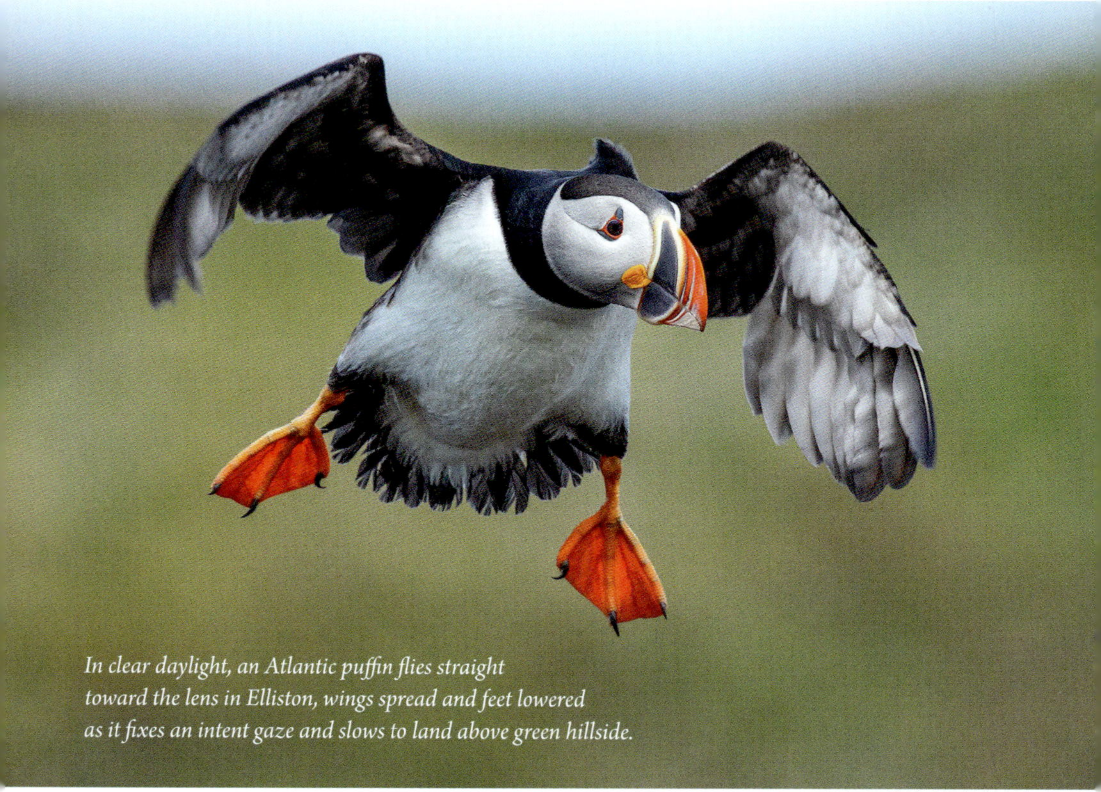

In clear daylight, an Atlantic puffin flies straight toward the lens in Elliston, wings spread and feet lowered as it fixes an intent gaze and slows to land above green hillside.

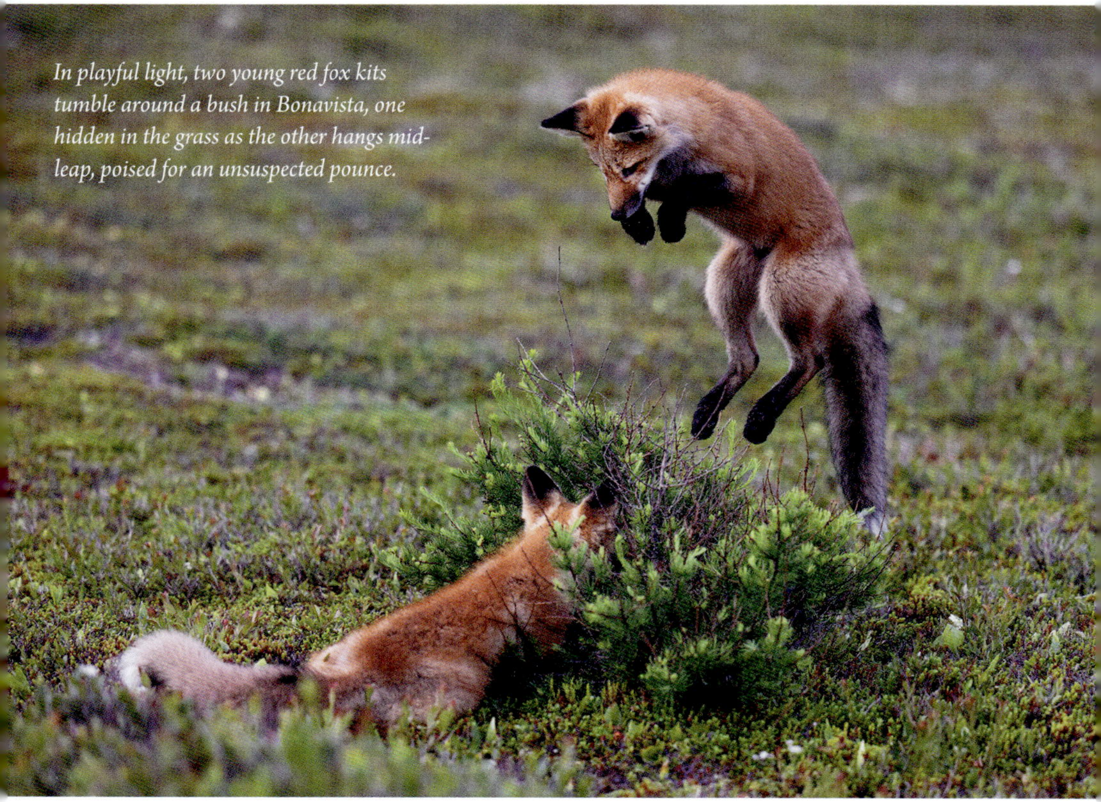

In playful light, two young red fox kits tumble around a bush in Bonavista, one hidden in the grass as the other hangs mid-leap, poised for an unsuspected pounce.

(right) In clear daylight, vivid blue water fills Windex Lake in the Torngat Mountains, its mineral-rich surface contrasting sharply with the bare rock and barren terrain rising far above the treeline.

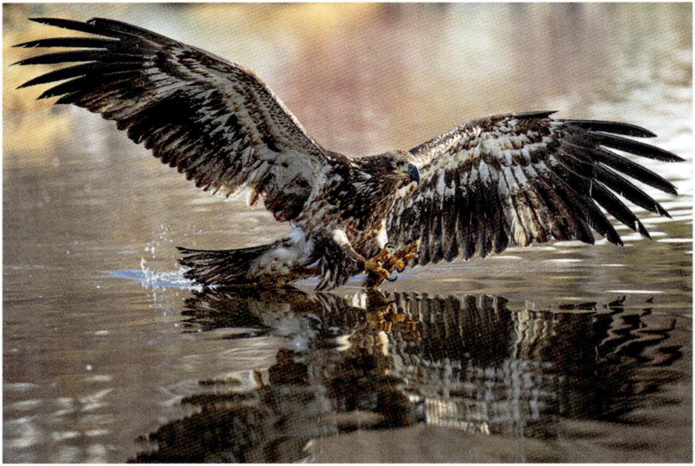

(above) In calm light, a juvenile bald eagle descends toward the water at Quidi Vidi, wings spread and talons extended as its reflection mirrors the moment just before the strike.

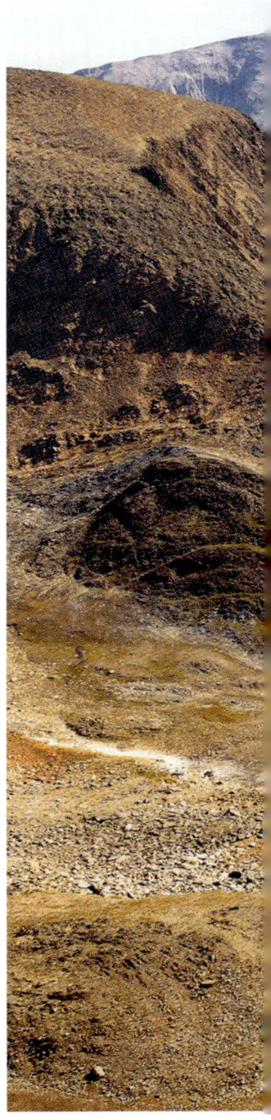

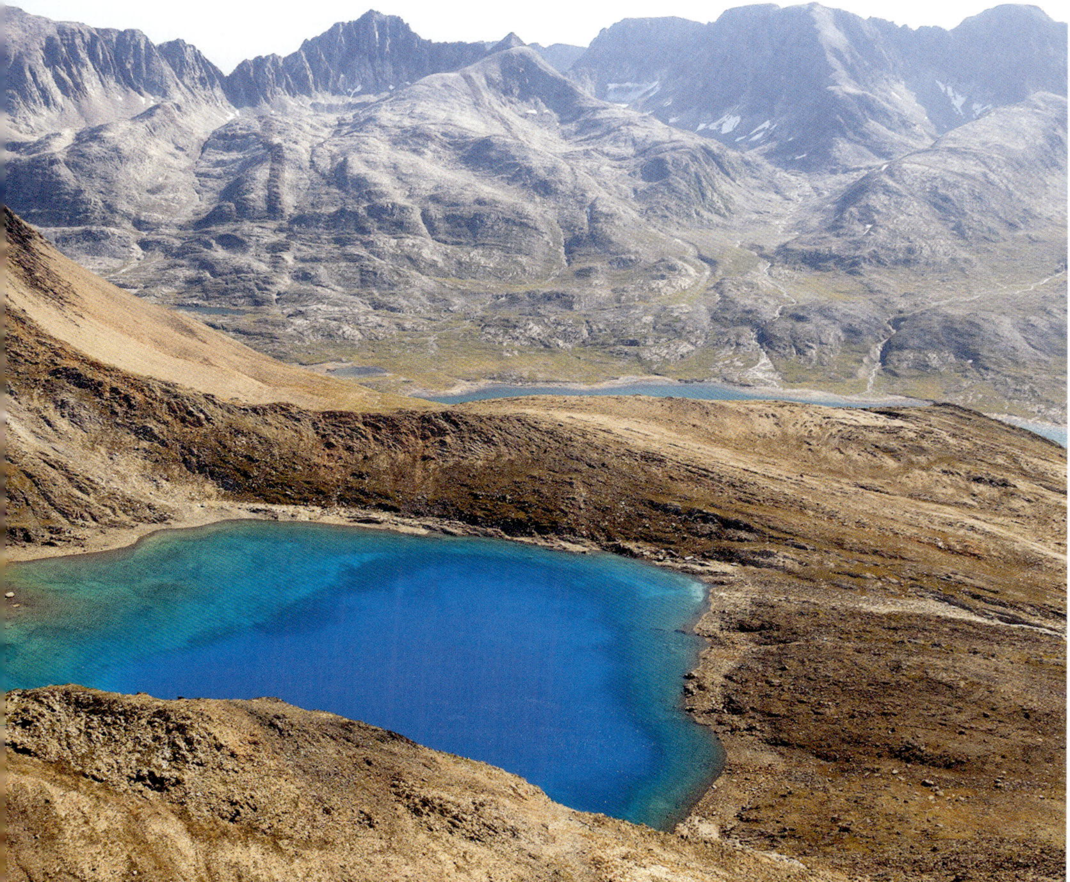

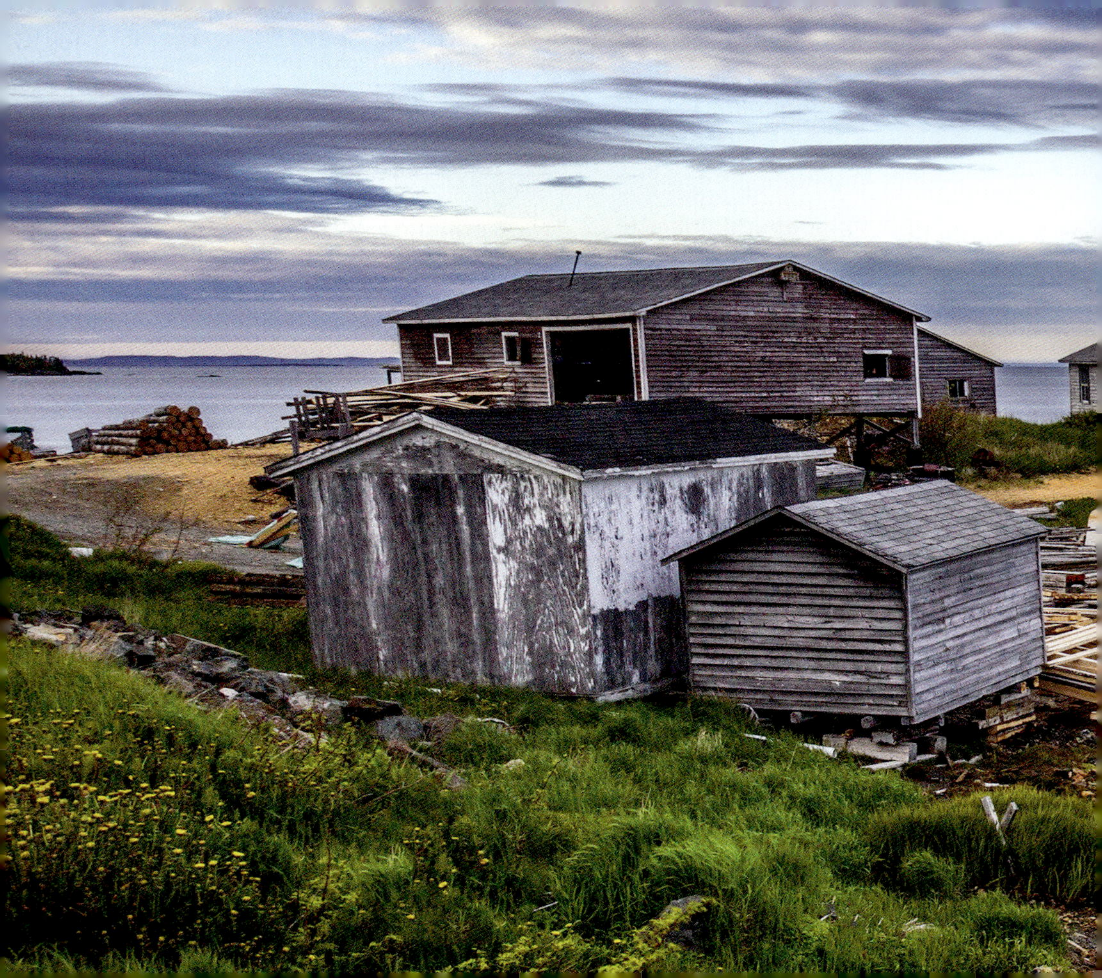

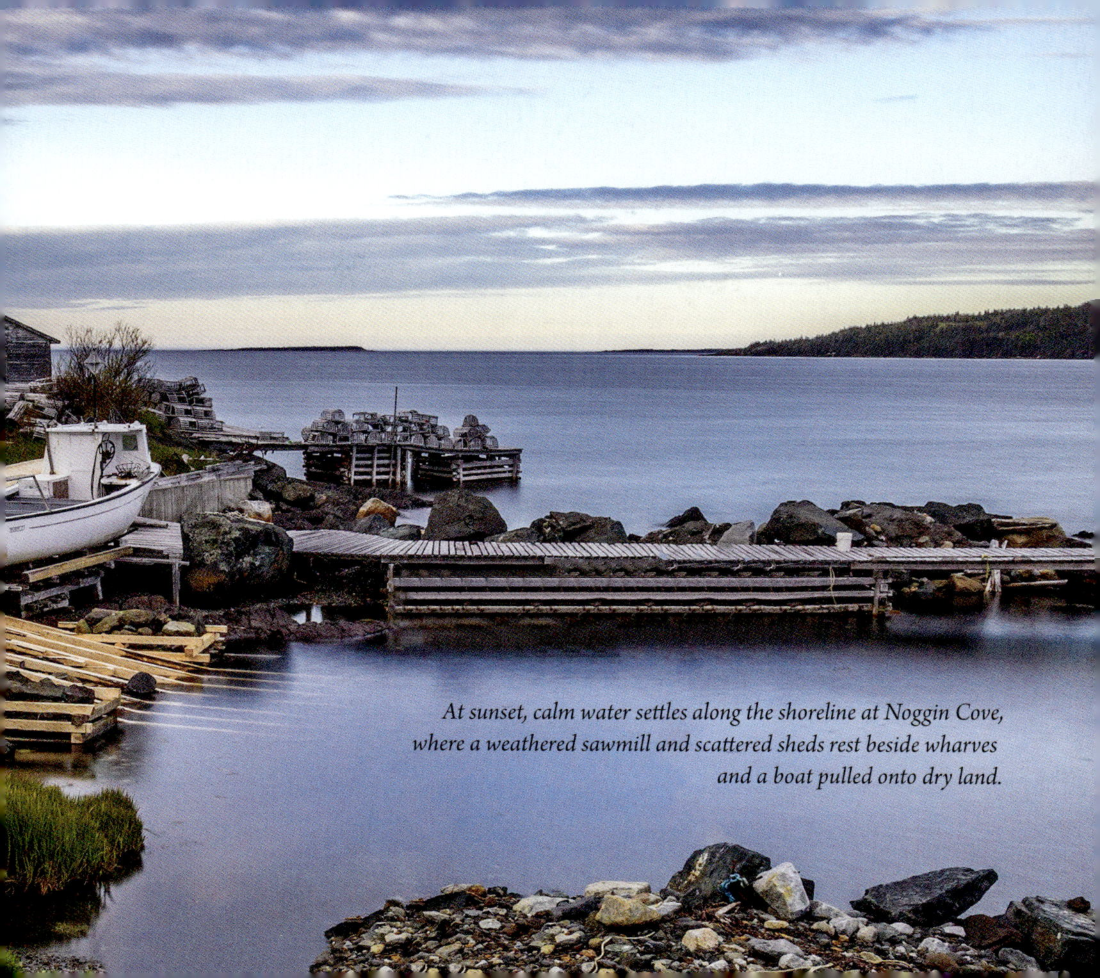

At sunset, calm water settles along the shoreline at Noggin Cove, where a weathered sawmill and scattered sheds rest beside wharves and a boat pulled onto dry land.

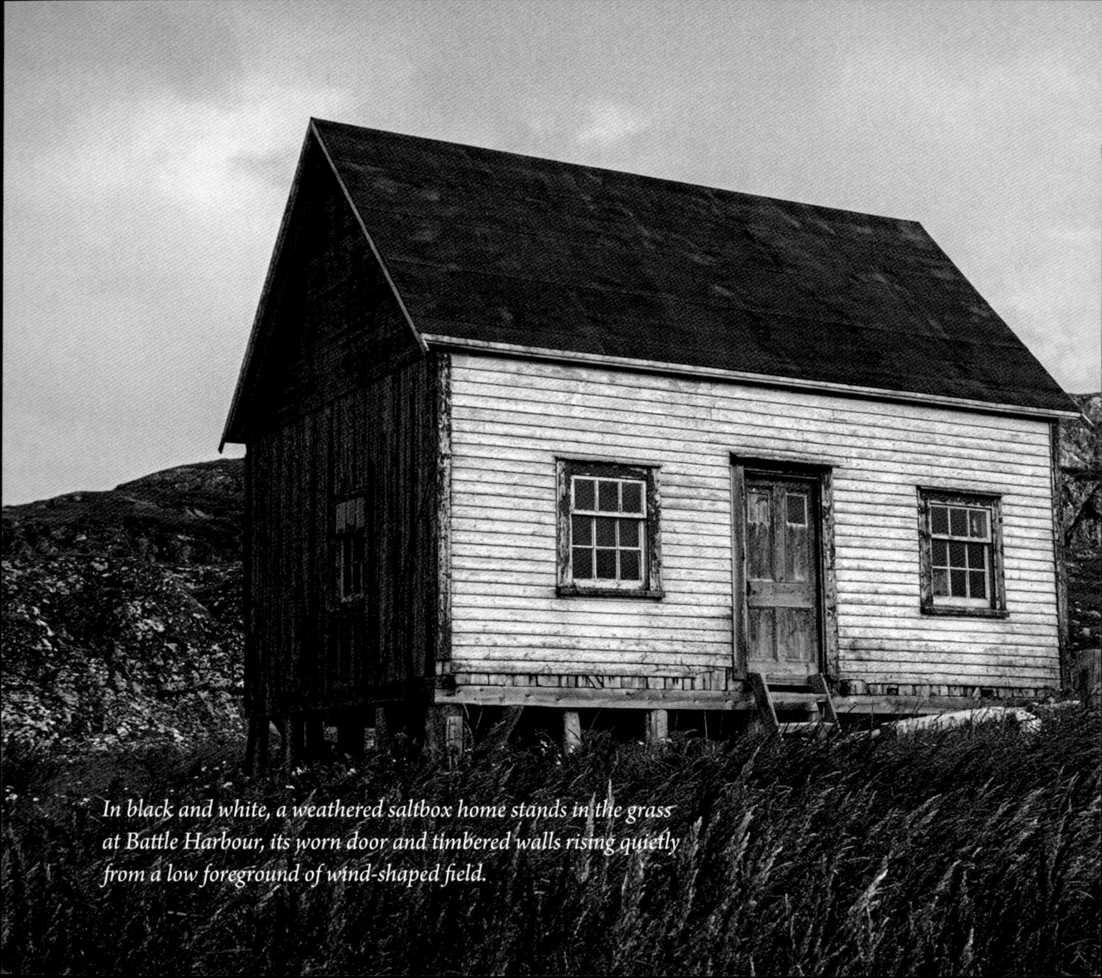

In black and white, a weathered saltbox home stands in the grass at Battle Harbour, its worn door and timbered walls rising quietly from a low foreground of wind-shaped field.

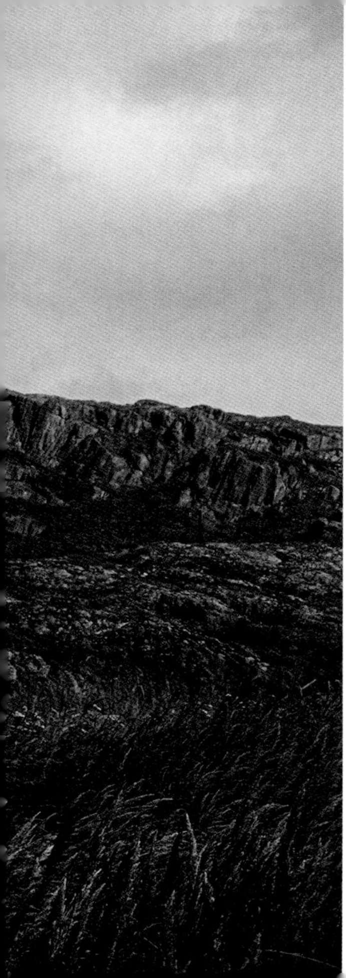

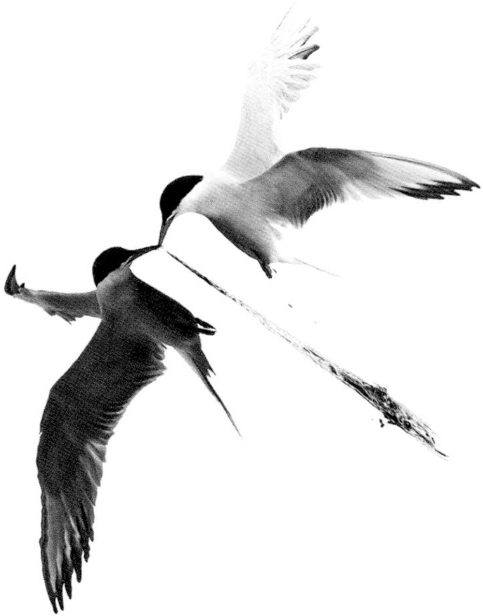

In a high-key, abstract frame, an Arctic tern pauses to drink; as the image turns and softens, the bird's figure transforms into a shape that echoes the delicate symmetry of a butterfly.

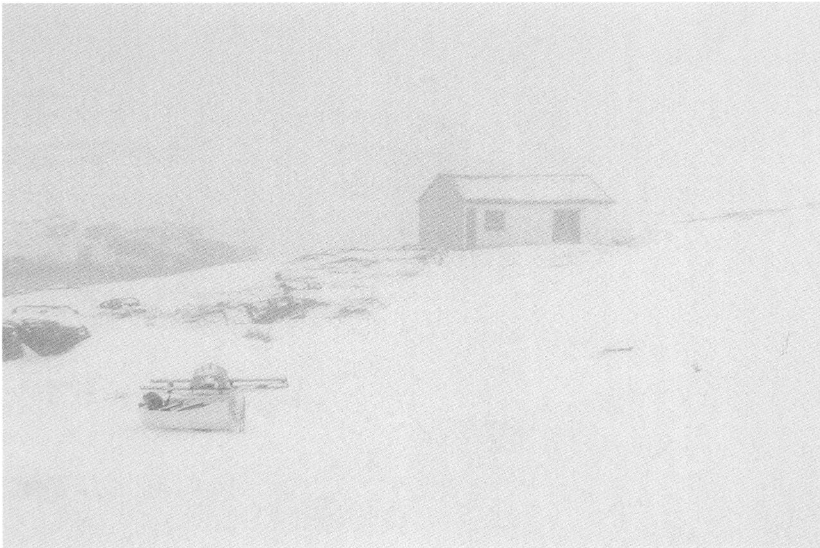

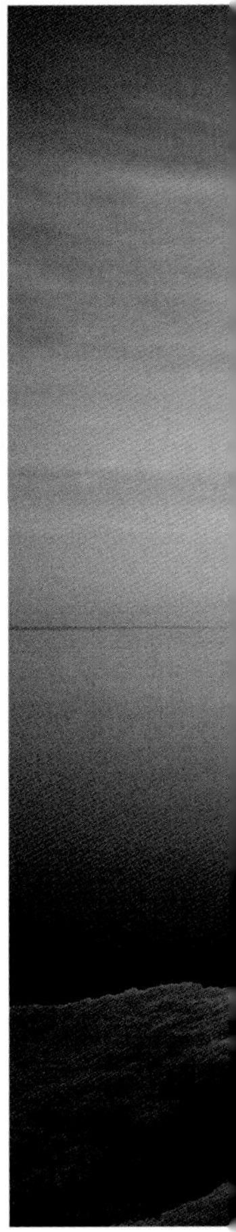

In early spring on the Northern Peninsula, thick white fog envelops the coast, reducing sheds, boats, and shoreline to faint sketches in a scene almost entirely lost to light.

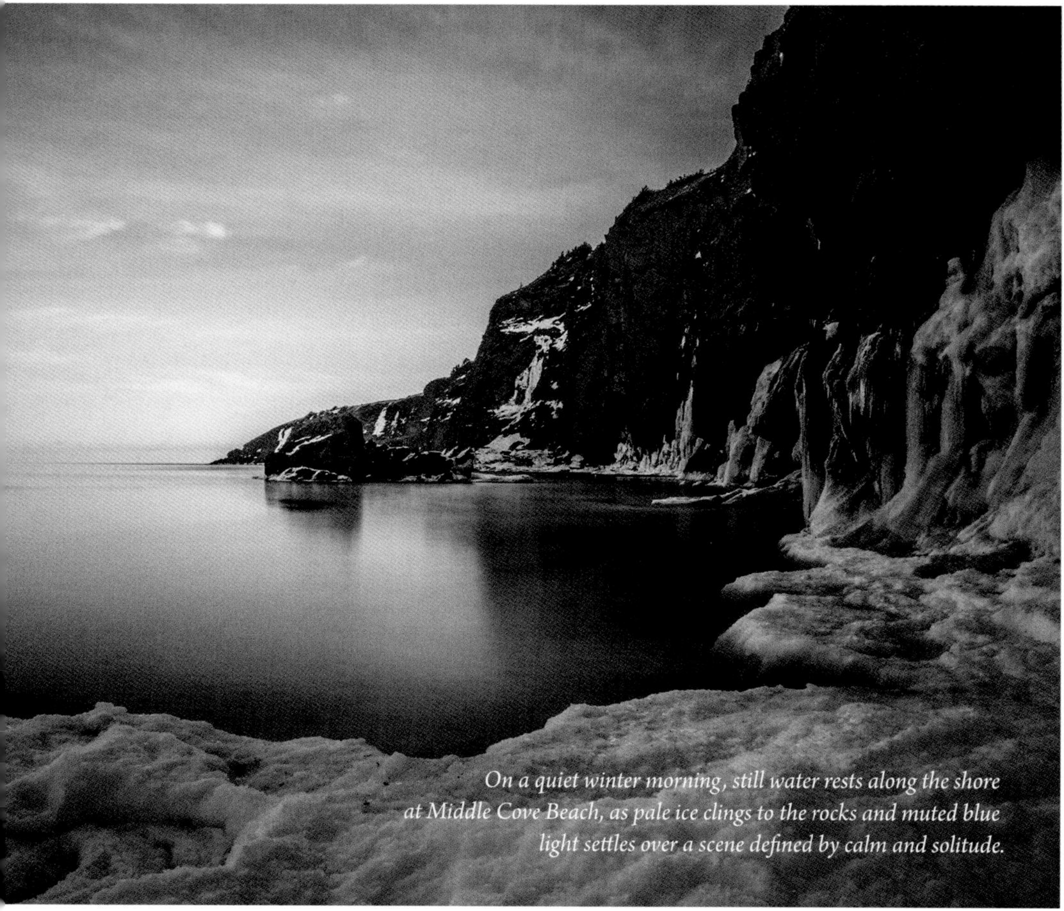

On a quiet winter morning, still water rests along the shore at Middle Cove Beach, as pale ice clings to the rocks and muted blue light settles over a scene defined by calm and solitude.

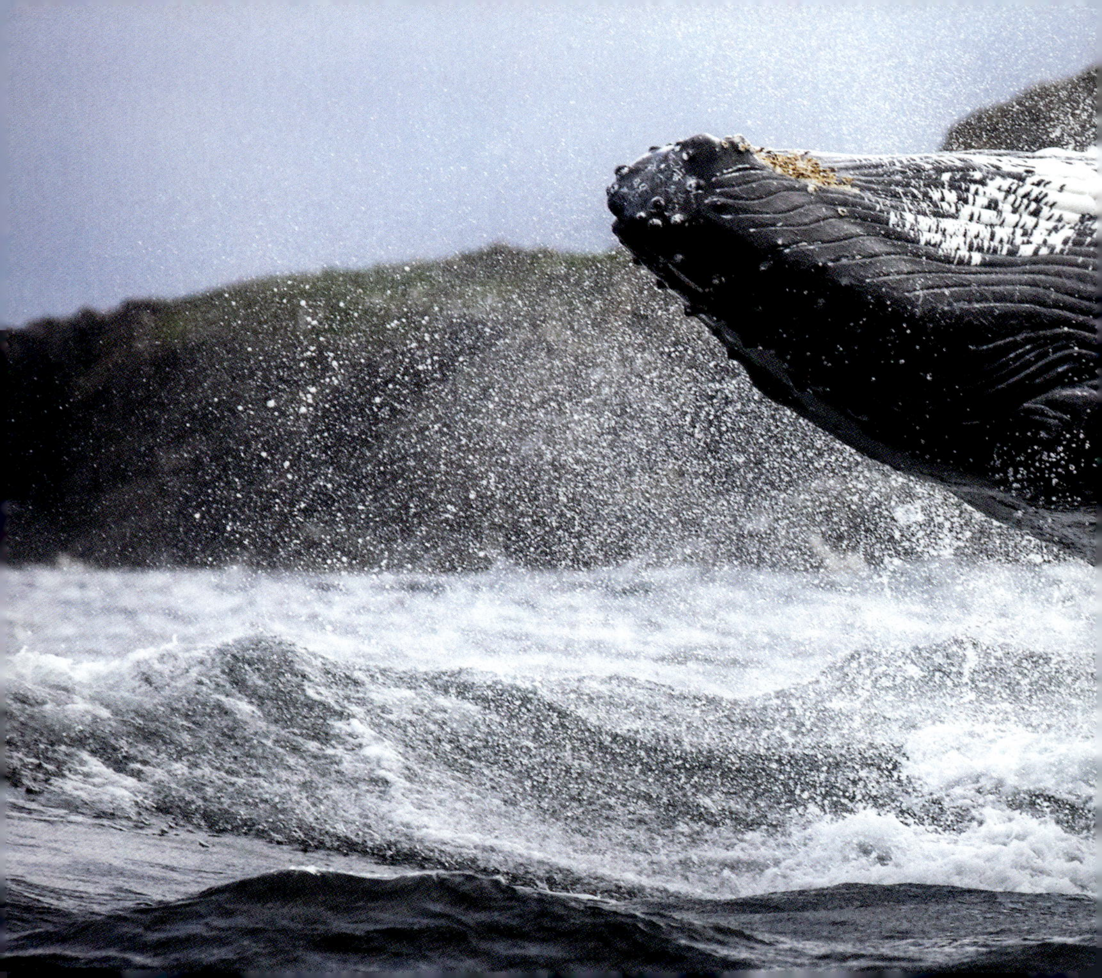

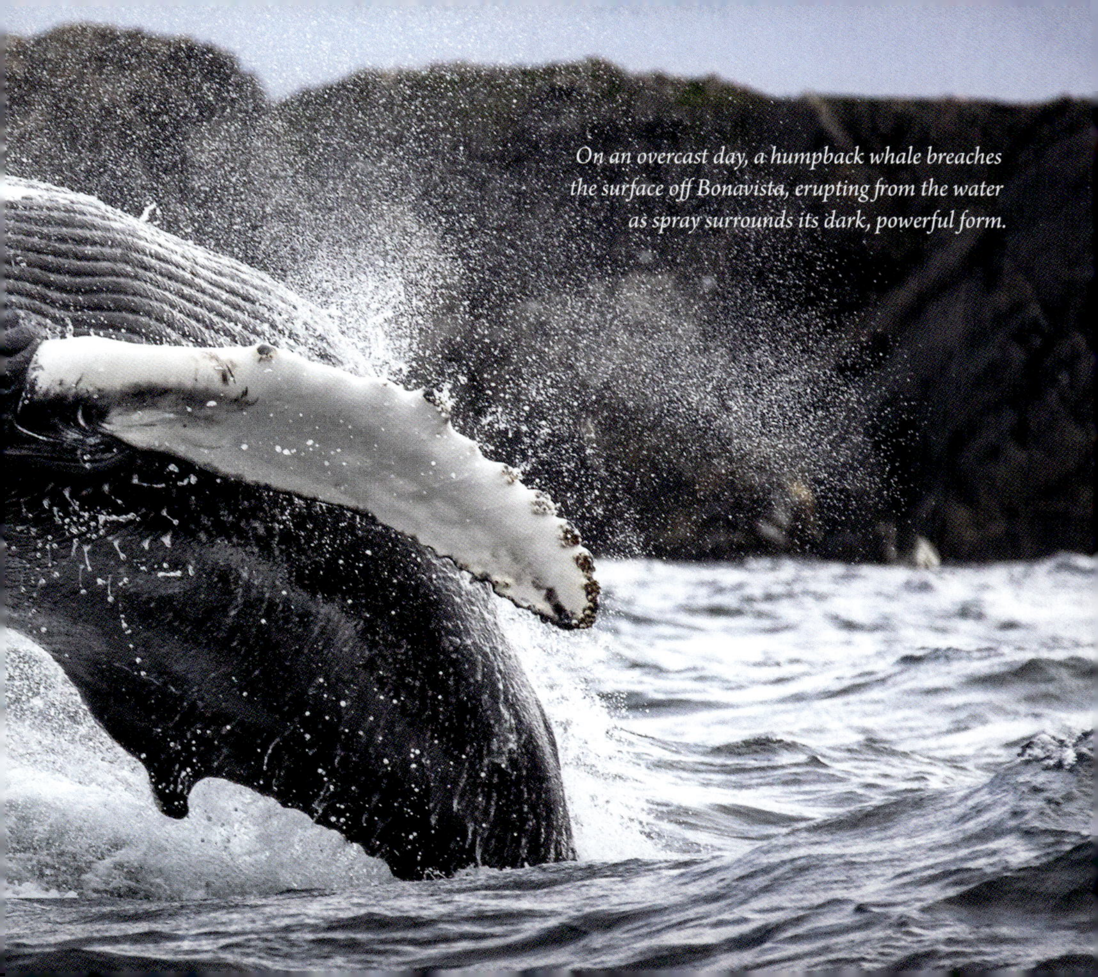

On an overcast day, a humpback whale breaches the surface off Bonavista, erupting from the water as spray surrounds its dark, powerful form.

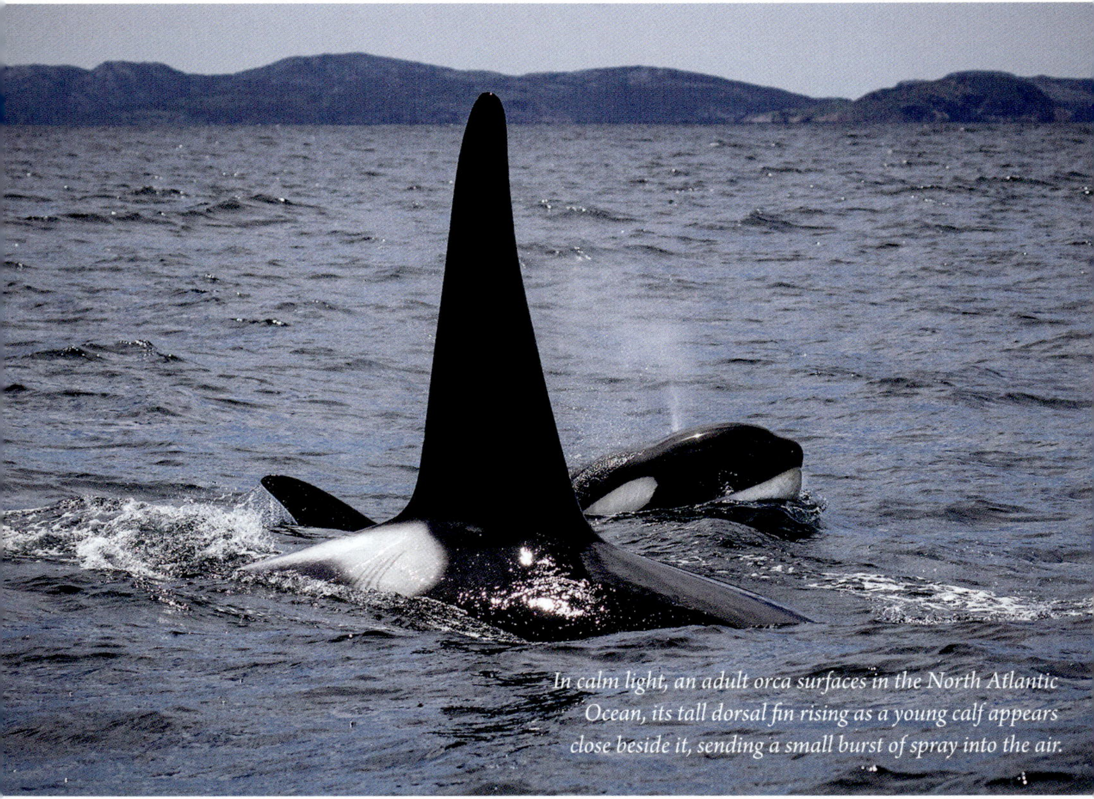

In calm light, an adult orca surfaces in the North Atlantic Ocean, its tall dorsal fin rising as a young calf appears close beside it, sending a small burst of spray into the air.

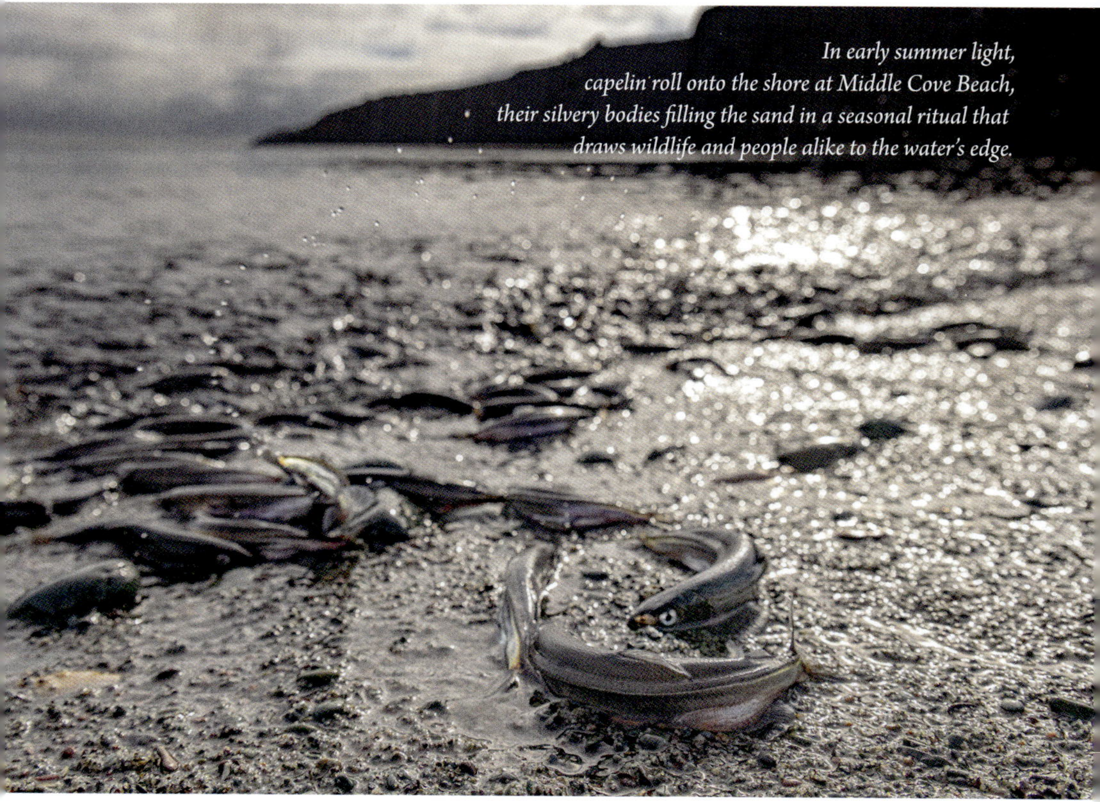
In early summer light,
capelin roll onto the shore at Middle Cove Beach,
their silvery bodies filling the sand in a seasonal ritual that
draws wildlife and people alike to the water's edge.

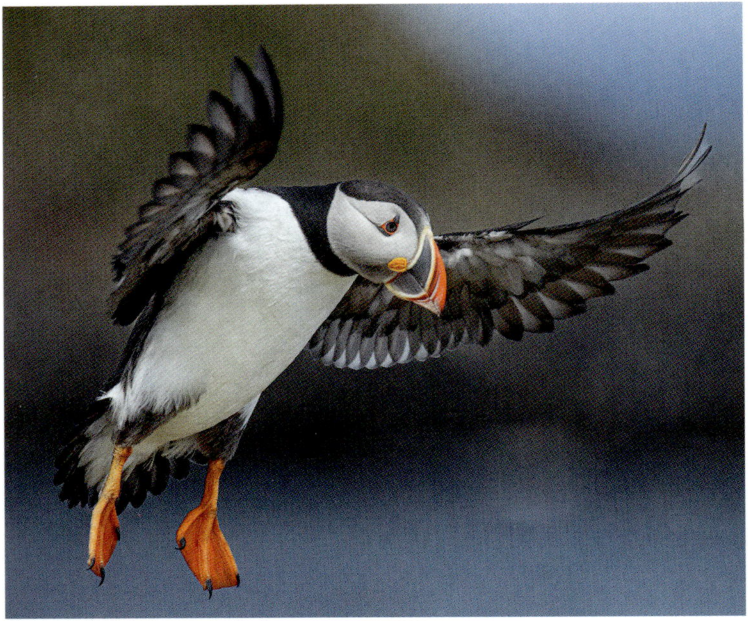

A lone Atlantic puffin descends toward the cliffs of Elliston,
wings wide and small talons extended,
a distant island softly out of focus behind it.

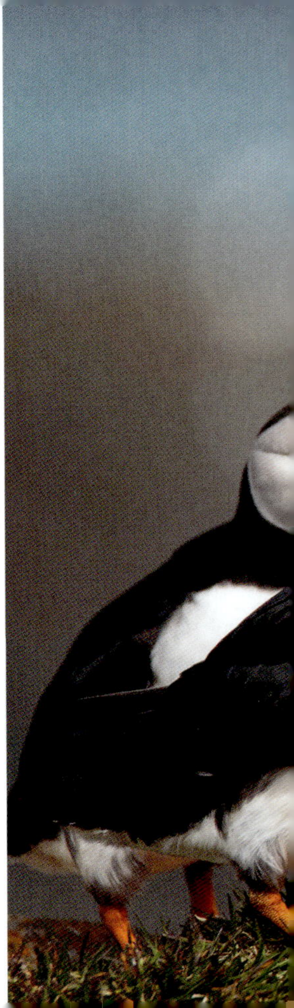

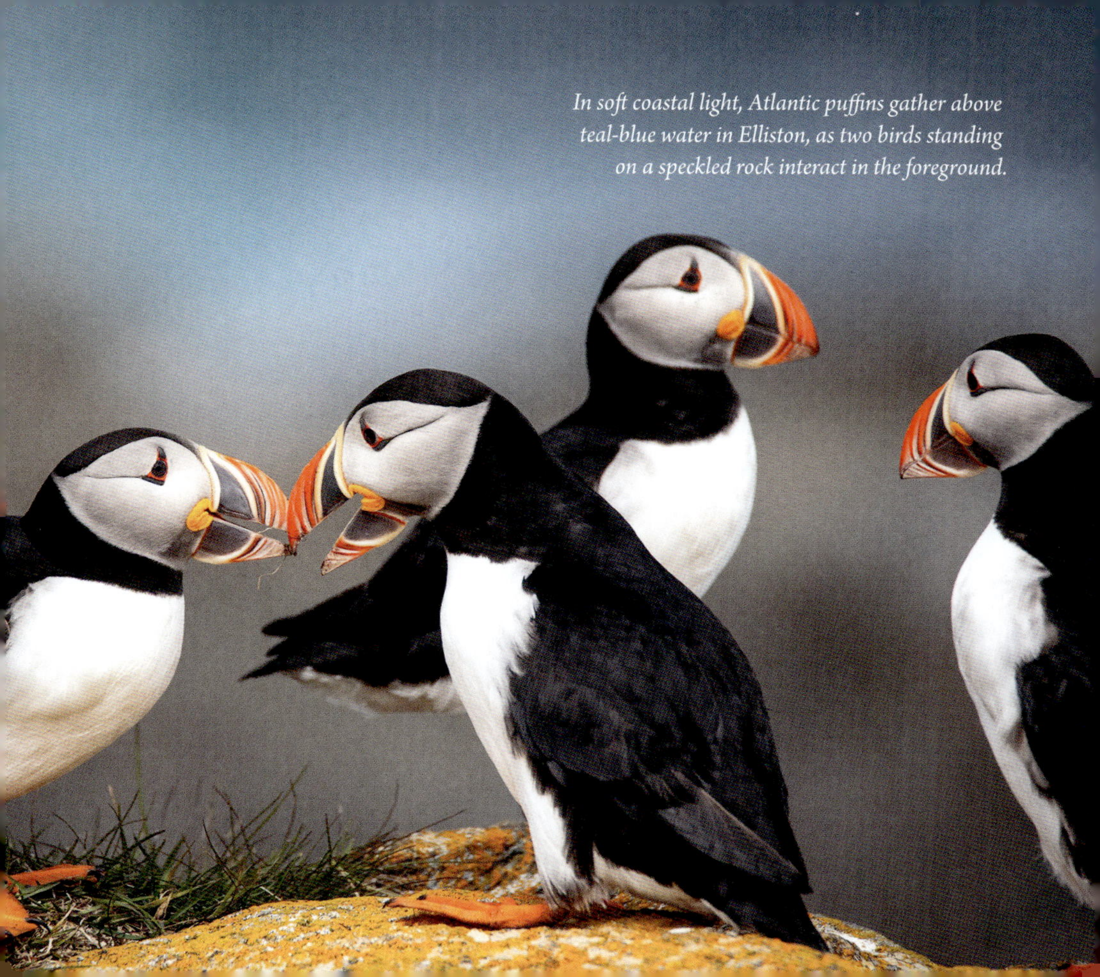

In soft coastal light, Atlantic puffins gather above teal-blue water in Elliston, as two birds standing on a speckled rock interact in the foreground.

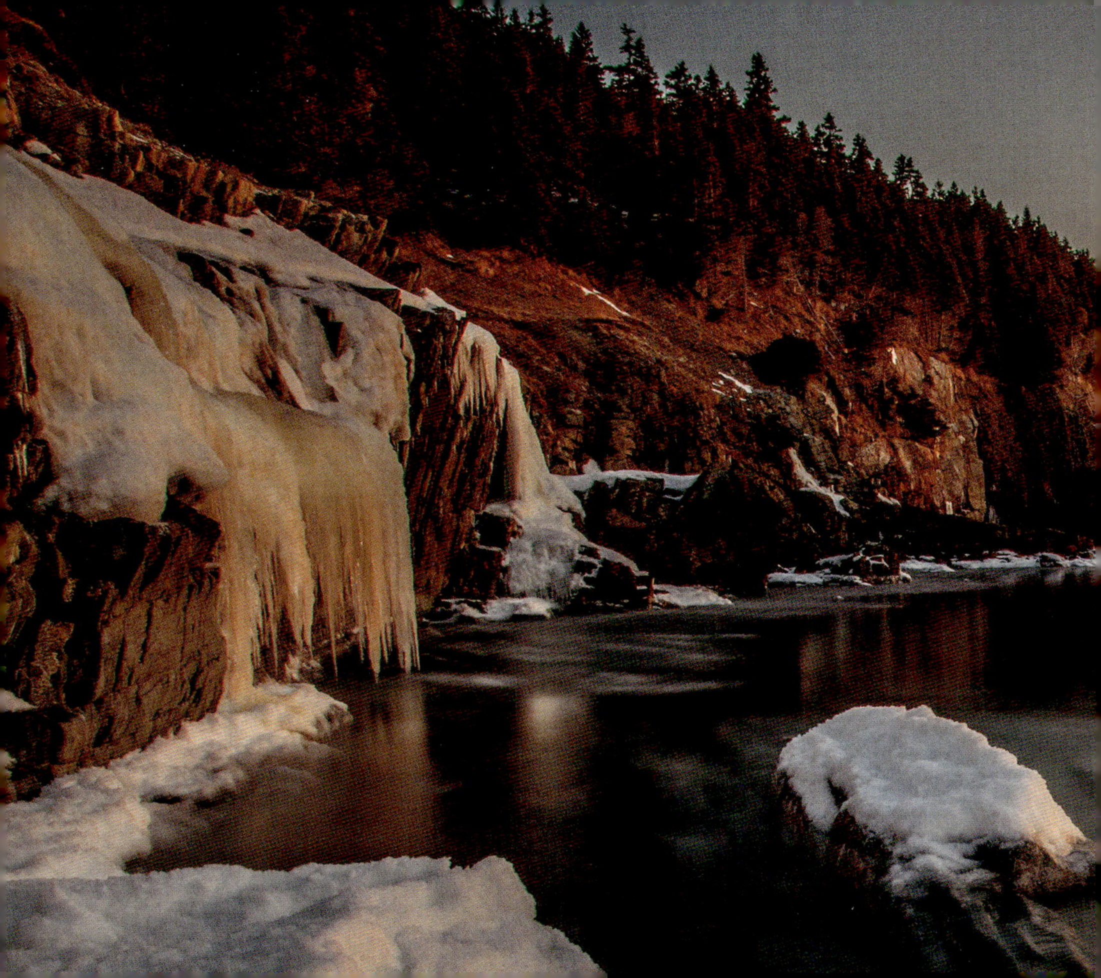

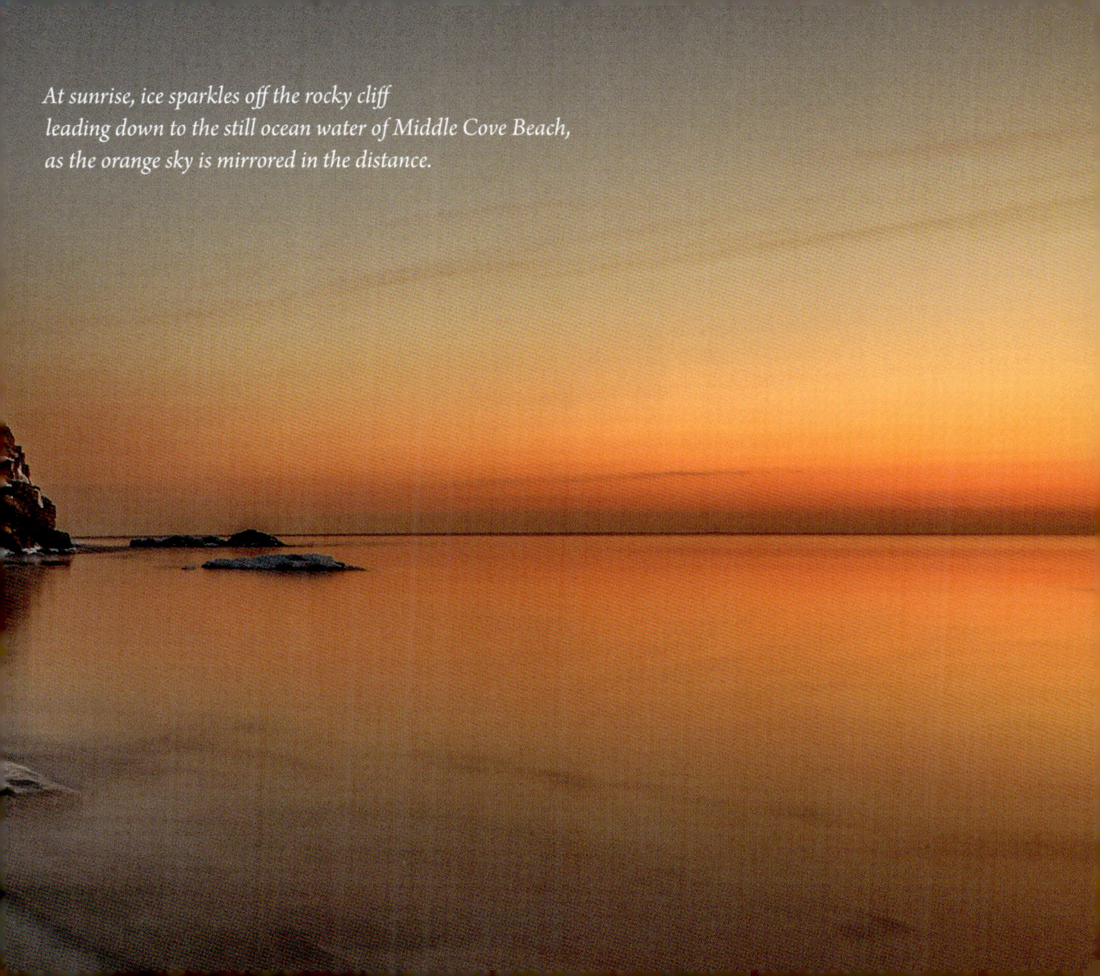

At sunrise, ice sparkles off the rocky cliff leading down to the still ocean water of Middle Cove Beach, as the orange sky is mirrored in the distance.

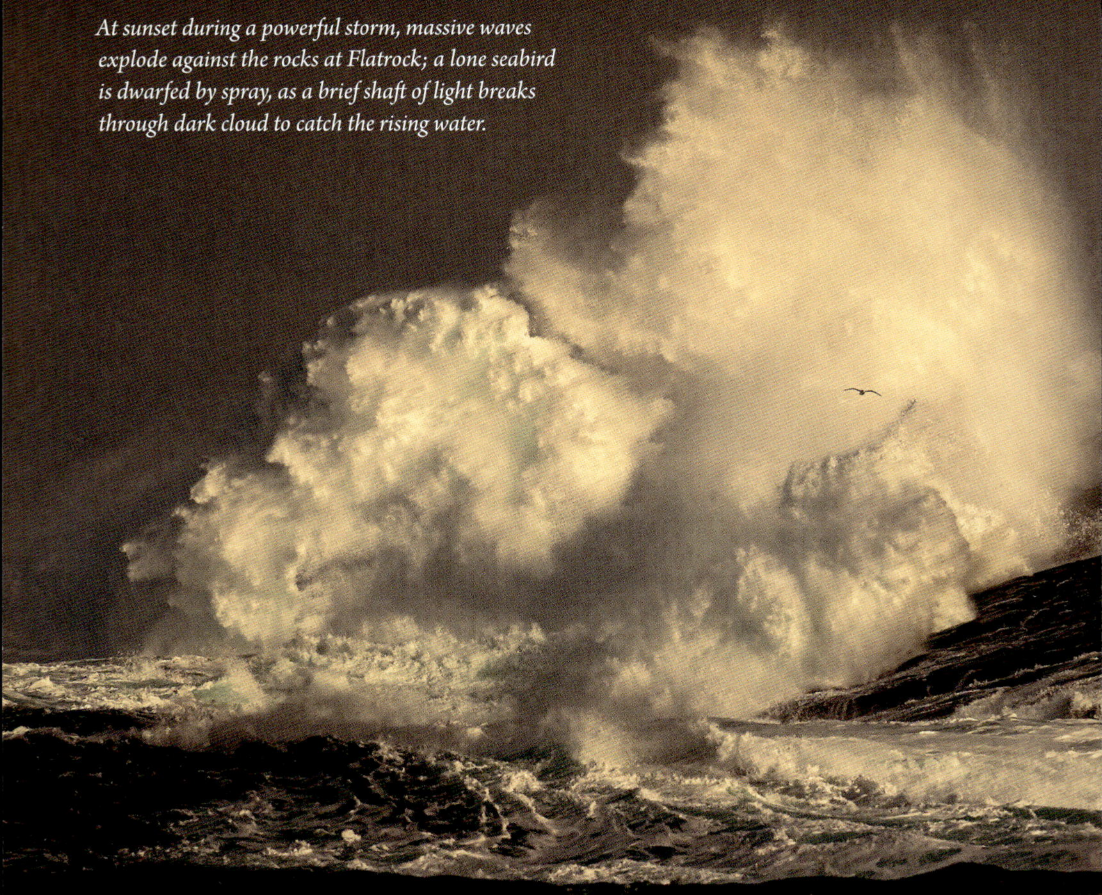

At sunset during a powerful storm, massive waves explode against the rocks at Flatrock; a lone seabird is dwarfed by spray, as a brief shaft of light breaks through dark cloud to catch the rising water.

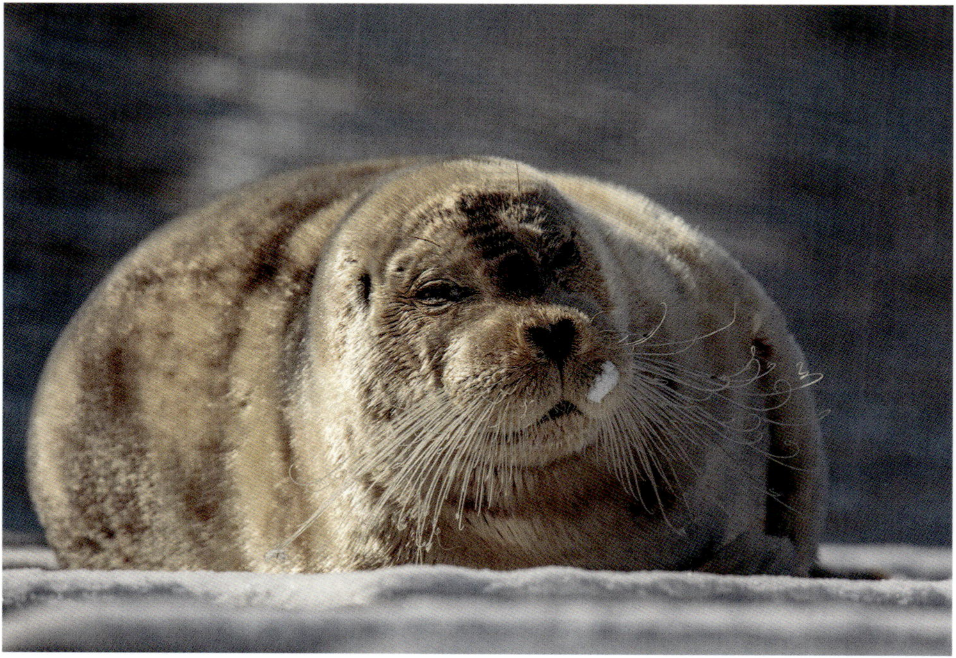

In early winter light, a harbour seal rests on the slipway at Quidi Vidi, snow dusting its whiskers as it basks quietly in the morning sun.

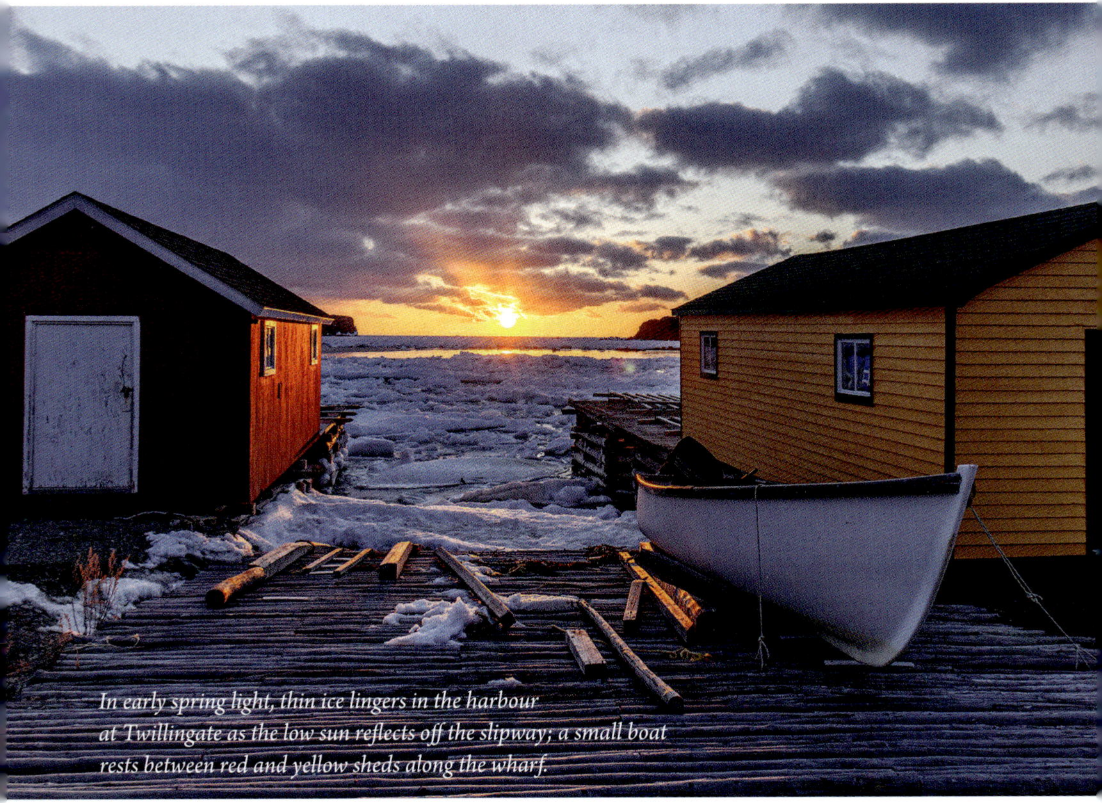

In early spring light, thin ice lingers in the harbour at Twillingate as the low sun reflects off the slipway; a small boat rests between red and yellow sheds along the wharf.

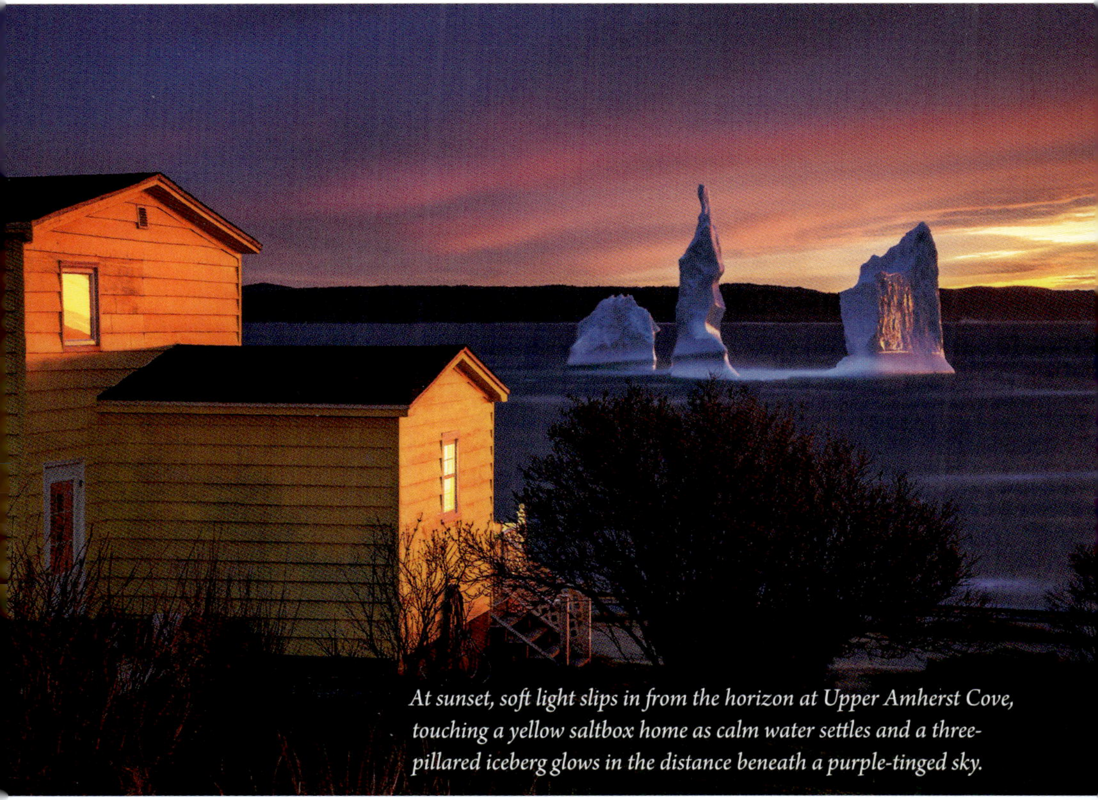

At sunset, soft light slips in from the horizon at Upper Amherst Cove, touching a yellow saltbox home as calm water settles and a three-pillared iceberg glows in the distance beneath a purple-tinged sky.

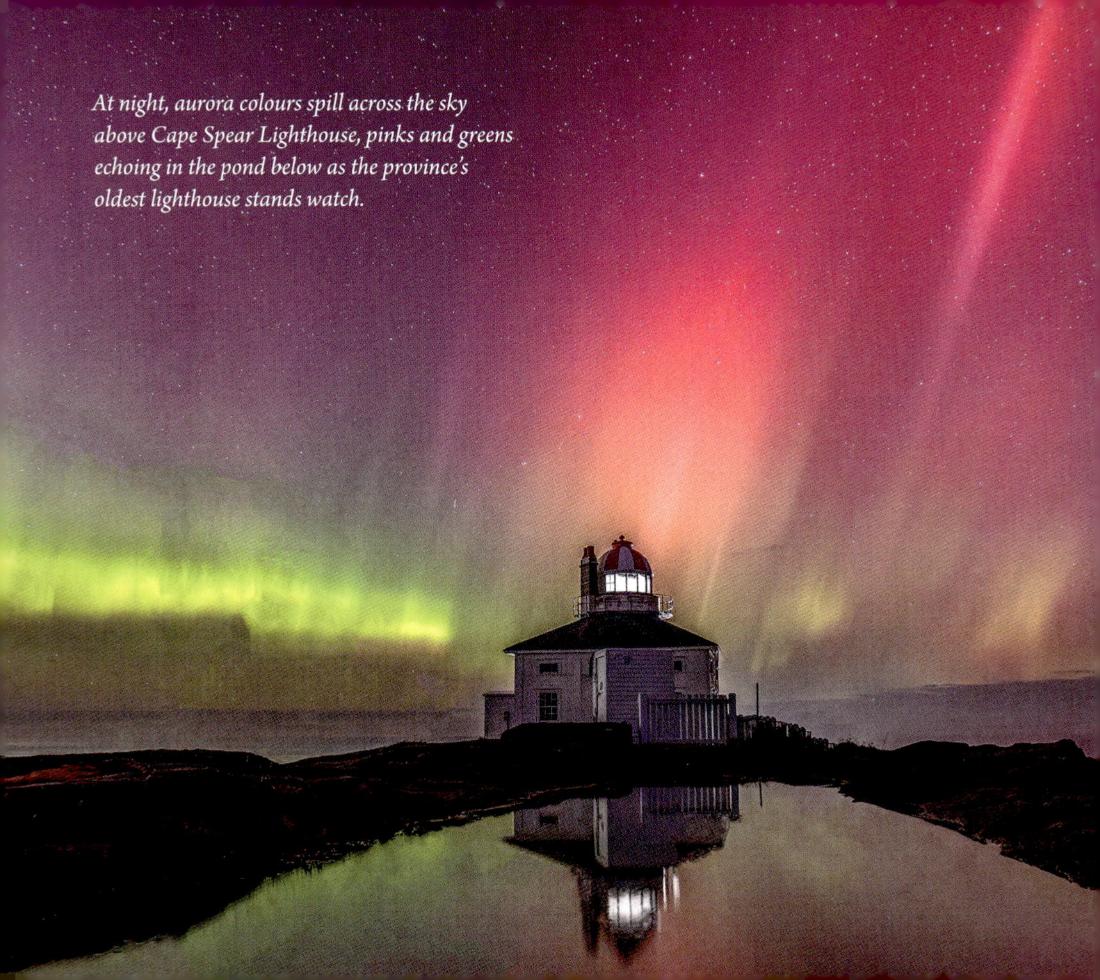

At night, aurora colours spill across the sky above Cape Spear Lighthouse, pinks and greens echoing in the pond below as the province's oldest lighthouse stands watch.

At night, green and purple northern lights drift above a still pond in the Torngat Mountains, their glow settling softly over the dark, remote Arctic landscape.

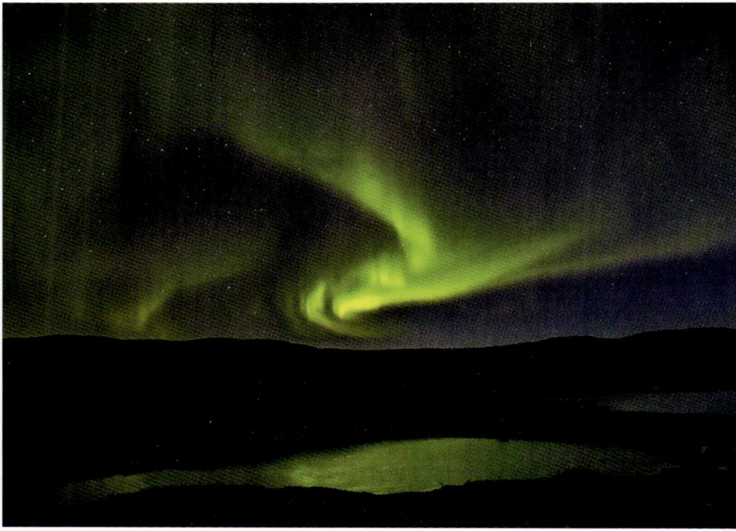

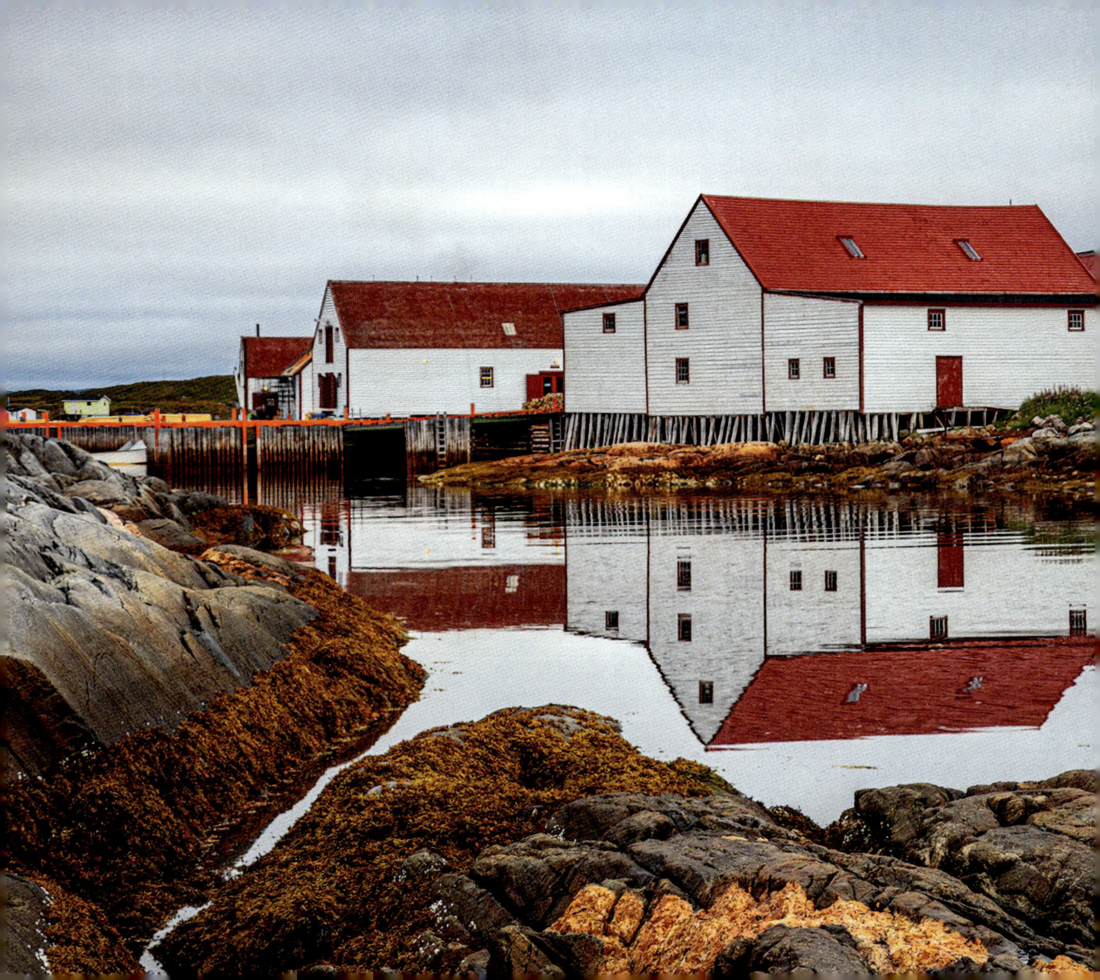

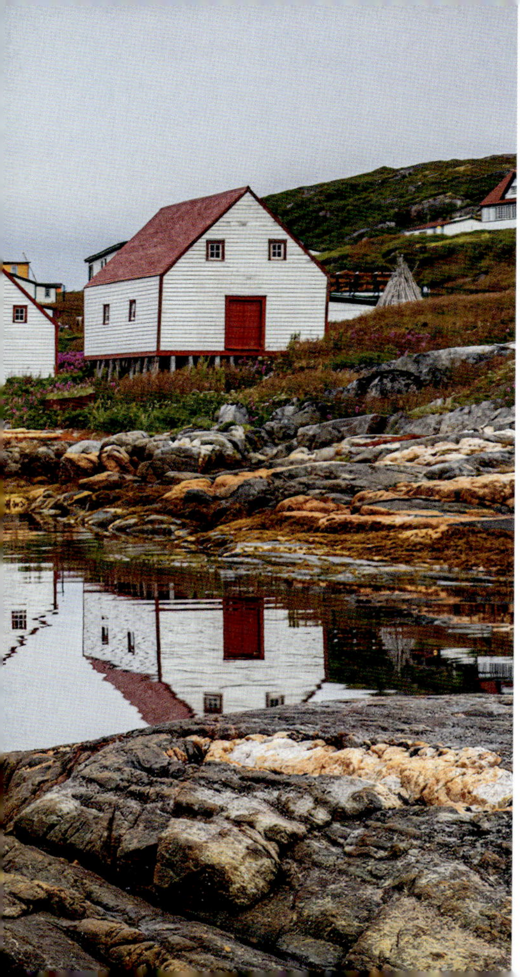

In calm light, the historic buildings of Battle Harbour rest along the shoreline, their reflections holding the memory of generations when fish were brought here and time moved with the tide.

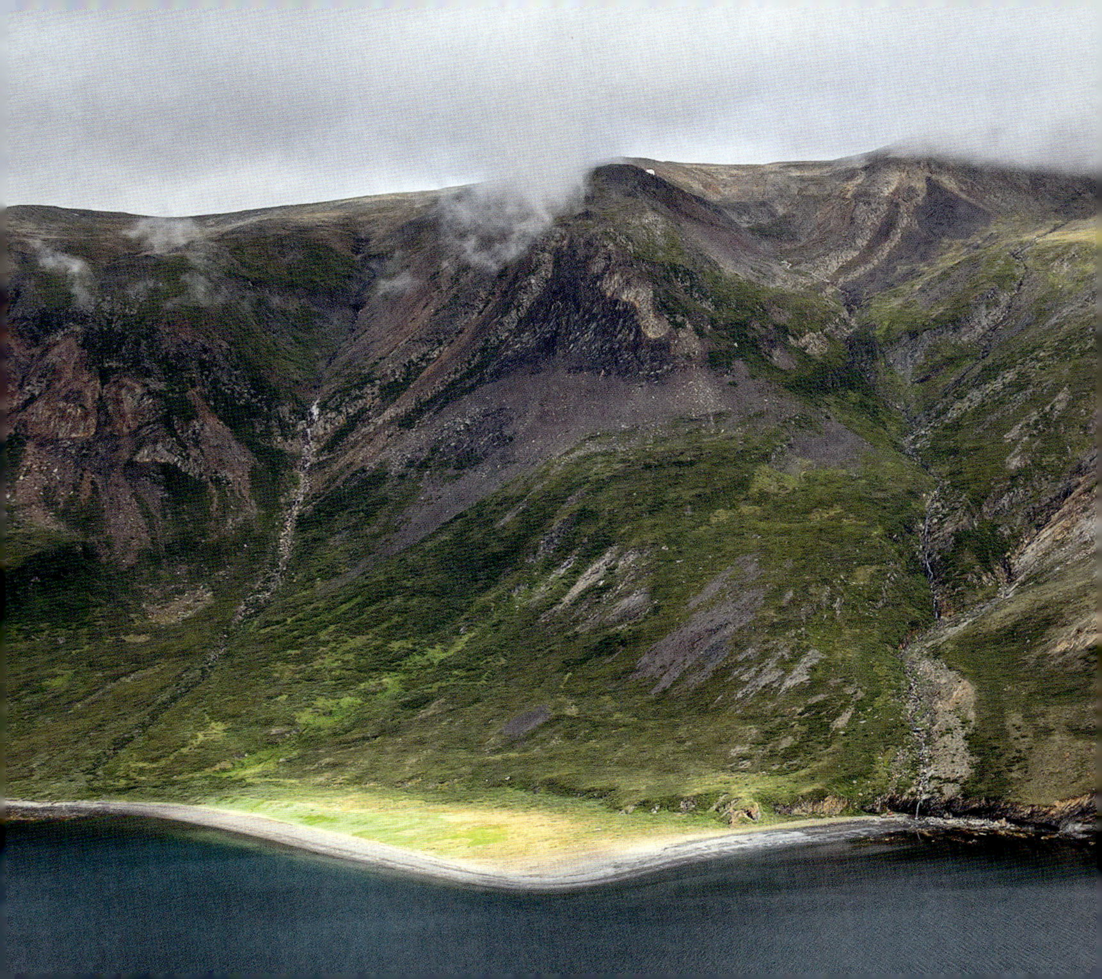

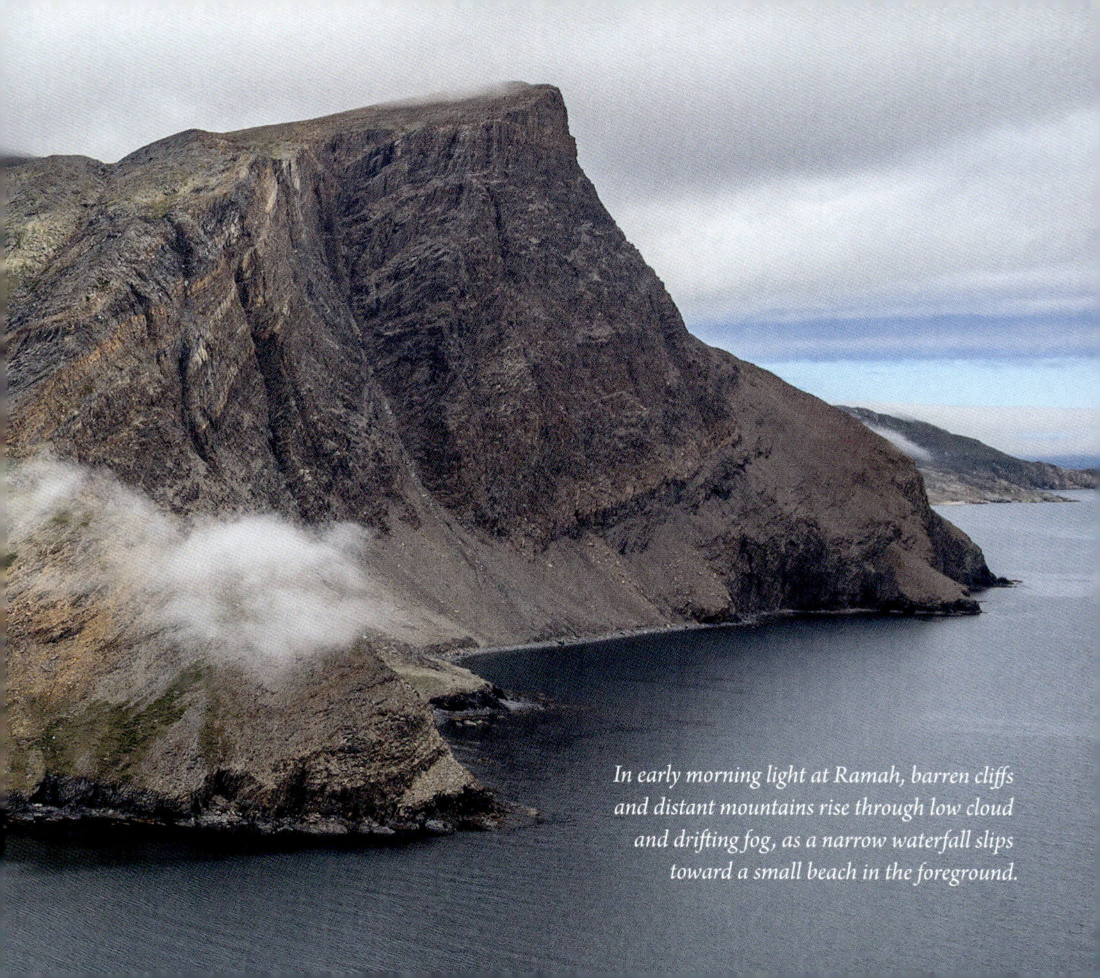

In early morning light at Ramah, barren cliffs and distant mountains rise through low cloud and drifting fog, as a narrow waterfall slips toward a small beach in the foreground.

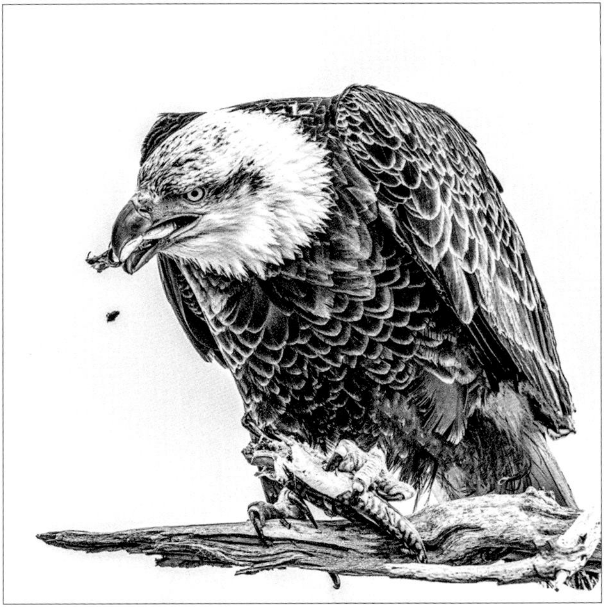

In high-key black and white, a bald eagle feeds while perched on a branch at Quidi Vidi Lake; a fragment of its catch falls away.

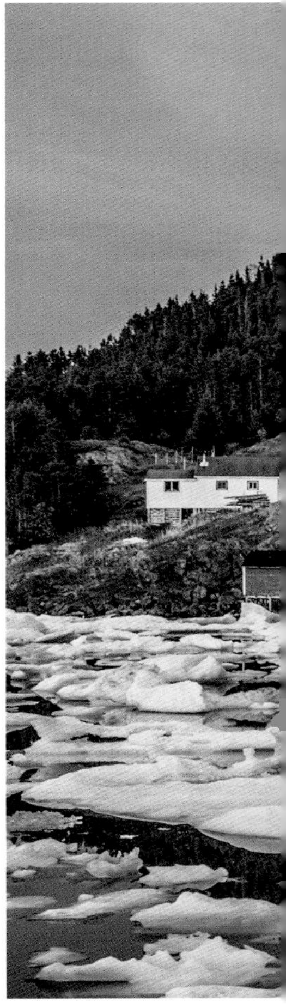

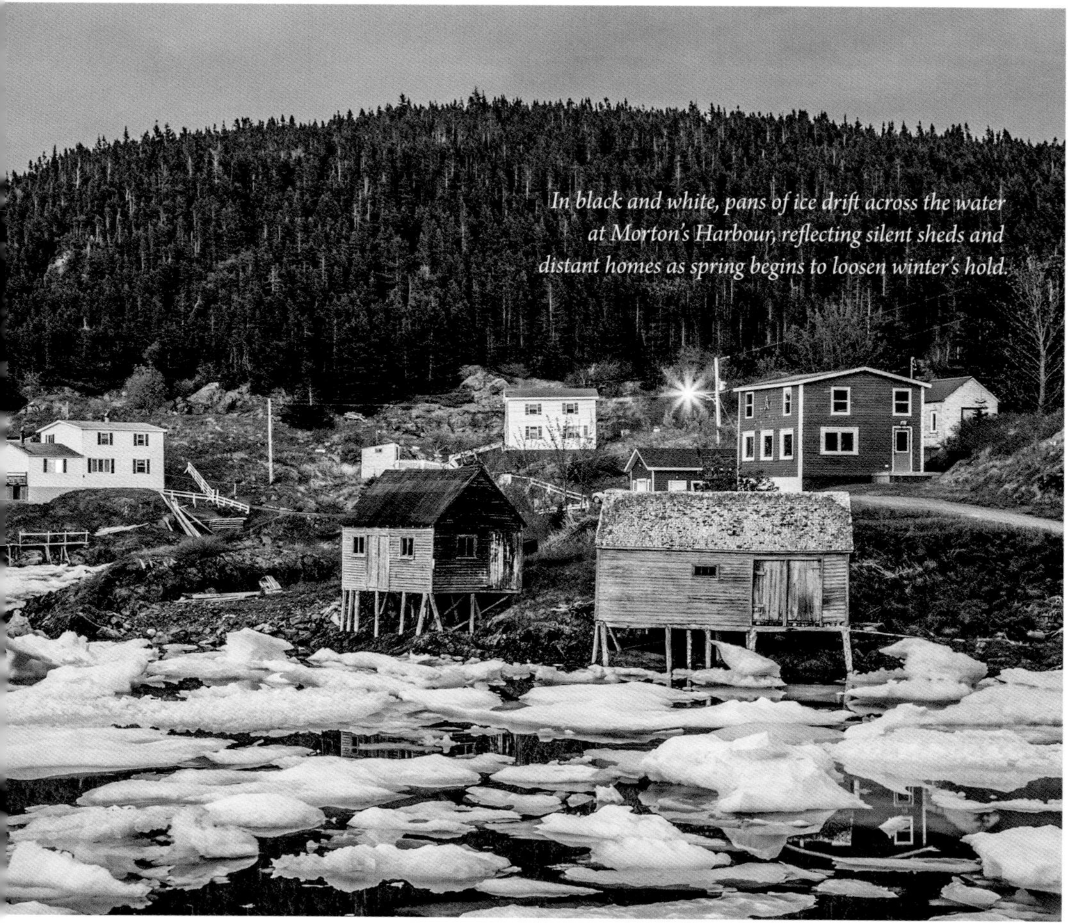

In black and white, pans of ice drift across the water at Morton's Harbour, reflecting silent sheds and distant homes as spring begins to loosen winter's hold.

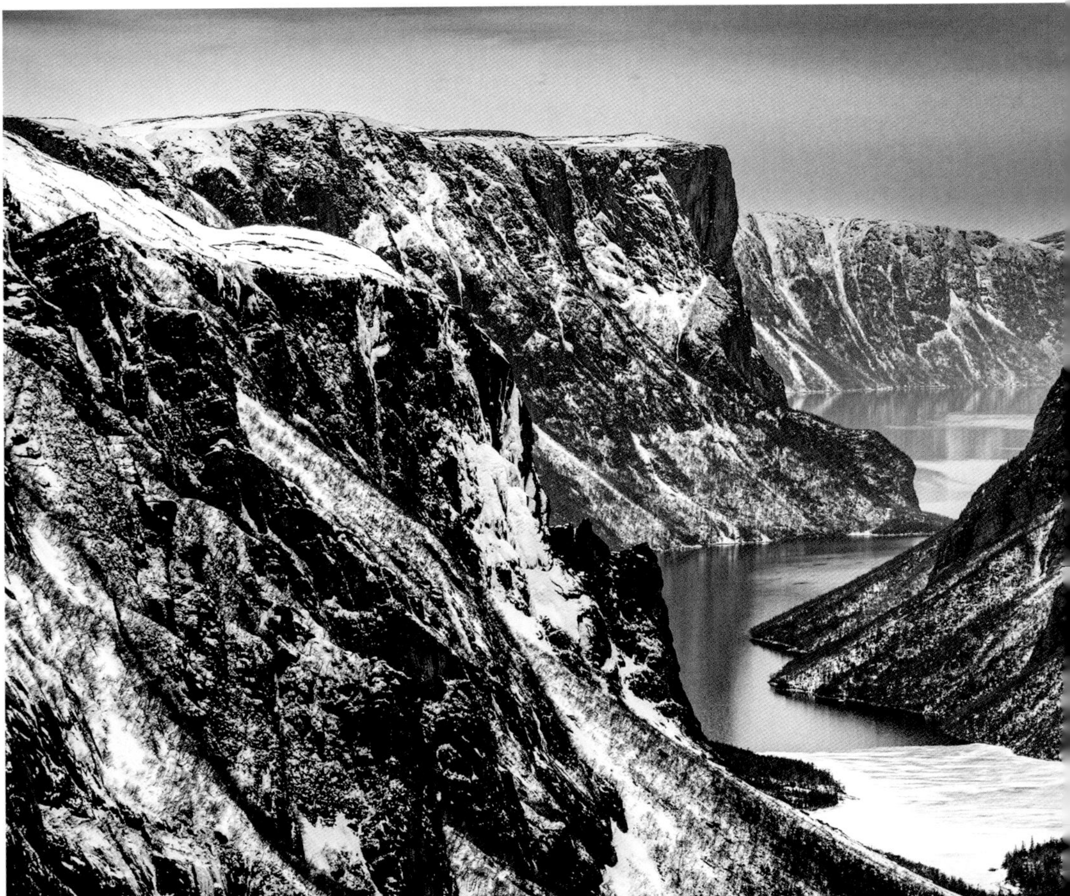

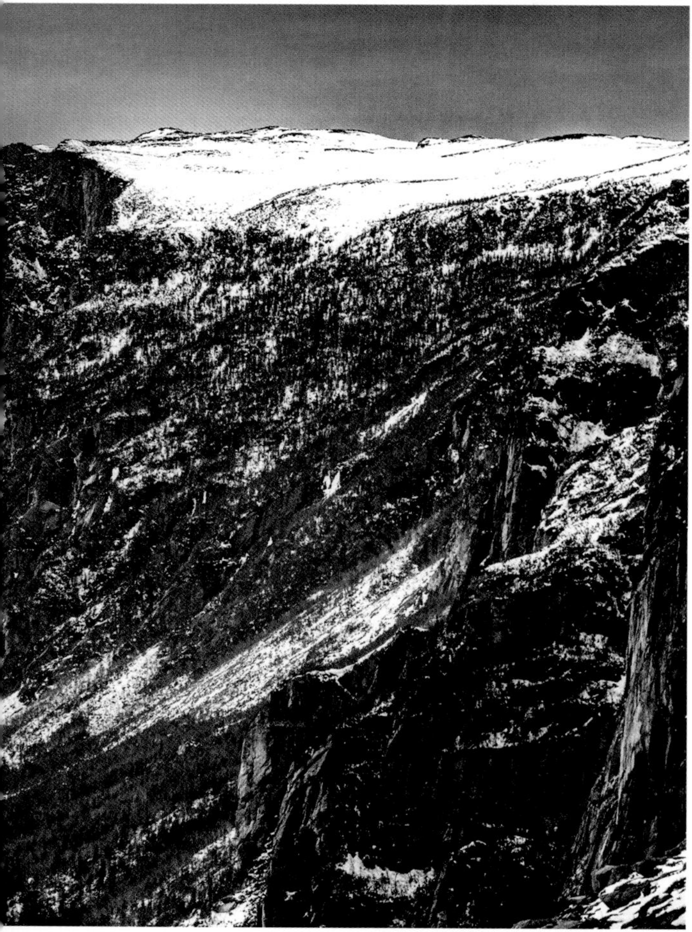

In black and white,
winter snow clings
to the cliffs at
Western Brook Pond
as calm water rests below,
and layered rock rises
like dark cake edged
with white icing.

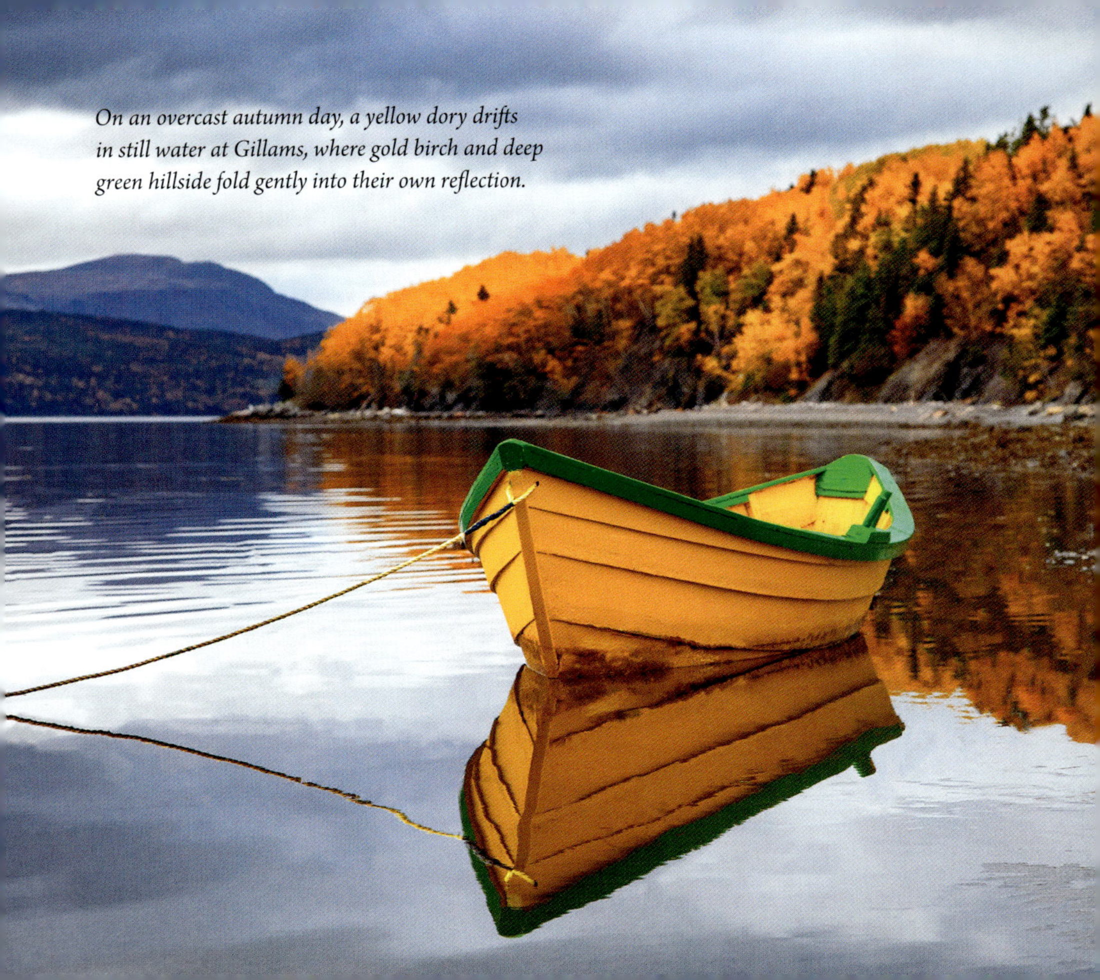

On an overcast autumn day, a yellow dory drifts in still water at Gillams, where gold birch and deep green hillside fold gently into their own reflection.

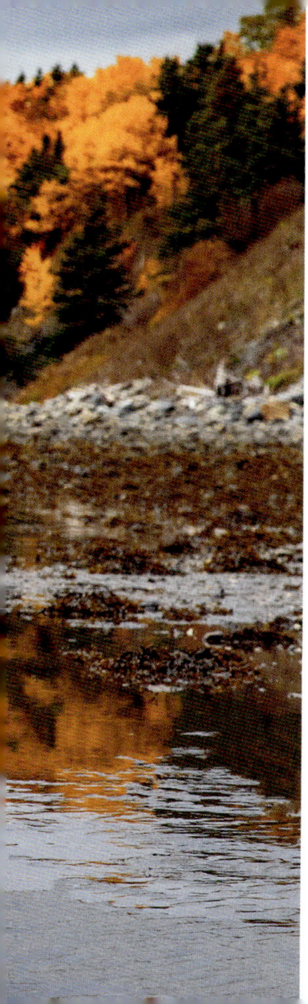

In autumn light, a brown wooden shed
with a yellow door stands in Quidi Vidi,
as golden birch trees line the cliffs beyond and
waterfalls descend through the landscape to the right.

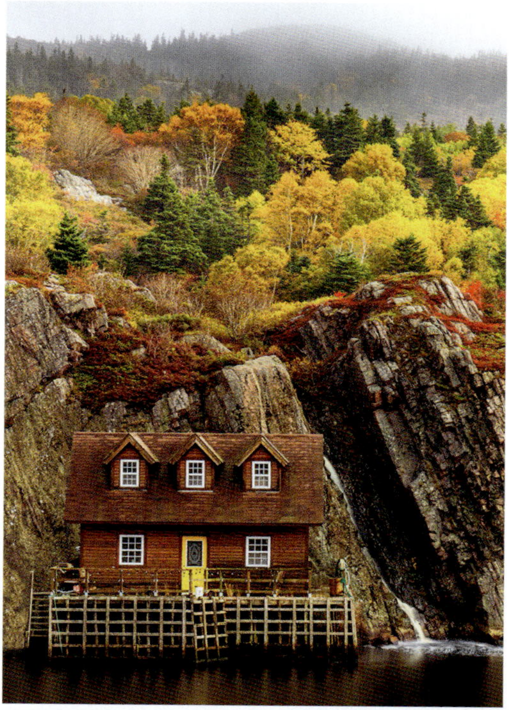

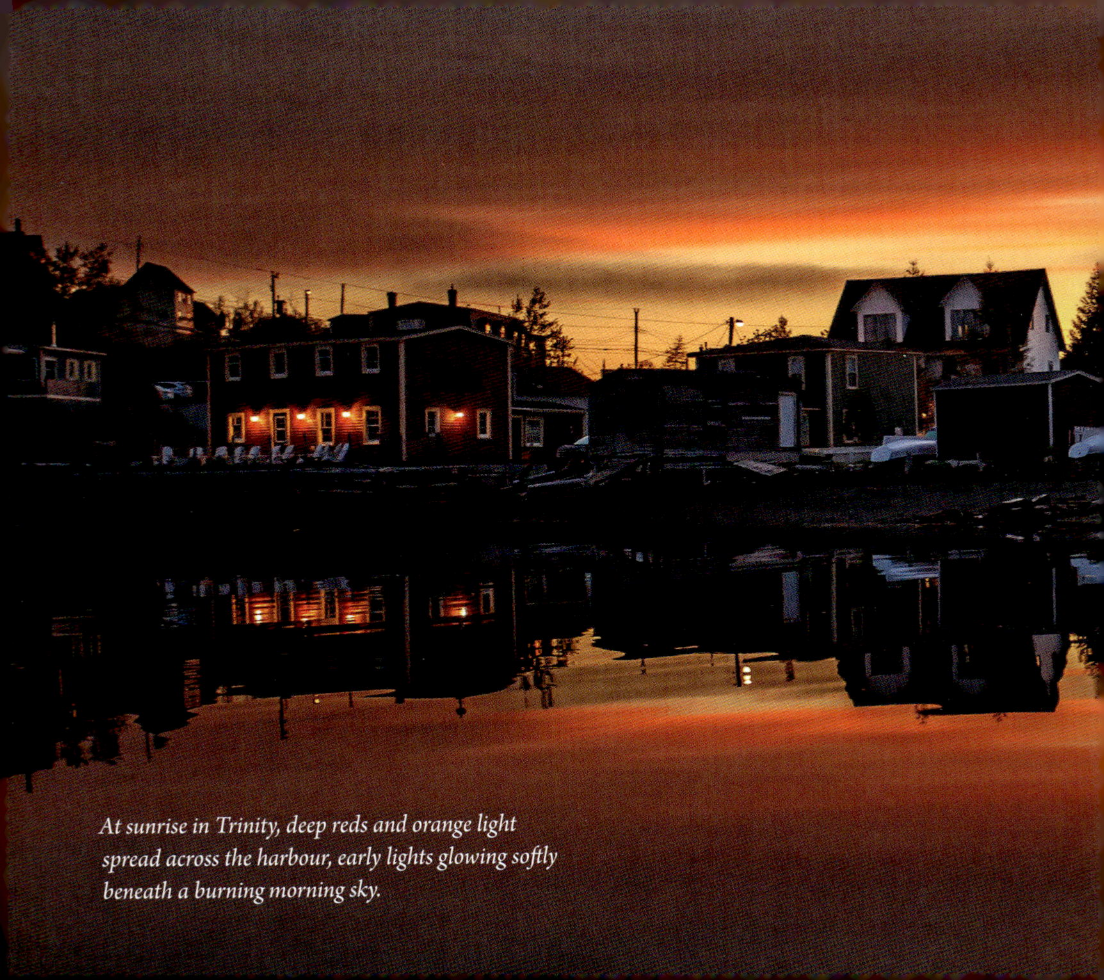

At sunrise in Trinity, deep reds and orange light spread across the harbour, early lights glowing softly beneath a burning morning sky.

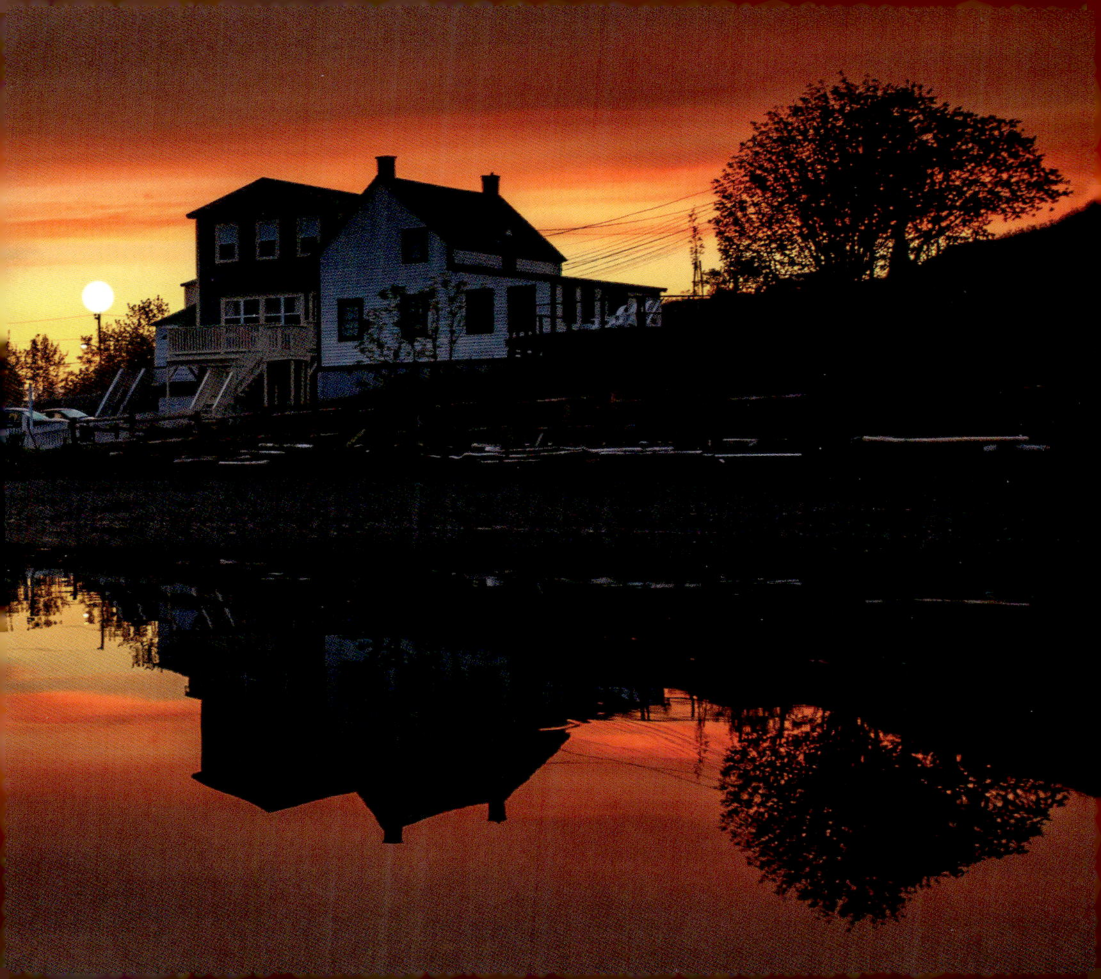

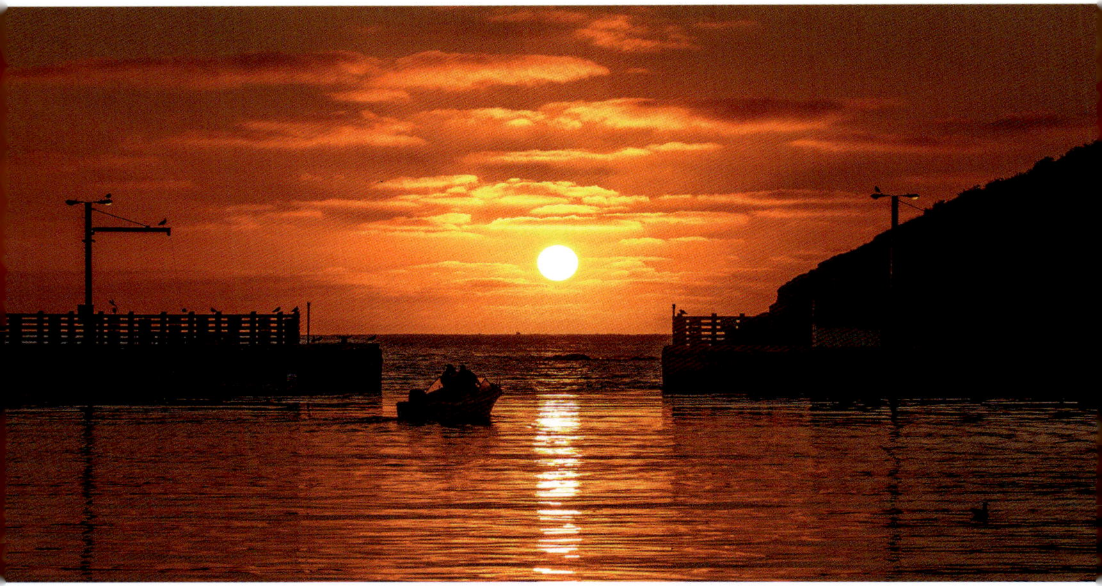

At sunrise, a fishing boat leaves the safety of the narrows at Petty Harbour, orange light spilling across the water as seabirds perch quietly along the wharf poles.

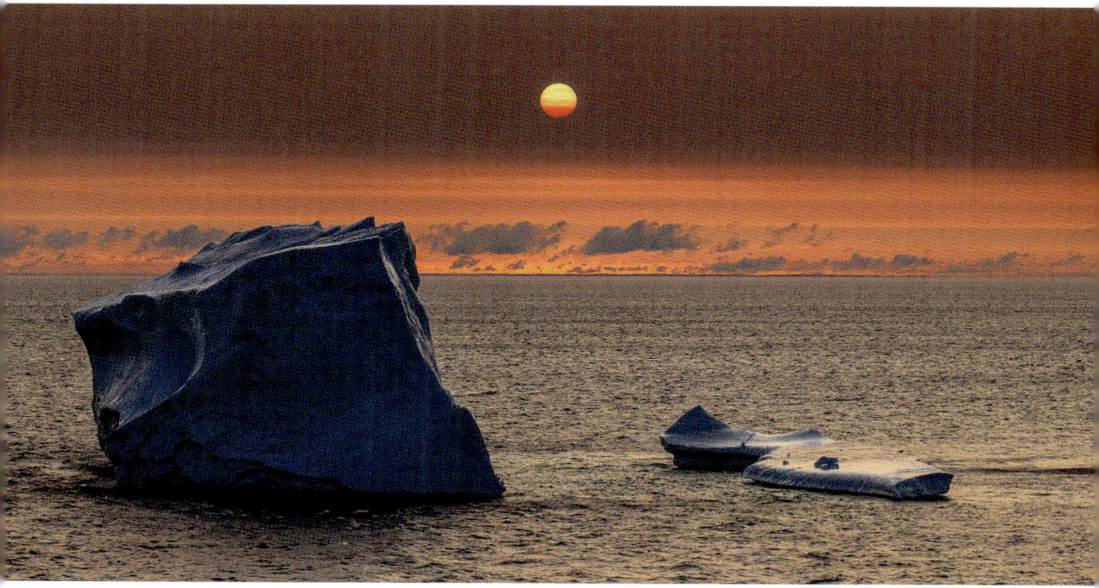

At sunset in Twillingate, warm orange light meets cool blue ice in the North Atlantic, as a deep blue iceberg reflects the fading glow of the sky.

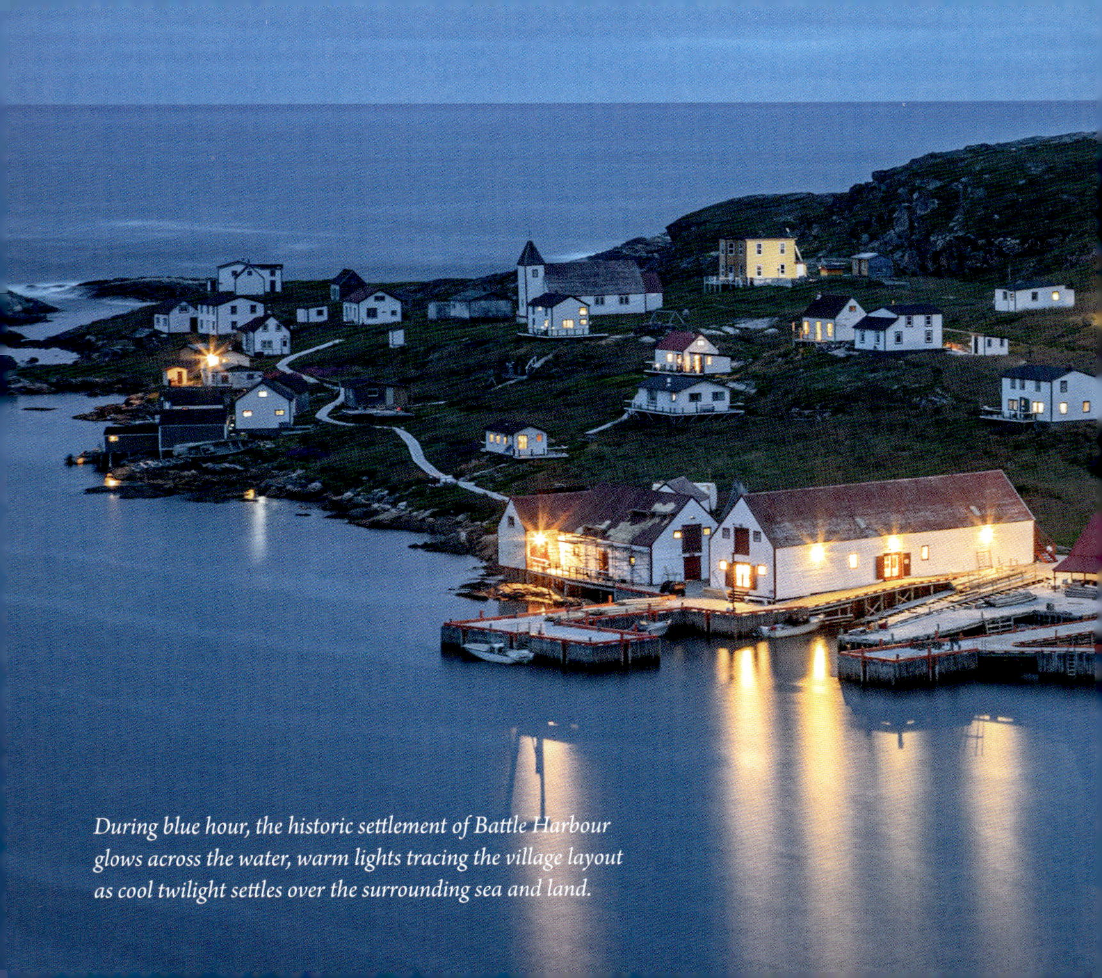

During blue hour, the historic settlement of Battle Harbour glows across the water, warm lights tracing the village layout as cool twilight settles over the surrounding sea and land.

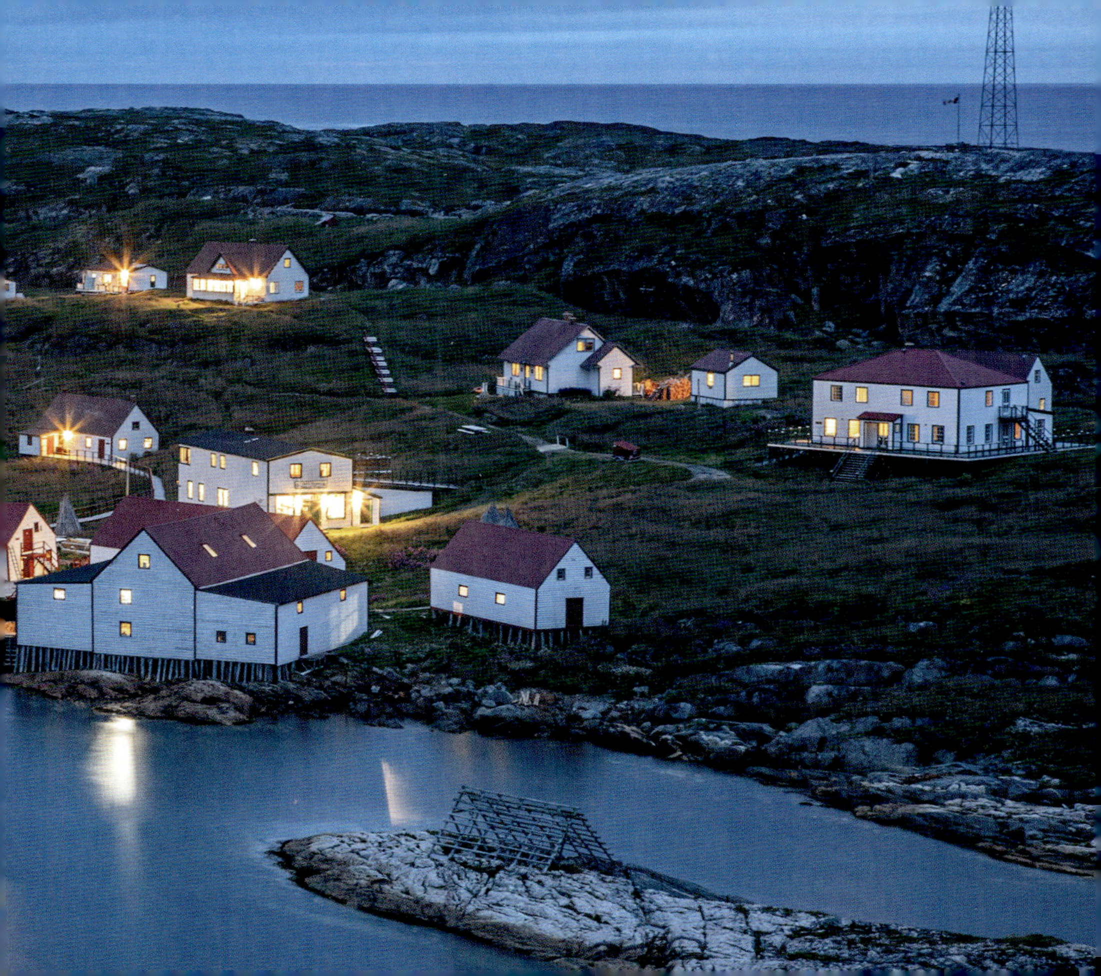

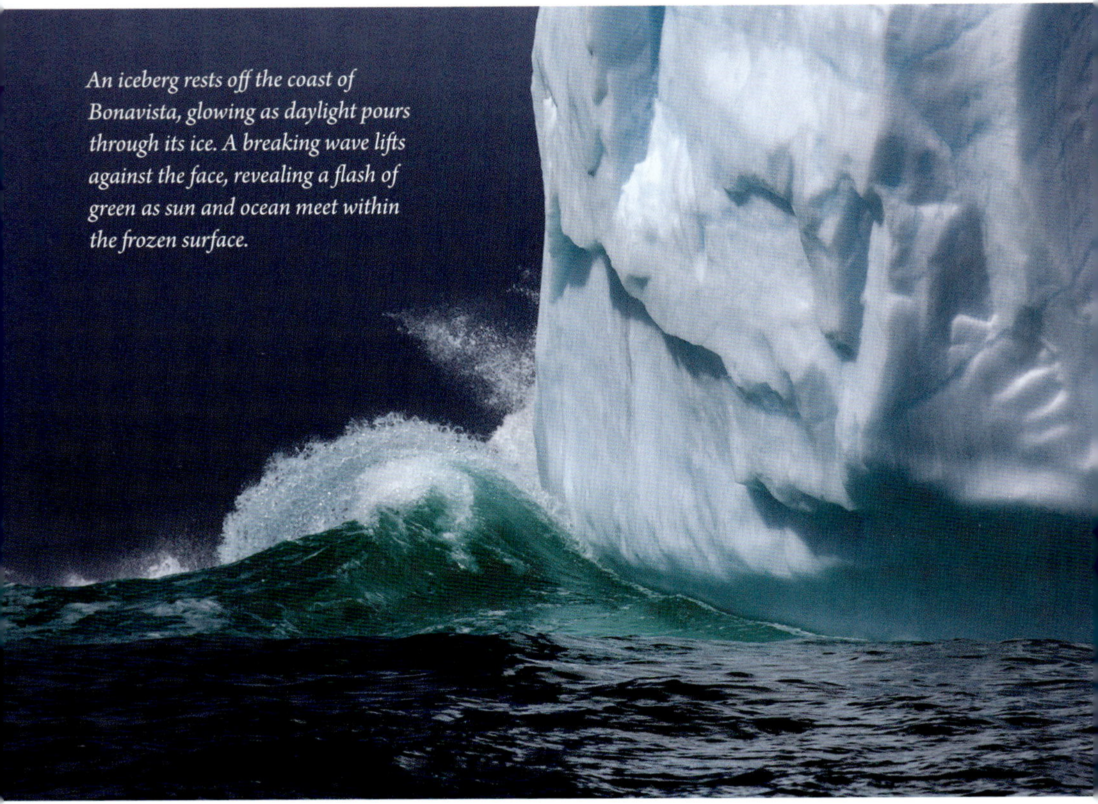

An iceberg rests off the coast of Bonavista, glowing as daylight pours through its ice. A breaking wave lifts against the face, revealing a flash of green as sun and ocean meet within the frozen surface.

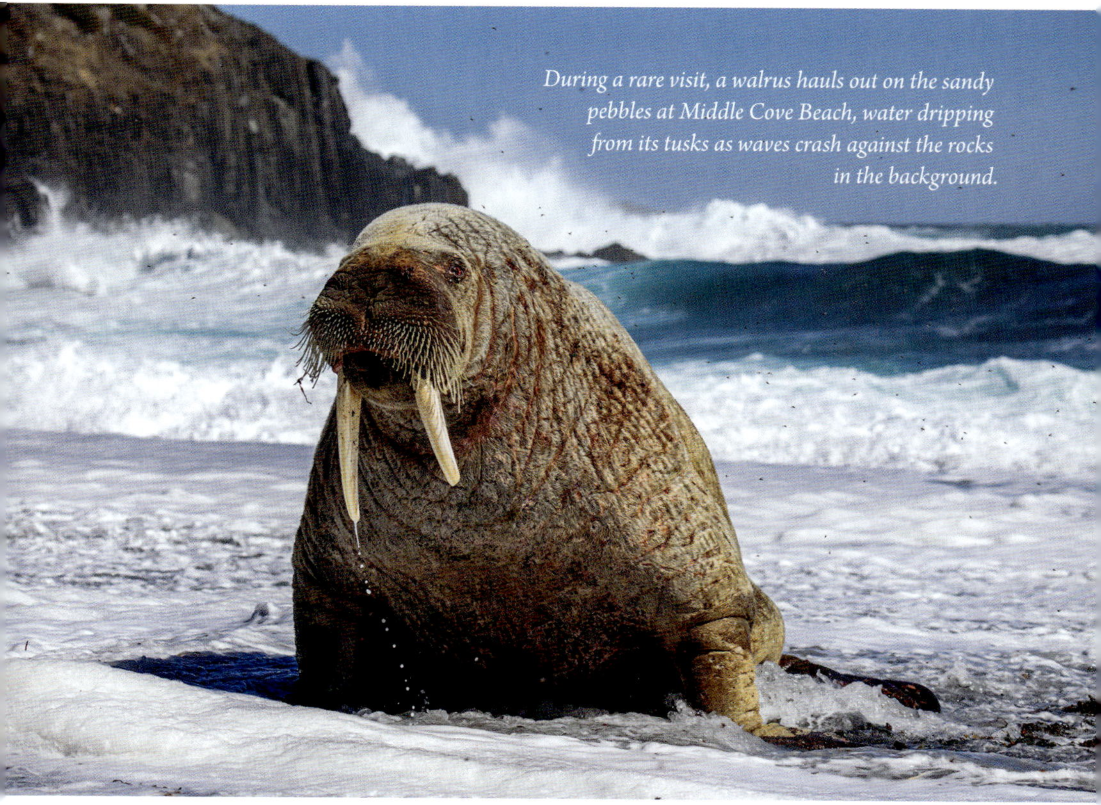

During a rare visit, a walrus hauls out on the sandy pebbles at Middle Cove Beach, water dripping from its tusks as waves crash against the rocks in the background.

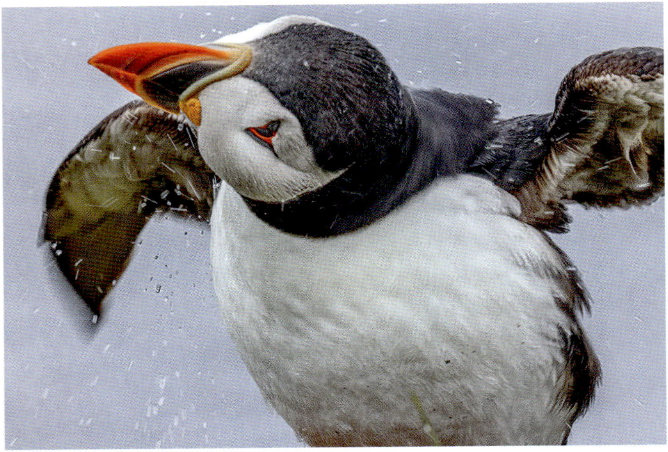

In soft light, an Atlantic puffin shakes rain from its feathers in Elliston, droplets lifting into the air as the bird settles after the storm.

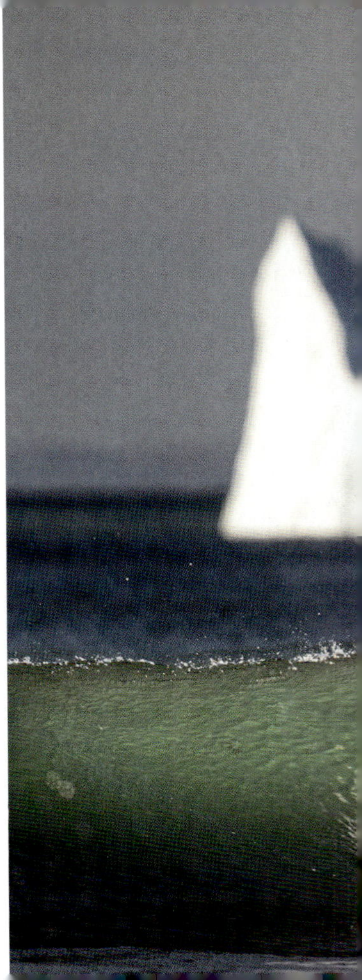

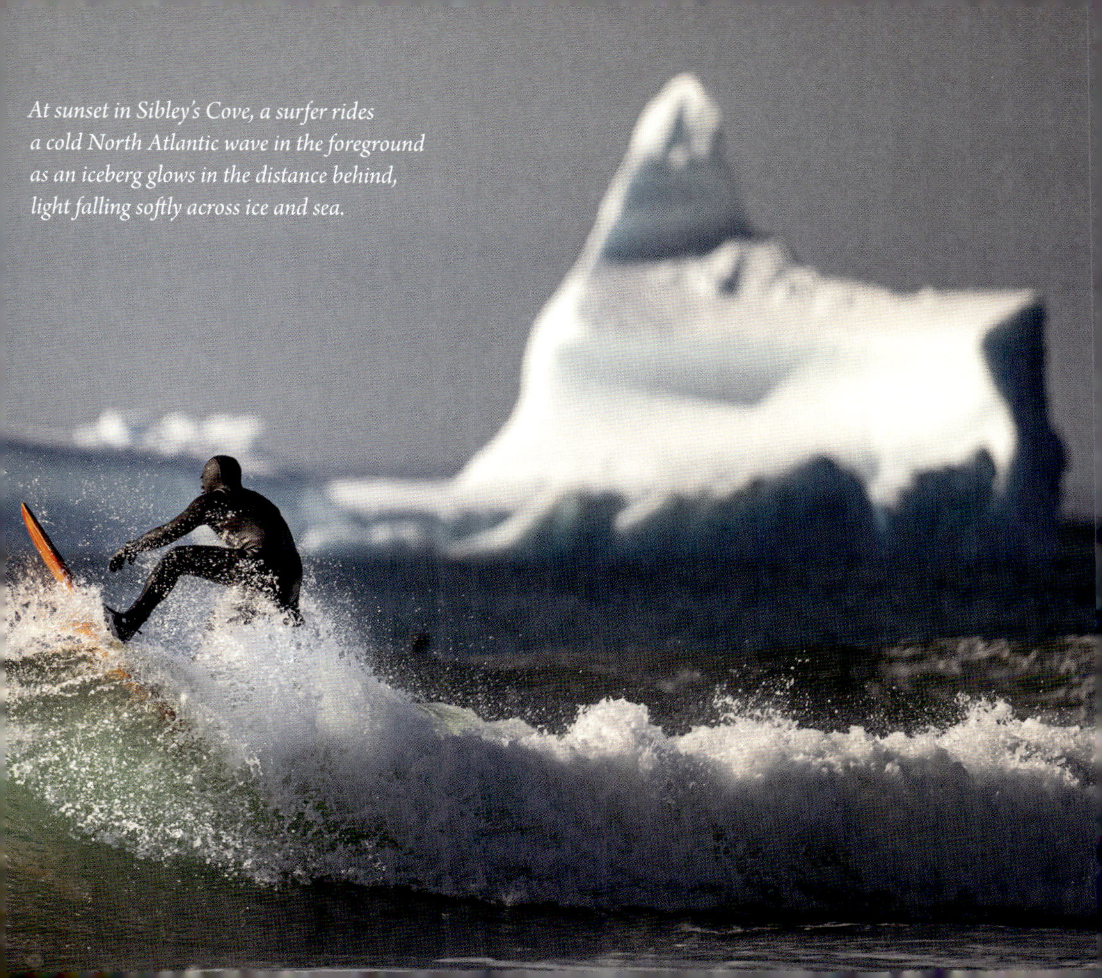

At sunset in Sibley's Cove, a surfer rides a cold North Atlantic wave in the foreground as an iceberg glows in the distance behind, light falling softly across ice and sea.

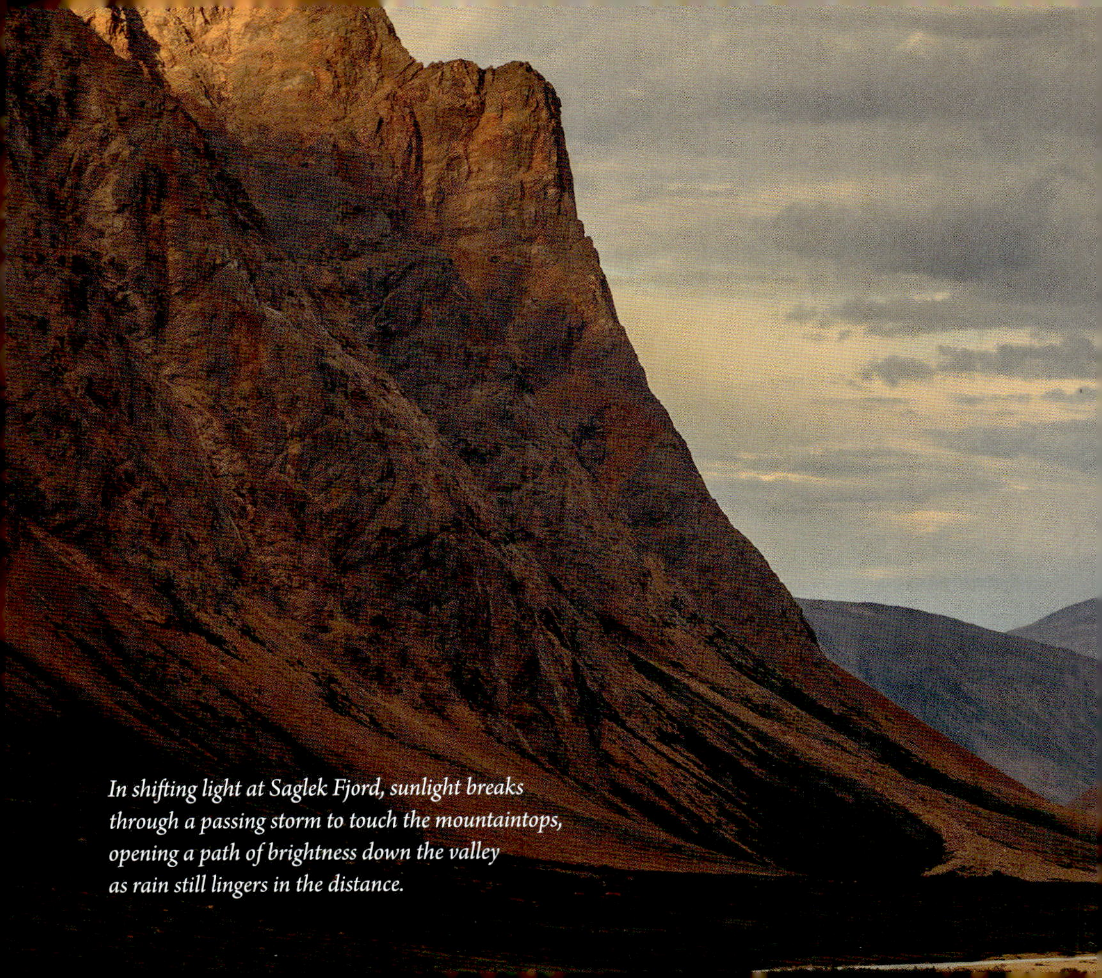

In shifting light at Saglek Fjord, sunlight breaks through a passing storm to touch the mountaintops, opening a path of brightness down the valley as rain still lingers in the distance.

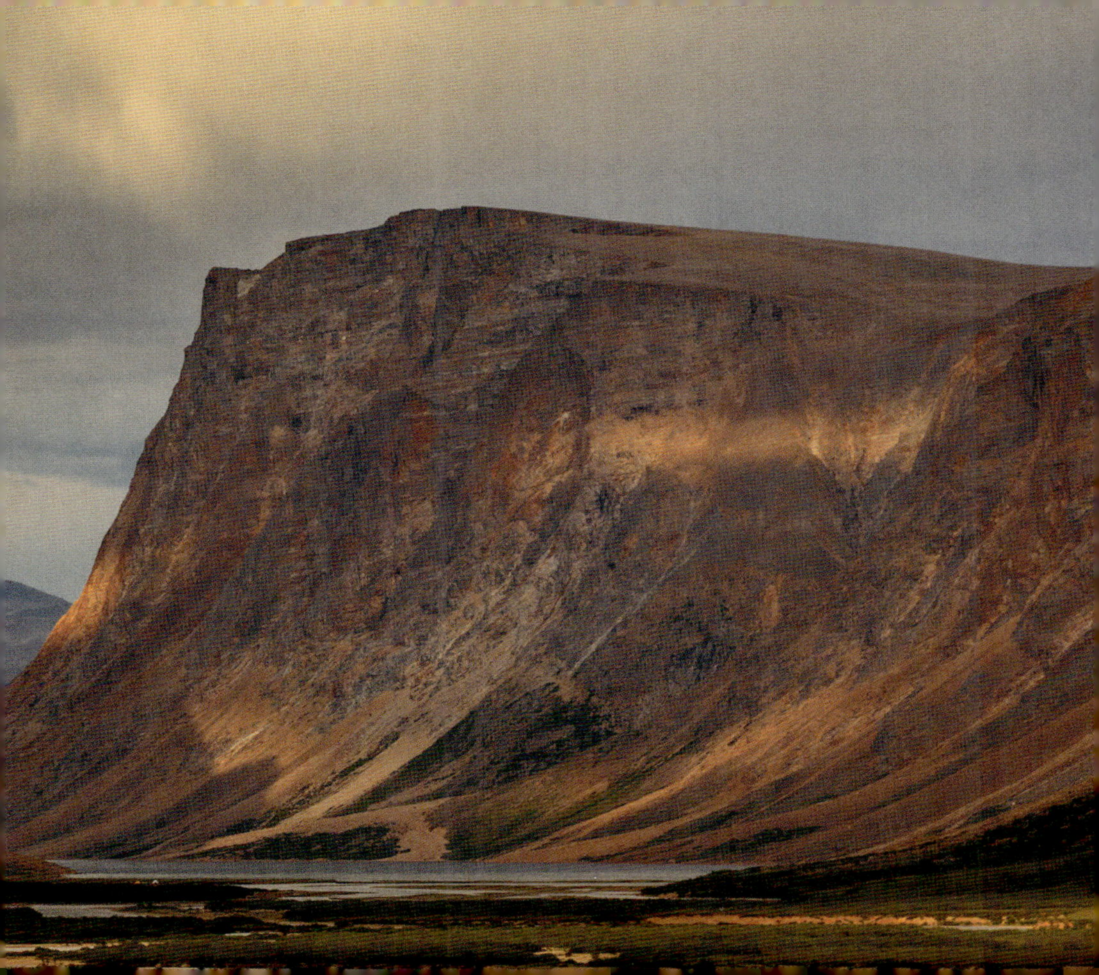

BREAKWATER BOOKS LIMITED
www.breakwaterbooks.com

CERTIFIED CANADIAN PUBLISHER

LIBRARY AND ARCHIVES CANADA CATALOGUING IN PUBLICATION
Lost in Newfoundland. Volume 2 / with photographer Michael Winsor.
Winsor, Michael, photographer
Canadiana (print) 20260137448 | Canadiana (ebook) 20260137464
ISBN 9781778530852 (hardcover) | ISBN 9781778530869 (EPUB)
LCSH: Newfoundland and Labrador—Pictorial works. | LCGFT: Photobooks.
LCC FC2162 .W56 2026 | DDC 971.8/050222—dc23

IMAGE CURATION; BOOK LAYOUT: Beth Oberholtzer, Oberholtzer Design Inc.

THE PUBLISHER GRATEFULLY ACKNOWLEDGES THE SUPPORT OF
The Canada Council for the Arts; The Government of Canada through the Department of Heritage; and The Government of Newfoundland and Labrador through the Department of Tourism, Culture and Arts.

Canada Council for the Arts | Conseil des arts du Canada

Canada

Newfoundland & Labrador CANADA

FSC www.fsc.org MIX Paper | Supporting responsible forestry FSC® C103567

PRINTED AND BOUND IN CANADA.

Breakwater Books is committed to choosing papers and materials for our books that help to protect our environment. This book is made of material from well-managed FSC®-certified forests and from recycled materials.